DATE

Published by Siduri Books 2009

2 4 6 8 10 9 7 5 3 1

First published in Great Britain in 2009 by
Siduri Books
3 Nyland View, New Road
Draycott, Somerset BS27 3SG
UK

www.siduri.co.uk

A CIP catalogue record for this book is available from the British Library

ISBN 978-0-9562052-0-9

Printed by
TJ International Ltd
Padstow, Cornwall, UK

THE WORLD AND WIKIPEDIA

HOW WE ARE EDITING REALITY

ANDREW DALBY

CONTENTS

Prologue

I use Wikipedia. So do you, I suspect. Wikipedia is a vast online encyclopedia – ten million articles in 270 languages – used daily by millions all over the world. Most of them would never have thought of looking at a printed encyclopedia.

Because I use Wikipedia, any errors in Wikipedia articles that I happen to mention in this book are my fault. I noticed them; therefore I could have corrected them. Any errors you have seen and not as yet corrected are your fault too. In this way, Wikipedia is unlike any other encyclopedia and any other web fact source that we are currently likely to use. We don't just read it; we write it. If we didn't, it wouldn't exist at all. Because we do – and because it's free, and is bigger than any encyclopedia before it, and is still growing – at least three years ago researchers in many fields found themselves using it as one of their mainstays. One year ago, in a process that is now gathering pace, it began to drive other fact sources out of business. 'Was this a good thing?' is a good question, but not one to lose sleep over. Like many of the statements in Wikipedia, it's a fact.

Wikipedia has almost become the one great big reference source that everyone always relies on. We have almost reached the point where there's no serious choice.

Now come the really interesting questions.

Chapter 1
Wikipedians at work

A POWERFUL EARTHQUAKE struck central Italy at 1.32 GMT on Monday 6 April 2009. At 2.20 there was a Wikipedia article about it.

A 19-year-old law student at the University of Chile, Warko is a fan of U2, the Simpsons and the Spanish Wikipedia, to which he has made 15,000 edits in three years. For him it was still Sunday evening. He made a small correction to the article on a young Chilean actor, killed two days earlier in a motorcycle accident. Then he heard breaking news of the earthquake. Finding a report on the online version of the Rome newspaper *Il Messagero*, Warko wrote a two-line article on the earthquake in Spanish, added a footnote citation to *Il Messagero*, and saved the article as **Terremoto de Italia de 2009**. Over the next half-hour he improved the article, categorised it under 'Terremotos de 2009' and 'Italia en 2009', and added links to new reports he'd found at Reuters and the US Geological Survey. At 2.53 he let it go.

Meanwhile Candlewicke, who usually contributes on Irish broadcasting and popular music, saw the first reports of the earthquake on the BBC website, typed out a five-line article for the English Wikipedia, with a citation of the BBC report, and saved it under the title **2009 Italian earthquake**. This appeared instantly in the English 'New pages' list, and the server clock still read 3.17 when Purplebananasandelephants, a self-appointed New Page Patroller, glanced at Candlewicke's work, decided it was too brief, and flagged it as a stub. But this was soon to change.

Warko came back to the Spanish Wikipedia at 19.11 GMT. He made two small improvements to the biography of a Chilean youngster who died while waiting for a heart transplant. Then he looked for his **Terremoto de Italia de 2009** and found it completely transformed. Vrysxy had taken it in hand; five other named users and several anonyms had chipped in. It was now ten times the length, full of cogent detail, with many more sources cited. Links to corresponding articles in 13 other languages were visible in their proper place. Five minutes earlier a careless anonym had spoiled the formatting. Warko corrected this – the work of a moment – and moved on, just too soon to observe the arrival of another interwiki link, this time to the Welsh Wikipedia.

By the end of the day the English and Spanish articles had been retitled (allowing for more than one earthquake in Italy in 2009). Both had already exceeded 1,000 words in length, complete with maps and tables; the English article had 14 footnote citations and had been edited precisely 200 times. Of the 265 language wikipedias a total of 20 already had articles on the subject: French, Italian, Polish, Danish, Chinese, Romanian, Portuguese, Serbian, Catalan, Hungarian, Dutch, Czech, Russian, Basque and Norwegian had all been added in the course of the day.

The news has moved on, and so have the newspapers. The BBC page consulted by Candlewicke is long gone, overwritten by later, fuller reports on the same day. The news that laboratory technician Giampaolo Giuliani had 'predicted the earthquake' made momentary headlines and was forgotten. The death toll rose, then levelled out and ceased to be reported. Wikipedia is still working multilingually towards the perfect article on **2009 L'Aquila earthquake**: tables of affected villages; statistics of victims by nationality; detailed lists of foreshocks and aftershocks; the claims and dismissals surrounding Giampaolo Giuliani; citations of earlier scientific papers on tectonic faults in the L'Aquila district; all readable, all documented, each addition judged by the consensus of later readers, and every previous version still available to be consulted and compared, all the way back to the pioneering texts of Candlewicke and Warko.

At 6.32 GMT on 25 March 2009, somewhere in the world, Keykingz13 set up a Wikipedia account. At 6.38, while studying the **List of hentai anime**, this Keykingz13 changed the title *After Class Lesson* to *After Church Sex*; then moved on to the long and serious article **History of Brunei** and made a series of small alterations based on free association: *golden age* to *platinum age*; *Sarawak* to *kalimantan*; *Sulu archipelago* to *malay peninsula*; *Ferdinand Magellan* to *christopher columbus*; *British protectorate* to *italian protectorate*,

and *the newly formed Malaysia* to *the newly formed brunei*. Six hours later, Keykingz13 reappeared in cyberspace, made several similar changes to **Brunei** including one sentence long enough to betray an inability to write grammatical English... then signed off and has not been seen again.

This is the most insidious kind of vandalism. It requires knowledge and careful reading to realise what, exactly, is wrong. **List of hentai anime** was corrected two days later by an anonym. The most obvious nonsense at **Brunei** was quickly noticed and reverted by Haleth. Unluckily it did not occur to Haleth to check further; so the other changes, including those to **History of Brunei**, persisted. After six hours, an anonym corrected *christopher columbus* to *Megellan*, and, a minute later, *Magellan*. After two days another anonym changed *the newly formed brunei* to *the newly formed Brunei* (which was no help at all).

Five days after Keykingz13's interventions, an editor from the Latin Wikipedia (it was Andrew Dalby) happened to look at **Brunei** in the course of checking whether or not there is a Latin name for Brunei. I noticed some strange errors on the page, found from the history that they had been introduced by Keykingz13, went on to see what else Keykingz13 had done, and finally completed the slightly complicated task of restoring the two major articles **Brunei** and **History of Brunei** to the near-angelic state from which they had fallen five days earlier.

Like most people you have heard of, **Jimmy Wales** is the subject of a biography on Wikipedia. Like most active editors of Wikipedia, the same Jimbo Wales has a busy talk page (and a blog, and a presence on Facebook and Flickr and Twitter). Unlike all other active editors and unlike almost anyone you have heard of, he co-founded Wikipedia and still watches over it. This brings him advantages and disadvantages. An advantage is that he holds dictatorial powers to ban users, delete pages and erase page histories (powers rarely used and often for a good reason). A disadvantage is that he does not know, or even want to know, most of the people who write to him on his talk page.

He did not want to know little AgentSpy101, who was working on a school project and claimed (on 19 March 2009) to have *read in a lot of articles* that Larry Sanger did the work while Jimmy Wales took the credit... but still did not seem to understand *1. what things have you done that involve leadership; 2. what struggles did you fight to acolmplish a goal.*

He probably did not want to know ChildofMidnight, an ironic Wikipedian who (on 4 April 2009) drew his attention to the article **Bacon mania** (and, while doing so, hinted that an airline ticket and hotel vouchers to attend the Buenos Aires Wikimania conference would not come amiss). The Child had set out on this leg of the bacon crusade ten days earlier at 22.56 on 24 March, with an essay on **Bacon in popular culture** that opened with the claim: *Bacon is celebrated as a joyous and gluttinous food in popular culture, especially in the United States where high protein foods are considered an important part of a balanced and healthy diet (see Atkins diet) and fitness is paramount*: in a brief space it had many of the faults of American food writing and few of the merits of an encyclopedia article. Within the hour, Kelapstick had categorised it unarguably as 'Pork', while Aleta, evidently not much of a baconian, had recommended *merging* the material in the general article **Bacon**. The Child returned, after midnight, to tweak the first sentence, which was now to begin: ***Bacon in popular culture** is celebrated as a joyous and gluttinous food.* This was a crucial defensive move because a text begins to look like a proper self-standing Wikipedia article when its first words are bolded and repeat its title. Aleta riposted with a peremptory *citation needed* placed immediately after *fitness is paramount*: potentially a killer, because how could the assertions in the first sentence possibly be documented? Aleta then (at last, thank heaven) corrected *gluttinous* to *gluttonous*, and added the category 'In popular culture', thus usefully aligning the bacon essay with **Christian demons in popular culture** and **Tufts University in popular culture**. The Child reappeared after a hasty online search to adjust the first sentence with *high protein foods are sometimes considered...* and *...fitness is not always paramount* (leaving nothing worth documenting) and, more usefully, to add to the body of the article a plethora of well-referenced details from newspapers and websites. It began to look like something almost worth reading. One of the new citations threw up the phrase 'Bacon mania', which the Child suddenly saw to be the article's redemption. The exhausted first sentence was reawakened one last time. ***Bacon mania***, it henceforth claimed, *is the joyous and gluttonous celebration of all things bacon, especially in the United States...* Happy in the knowledge of four hours well spent, ChildofMidnight went to bed.

Why tell this story? Because it is evidence of the awesome power wielded by those who write on Wikipedia. Whatever they write. ChildofMidnight had started an article that just two weeks later extended to 2,200 words, with 34 footnote references, and really does document a significant aspect of United States food culture; it had acquired an almost perfect title, one that might never have been found without the citation imperative and the menace of merger. Over that short period the article had been edited 200 times by 15 Wikipedians. The discussion page was longer than the article, with 13 contributors; there was further discussion at **Talk:Bacon**. Within hours after the change of title, anyone searching Google for 'Bacon mania' would have found this Wikipedia page nudging the original inventor of the phrase for top ranking. Just ten days later Tovin Lapan, a writer on *Street* (the online incarnation of the *San Diego Union-Tribune*) reported his investigation of inflated claims for bacon consumption in the United States, and, as a sort of backhanded acknowledgement, since he took several facts from ChildofMidnight's work, he noted that 'Wikipedia has an entire page dedicated to the topic of recent "bacon mania".'

As it happens, ChildofMidnight writes on other matters more contentious than bacon. The Child is one among some hundreds of Wikipedia editors who make frequent and serious edits to articles on United States politicians. This field is bitterly fought over, and it appears, to a mere outsider reading the endless discussions and their less-than-exciting results, that the rules of engagement changed somewhat when Barack Obama was elected to succeed George W. Bush. For example: ever since 2 January 2006 Wikipedia had a page **Criticism of George W. Bush**, begun by CastAStone *as a part of an effort to reduce the size of the George W. Bush main page*. Several thousand revisions later, on 13 March 2009, it was a taut piece containing 8,500 duly-referenced words (and there was even an equivalent article on the Arabic Wikipedia), but for some reason dissatisfaction was beginning to arise. On that day Sceptre proposed a merger with **Public image of George W. Bush**, a tangentially related topic; three days later QueenofBattle even waded in with a *speedy delete* tag, a rare move for a hard-working page that had given pleasure for three years. This did not stick, but the merger went ahead on 19 March and lots of juicy details concerning various attacks on Bush's personality and behaviour disappeared in the process; ChildofMidnight tried to rescue one such, but could not find the necessary citation in time.

Considering the strength and apparent popularity of the article, discussion of its impending merger/deletion was astonishingly muted. One note is heard in the distant background. *It shows you show badly slanted the admins really are. If you don't believe me, ask yourself, where is the 'Criticisms of Barack H. Obama' page?* a newbie asked rhetorically. *'Criticism of Barack Obama' was speedily deleted*, an older hand replied, and a prefect immediately chipped in with the decree that all 'Criticism of...' pages are the result of *lazy editing or agenda-based editing*.

The prefect didn't want to admit it, but the newbie was on target. The rules that allowed **Criticism of George W. Bush** for three years have been hastily reinterpreted and the page has been dismantled, all in order to head off demand for a parallel page 'Criticism of Barack Obama'.

Now this reinterpretation of the rules is a bad thing. A historian would argue that the existence and nature of criticism of a head of state is important. An article surveying contemporary criticism of Augustus, or Nero, or George III, would be really useful; it would be more instructive than one surveying contemporary praise, and in any case there is no moral imperative to balance the two. I would argue that, anyway. But, I admit, it's hard to compose such an article dispassionately when the subject is a person for whom, or against whom, one is personally voting.

As I write this no one is allowed to create 'Criticism of Barack Obama', although a potential article is being drafted on a user talk page. Meanwhile there are two possible ways to insert information on negative perceptions of Barack Obama into Wikipedia. One alternative is to get the material into newly created articles that will survive. Few of them do; but, for example, Grundle2600 created the article **Obama Bear Market**, a jargonish but well-documented idiom denoting the stock market's behaviour during Obama's early days. Within two days the information was merged into a new, more generalised (and admittedly better) article **US bear market of 2007–2009**. Wikipedia conveniently forgot the uncomplimentary phrase 'Obama bear market'.

The other way is to slot the information into articles that exist, currently **Barack Obama**, **Public image of Barack Obama**, **Presidency of Barack Obama** and **First hundred days of Barack Obama's presidency** (a page that, like a naughty child, is currently said to have *multiple issues*). ChildofMidnight, whom we met above, is one of the more persistent among the editors who squeeze negative viewpoints into these articles. It isn't easy. By mid April the Child had made 53 moves on **Barack Obama** and 13 on the 'Hundred days'; Grundle2600, a less skilful player than the Child, had led 22 attacks on the 'Presidency' page and nine on the 'Public image'. The tactics of Scjessey, Grsz11, Wikidemon and others defended Obama from most of these critical jabs.

Such games carry risks. For maintaining his arguments concerning Barack Obama and Nancy Pelosi just a little too long, the foolhardy Grundle received four *warnings* and three *last warnings* (not in any logical order), most of them delivered by Scjessey, followed, on 4 April, by a painful one-day *block*. ChildofMidnight immediately intervened to dispute the propriety of this punishment, adding, to comfort the disconsolate Grundle, *there are those who game the system and violate the guidelines in order to advance political agendas. Don't get baited into responding and losing your cool. Wikipedia is just like the real world.*

ChildofMidnight, though never yet blocked, was pinned to the **wp:Administrators' noticeboard** soon after midnight on 7 April by Banjeboi, who had put together a long list of the Child's alleged contraventions, fully documented with links, relating to the page on **Barney Frank**. For those currently on other planets, Barney Frank is a Democrat representative from Massachusetts, Chair of the House Financial Services Committee, and a prominent gay politician. ChildofMidnight, in common with some other editors, wanted the page to be clearer and fuller from the start about Frank's mildly exciting earlier life, his notably liberal agenda and his interesting interactions with Fannie Mae and Freddie Mac before those moneylenders went into meltdown. The Child had, it must be added, teased his opponents on the Barney Frank talk page by suggesting, disingenuously, that their discomfort at his frequent references to Frank's gay politics stemmed from their own homophobia. This really hurt. *Would a pageban make sense?* Banjeboi concluded plaintively. Within 40 minutes those complaints had been echoed by Scjessey and Wikidemon: the Child had even been *coaching and inciting other disruptive users* (well, one user, maybe). The discussion did not go all the critics' way. ChildofMidnight fought back vigorously. Aleta, the moderate baconian, breezed in and advised participants to cool off and talk it over at **Talk:Barney Frank**; yet, as I write this, Wikidemon is still urging that the Child be banned from all politics articles and the matter is unresolved.

A page on the New Zealand National Party politician **Richard Worth** has existed on Wikipedia since October 2004, when the self-effacing Vardion (who generally works *in the quieter areas of Wikipedia*) added an initial biographical outline, citing no source. Like the rest of Wikipedia, this particular article has steadily improved: it now provides a full sketch of Worth's political career (with footnotes) and an action photograph of him about to say something amusing at a launch party. The photograph was taken and uploaded by Stuart Yeates; it was the first such image he had handled, and it took Gadfium's help to get it to appear on the page.

Thanks to text and picture you almost know Richard Worth; you can almost feel the modest conflicts of interest in which he has once or twice been entangled. Because he, like Wikipedia, has steadily improved his standing since 2004. He is now New Zealand's Minister of Internal Affairs.

One such alleged conflict of interest, concerning a trip to India that apparently combined private with national business, became newsworthy on 30 March 2009. At 15.01 GMT an anonymous Wikipedia editor added a complicated sentence about it, with a rough footnote to an online news source. At 19.25 Gadfium, who watches this and many other New Zealand pages, reworded the sentence and improved the reference. And then, at 21.59, a very occasional editor named Richard W Worth made an emendation which reduced *a potential conflict of interest* (followed by the details) to *a perception of a potential conflict of interest* (followed by very little). The same edit clarified that Richard Worth was no longer chairman of certain relevant organizations, and, unintentionally or not, deleted the footnote.

Was the editor Richard W Worth the same person as the subject of the article? In the nature of things, this isn't certain. Most people use aliases when editing Wikipedia, but some prefer real names, and normally Wikipedia doesn't verify editors' identities: this is an essential element of the freedom to edit. You may choose almost whatever name you wish, unless it's offensive or already in use. So, theoretically, the editor called Richard W Worth might really have that name, or might be impersonating Richard Worth (such things have happened), or might have chosen the name at random. But in this case the only edits made by Richard W Worth had been to the page about the politician **Richard Worth**, and they had been favourable to the subject. Others concluded – rightly, I believe – that the editor was the politician.

The story moves from conflict of interest in New Zealand politics to conflict of interest in editing Wikipedia. There are guidelines, and they include the strong recommendation that you should not edit a page about yourself except to remove vandalism or to correct obvious errors.

Within 15 minutes Gadfium had noticed the change and restored the footnote. At this point Gadfium and Stuart Yeates, the same editor who had photographed Worth at the launch party, looked at the history and noted that this was not Richard W Worth's only contribution to the page. Back in December 2008 he had added numerous details (including one of those same chairmanships now seen as a potential conflict of interest). Although far from scandalous, this editing was perhaps self-interested. At any rate it broke the usual rule. And so, at 5.25 on 1 April, Gadfium left a message for Richard W Worth advising him to look at the conflict of interest guidelines, to abstain from making further similar changes himself but to propose them on the article talk page; at 7.53 Yeates set out all the information on the talk page and promised to revise the biography, removing conflict of interest. Bactoid, a New Zealander who seems from other edits to have political views opposed to those of Richard Worth, took the opportunity to add: *If the user continues I would recommend a ban*. Gadfium responded quickly (and correctly) that a ban would be an over-reaction.

And now, the reach of Wikipedia. Less than 24 hours after Gadfium's message, at 5.23 GMT on 2 April, the online news source *TVNZ* reported that the New Zealand prime minister had described Worth's actions as 'not sinister but stupid'. The report added that Worth 'edited the Wikipedia website to record instead of a "potential" conflict of interest that there was only a perception of one. That earned him another telling off – not from the Prime Minister this time, but the website editors.' At about the same time Worth was facing parliamentary questions about his compliance with the rules of the New Zealand *Cabinet Manual*: 'Why did the Minister tamper with his own Wikipedia entry earlier this week, and does he intend to take the advice Wikipedia gave him yesterday afternoon [New Zealand time] that he should consult Wikipedia's conflict of interest guidelines?' The Speaker could not at first be sure that the question was relevant, but was sufficiently persuaded to permit the tabling of documents on 'Dr Worth's view of himself on Wikipedia, and Wikipedia's comments to Dr Worth in response'.

Let's be clear about this. Worth invited the warning from Gadfium, the exaggerated threat from Bactoid, and the embarrassment of having the whole interchange rehearsed in the New Zealand Parliament, purely because he used his own name. Many people adopt pseudonyms to edit their Wikipedia biographies, and if it is done discreetly usually no one notices; often the self-interested edits survive. Worth's approach to Wikipedia was perfectly honest and open. That was his mistake.

On the best possible day for the creation of such a masterpiece (1 April 2009), Noroton completed the first draft of **Hotel toilet-paper folding** (1,500 words, 14 footnote references, a two-item bibliography) and saved it. But would it survive? As a potential 'good article' candidate it needed at least one illustration, and at 00.39 Kevin added a nice one. It still wanted incoming links; within four days suitable cross-references (which might or might not stay) had been inserted at **Hotel**, **Toilet paper**, **Origami** and **Hospitality**. More than anything, it wanted to be noticed. Half an hour after creating the page, Noroton showed up at the Jimbo Wales talk page and wrote:

Dear Jimbo, with the creation of Hotel toilet-paper folding it logically follows that Wikipedia must have covered all subjects worth encyclopedia articles, and the encyclopedia can now slowly wind down its operations as editors polish off the existing set with improvements and then find themselves with nothing more to do. (The historic moment took place at 00:03, April 1, 2009, GMT.)

Chapter 2
Where it came from

THERE ARE LOTS of reasons for reading. One of those reasons is to find out a fact known to the writer but currently unknown to the reader. Another is to understand something clear to the writer but currently opaque to the reader. All kinds of texts may occasionally help in those quests. The special feature of encyclopedias is that they are designed to help. This chapter traces three traditions of books specially designed to help in the quest for knowledge. The three traditions, plaited together, lead to where we are now: to Wikipedia and its surviving rivals.

The first tradition, the one to which the word encyclopedia properly belonged, is that of the survey of knowledge – the 'circle of knowledge'.

The most ancient book of this kind was compiled in Latin, in the days of the Roman emperor Vespasian, by Gaius Plinius Secundus. Pliny the Elder, as he is familiarly known, had fought on Rome's German frontier. He was now an admiral, a personal friend of the Emperor, an avid reader and an obsessive collector of knowledge.

'He made excerpts of everything he read [his nephew reminisced] and always said that there was no book so bad that some good could not be got out of it... A book was read aloud to him during dinner and he took rapid notes... In the country the only time in the day when he stopped working was while bathing, I mean, when actually in the water, because when he was being towelled and massaged he dictated notes or had a book read to him. When he was travelling he felt free to give every minute to work; he kept a secretary at his side with book and notebook, and this is why he used to be carried about Rome in a sedan chair. I remember that he told me off for walking: I could have put those hours to use, he insisted. This is how, among his many public duties, he managed to complete his many writings; this is why I have inherited from him 160 notebooks of excerpts, written in a minute hand on both sides of the page.'[1]

In AD 79, stationed with the fleet at Misemum, Pliny saw the eruption of Vesuvius from his villa. He led his ships across the Bay of Naples to hover just offshore near Pompeii and rescue the city's fleeing population. All went well; many lives were saved. But Pliny himself refused to leave. He had studied various natural disasters but he had never been close to a volcanic eruption. He walked back towards the stricken city. Somewhere along the beach near Pompeii, overcome by fumes, he died the death of a true vulcanologist. Eruptions of the Vesuvius kind are now called 'Plinian' in his memory.

Today Pliny would be Wikipedia's edit-count champion, its most modest disputant, its most loved and most versatile contributor. He would never be blocked for breaching the *three-revert rule* (which disallows reverting the same page three times in 24 hours): no edit, he would say, is so bad that some good cannot be got out of it.

Instead of this, after several other books on all kinds of topics, Pliny wrote the *Naturalis Historia*, 'Survey of Nature'. Shortly before his death he dedicated it to the emperor Titus, Vespasian's eldest son and destined successor. Quirkily but systematically, in 37 papyrus rolls Pliny surveys the world of knowledge from mathematics by way of geography, biology, anthropology, agriculture, pharmacology and mineralogy to sculpture and the graphic arts; the whole of Nature and what humans have built on her. If 37 seems an odd number, blame it on Pliny's second great innovation. Not only was he the first author in the world to attempt something like an encyclopedia; he was also the first author in the world to begin his work with a full guide to contents and list of sources. You do not need to unroll all of books two to 37 to find a particular topic; you glance through book one. After consulting (let's say) book 14 about wine, you do not need to guess which sources Pliny used when writing it; you look back at section 14 of book one and you find that they are all listed, those books that were forever being read to him, those excerpts that he never stopped scribbling or dictating. With encyclopedic modesty Pliny has named his sources; but, with the insouciance of a second-rate Wikipedian, he provides no *inline citations*.

Pliny's user page, as a Wikipedia editor, would make a special claim to fame. He is the first known author to have used the word *encyclopaedia*, 'full circle of knowledge'. He didn't give this name to his own work – *encyclopaedia* wasn't yet seen as the description of a book or as a potential title for a book

– but he used it to explain his purpose, which was to offer a full circle of learning, a complete system of knowledge laid out in a logical pattern.[2] The word is Greek, and Pliny tells us that it was actually used by Greek teachers or philosophers in his time. No doubt that's true, but we know the word only from him and from one other contemporary Latin author.

Pliny had successors. About the year 630, when Latin learning was in some danger of decadence, archbishop Isidore of Seville paused in his lifelong struggle against the Arian heretics to compile a modest encyclopedia. It covered a wide field of knowledge: grammar, rhetoric, law, religion, literature and language had not been part of Pliny's scheme but Isidore attempted them all. *Etymologiae*, the usual title of his work, betrays an obsession that was all his own. Isidore liked to trace the origins of words. He also knew that Christianity was right and that all heretics, as defined by the synods in which he had participated, were wrong. Isidore was an assiduous writer and, like Pliny, he would be an enthusiastic Wikipedian. He would scatter unsourced and nonsensical etymologies as widely as he could, defending them on talk pages, and some of them would not get deleted. He would insist on his message well beyond other users' patience, and would be blocked repeatedly for breaching the three-revert rule. Yet his world map demonstrates his flair for simplification: he would be an excellent contributor at Wikiforkids.com.

Isidore would not, like a bad Wikipedian, have tried to claim ownership of the articles he contributed. It seems he handed over his text, half-edited, to his younger colleague Braulio, Bishop of Zaragoza. It was Braulio who arranged it in 20 books and added a table of contents. There was no need for a list of sources: Isidore found some good fresh quotations but he was largely borrowing from and abridging predecessors like Pliny.

Four centuries later, on the other side of the world in China, another and greater one-man encyclopedia was in view. Its author, Shen Kuo, had had a military career as active as Pliny's and an appointment as Imperial astronomer during which one of his most important contributions was the pinpointing of the true celestial pole. His public career ended in disgrace and forced retirement. This was his cue to begin writing. Shen Kuo's *Mengxi bitan*, 'Dream brook brush talks', completed around 1088, has the oddest title of any encyclopedia (much odder, surely, than Wikipedia) and an unusually high proportion of original research and synthesis (which Wikipedia, incidentally, doesn't allow). Shen Kuo's structure of knowledge begins with government, law and literature; it ends with anthropology, archaeology, languages and music; and between these are the pure and natural sciences, in many of which the author himself was an observer and innovator.

Pliny completed his 36 volumes, worked up the table of contents and list of sources, and wrote the dedication. Isidore (apparently) did not. Whether Shen Kuo reached that final stage is not certain. Some form of his work was being quoted by another author three years after Shen Kuo's death, in 1095, suggesting that it was already published; but no such version survives today. Those who can read Chinese read Shen Kuo only on the basis of an 1166 edition, in which his original 30 sections were compressed to 26; those who only manage English can't read him at all. Shen Kuo, it seems, would be a mainstay of the Chinese Wikipedia, but his interest in ancient languages and forgotten scripts would surely impel him to range more widely. His well-labelled diagrams would earn him frequent credit in *Did you know?* on the Main Page. With enviable frequency they would be promoted to *good article* and onward and upward to *featured article*, than which no higher wiki-accolade exists.

Far bigger than Isidore's *Etymologiae*, the *Speculum Maius* ('Greater Mirror') that Vincent of Beauvais spent his whole life writing is the quintessence of the medieval European encyclopedia. Amateurs do it in their spare time; Vincent, 'reader' at the Dominican monastery of Royaumont around the year 1255, did it for a living (I mean, a monastic living: simple food and a hard bed). First from his pen came the *Speculum Naturale*, a so-called 'mirror' of natural history that is structured like chapter one of *Genesis*, beginning, therefore, with the natural history of the denizens of heaven. Then followed the *Speculum Doctrinale* on all the subjects that human beings teach one another, from logic and law to astronomy and medicine; then the *Speculum Historiale*, a world history. The total amounts to 80 books, each of them as long as one of Pliny's papyrus rolls. Vincent is hardly an original thinker, yet as an encyclopedist he ranged widely, citing Greek, Arabic and Hebrew sources almost as readily as Latin.

The religious structure of his work notwithstanding, Vincent would be a gooseberry at Conservapedia; a fish out of water at CreationWiki.

He would be an open-minded but conservative Wikipedian; a creator of many articles.

The second tradition that is plaited into the whole art of encyclopedia-making is the dictionary.

If it's a list of words in alphabetical order, it's a dictionary, and that's all there is to it. If it begins to tells you about the facts and ideas that go with the words – if it has entries for proper names, places, people, historical events – then it's halfway to being an encyclopedia. Pure dictionaries existed in Pliny's time, though not in Latin: encyclopedias of his type were appropriate for Latin, it seems, while dictionaries were appropriate for Greek. The oldest surviving Greek example, compiled in the fifth century by Hesychios of Alexandria, is known simply as *Lexikon* or 'word-book'. It runs to 50,000 entries, most of which are pure dictionary items, with a very few proper names and historical facts interspersed. Hesychios matters because he inspired the next stage: a true encyclopedic dictionary, a vast, anonymous tenth-century compilation called *Souda* ('The Fortress'), one of the great works of Byzantine scholarship. In the 30,000 entries of the *Souda*, just as in modern encyclopedic dictionaries, the biographies and the geographical articles are interspersed with the common-but-difficult words. It is a real encyclopedia in embryo. Author biographies in the *Souda* will often include a confused list of works – some titles duplicated, some omitted – just like a second-rate Wikipedia stub. There will be a note about other people with the same name, just like a Wikipedia disambiguation page.

In the years before search engines, you might easily have let your mind dwell on an alphabetical encyclopedia and reach the conclusion that from A to Z is the sensible, the obvious, the only way to go. In western Europe, in the years between 1499 and 1619, this is how people were thinking. I choose those dates because in 1499, in Milan, the Greek émigré scholar Dimitrios Chalkokondylis produced the first printed edition of the *Souda* (in Greek only). In 1619, in Geneva, the same Greek text was published in parallel with a Latin translation by Emilio Porto, making it accessible not just to classicists but to every well-educated European. Already in 1499 there had been some question as to whether huge medieval encyclopedic manuals like those of Vincent of Beauvais, however well equipped with guides and indexes, could really serve as reference sources in the modern world. People still went on writing such books, but no one claims that they were bestsellers. Thus, by the time that the 1619 *Souda* was issued in alphabetical order with handy Latin translation, fashion had completely dropped the old-style encyclopedias and was taking up the new alphabetical format.

At first these new encyclopedic dictionaries were in Latin. The first English alphabetical encyclopedia arrived in 1704: it was John Harris's *Lexicon technicum, or an universal English dictionary of arts and sciences explaining not only the terms of art, but the arts themselves*. The idea was so successful that it still survives. Look at Ephraim Chambers's *Cyclopaedia, or a universal dictionary of arts and sciences*, first published in 1728; look at the unbeatable 12 handy volumes of *Everyman's Encyclopedia*, begun in 1913, the brainchild of Joseph Malaby Dent; look at its American contemporary, the one-volume *Funk & Wagnalls Encyclopedia* first published in 1912; and then look at *The Cambridge Concise Encyclopedia* – 'instant access', 'like no other' – brand new in 1992. Perhaps the single most successful species in this genus was the large-scale German *Conversations-Lexikon*, begun in 1796, completed in 1808 under the eye of Friedrich Arnold Brockhaus. *Brockhaus* has been regularly revised and reissued ever since. It has spawned adaptations in other languages, including – in English – the *Encyclopedia Americana*, first published in 1829.

Twenty years ago I said, to anyone within reach of a reference desk whisper, that no one had yet invented a reference source faster than a printed alphabetical dictionary, and the *Encyclopaedia Britannica* salesmen were saying very much the same thing.[3] Twenty years ago it may have been true.

The third strand of the modern encyclopedia is the sourcebook.

We have seen approaches to this already. Pliny names his sources (but with no precise citations). Hesychios and the *Souda* quote sources (but not for encyclopedic information). And there was, even before these two, a tradition of listing books by topics to produce a subject catalogue or bibliography: this is what the poet Kallimachos did as librarian at Alexandria, the same Kallimachos who said that 'a big book is a big nuisance'. His catalogue is lost. The great medieval catalogue of al-Nadim, completed in 987 or thereabouts, can still be read by those who really want to. It is an astonishing survey of Arabic written culture, by one who was in an excellent position to compile it: a courtier (al-Nadim means 'the courtier'), son of a bookseller. Outlines of books on every subject, including many translations from Greek and Latin, jostle together with author biographies and brief, pointed quotations, because, in Arabic literature, authority rules.

And so it does in Chinese literature too; but in China, with its emperor-sponsored learning, its official libraries, its millennia of examinations and qualifications, size eventually proved not to matter. In China the just-about-manageable sourcebook (I need but mention *Song sidashu*, 'Four great books of the Song dynasty', compiled around the year 1000 by Li Fang, Wang Qinruo and others and running to 20 million characters or, say, 10 million words) was not enough. The far-from-manageable sourcebook (I will only name *Yongle dadian*, 'Great canon of the Yongle reign', completed in 1408 in 917,480 pages, roughly 50 million characters, never printed and now lost; and *Gujin tushu jicheng*, 'Complete collection of ancient and modern illustrations and books', completed in 1725 by Chen Menglei and Jiang Tingxi in 800,000 pages and 100 million characters; printed in an edition of 60 copies) seemed insufficient. Only in China were these surpassed (step forward, *Siku quanshu*, 'All books from the four treasuries', compiled in 1773–1782 by Ji Yun and Lu Xixiong in 2,300,000 pages and 800 million characters or, say, 400 million words; distributed in an edition of seven copies) by something that could never even have approached manageability until, nearly two centuries after its publication, computerised text searching was invented.

An encyclopedia structured on the 'circle of knowledge' principle, like those of Pliny, Shen Kuo and Vincent of Beauvais, may be very good at explaining any imaginable subject but it falls down because, the bigger the book, the more difficult it becomes to find an individual detail. An alphabetical encyclopedia may be nearly perfect as a means of finding facts quickly but it falls down because, the bigger it gets, the harder it is to pursue related facts and grasp a complete subject area. A sourcebook encyclopedia may be unbeatable in tracing statements to authorities but it falls down because, the bigger the book, the more difficult it gets to relate these statements to one another and to any set of generally accepted facts.

All three types of encyclopedia also have added problems as they get bigger and as the rate of human progress grows. Bigger books are more expensive to produce; they are more complicated to revise; they take up more space.

That's it, then. Now that we've identified the problems we can begin to see what form the solution will take. We must plait the three traditions together into a perfect encyclopedia, logically arranged, quick to access, properly sourced; we must compress all this into a manageable space; we must distribute it widely; we must find a simple way to update it. Then, at last, all knowledge will be at everyone's fingertips. OK. How will we do this?

The first serious attempt to do at least some of these things happened in France in the eighteenth century, under the title *Encyclopédie, ou dictionnaire raisonné des sciences, des arts et des métiers* ('Encyclopaedia, or a systematic dictionary of sciences, arts and professions'). What set out as a French translation of Chambers's *Cyclopaedia* became a far more ambitious undertaking in the hands of its publishers and editors (notably the gifted author Denis Diderot). The result was a set of big volumes that were beautifully laid out and illustrated; they were admired and prized even by the obscurantist churchmen who were attempting to stop their production, and they are still a pleasure to read. The main set is alphabetical, from A (in June 1751) to Zzuéné (volume 17, in December 1765), Zzuéné being the editors' chosen spelling for the historic city of Syene on the Nile. Then come the illustrations, 11 volumes of them, interspersed with explanatory text.

These were in turn followed by a five-volume supplement and a two-volume index. The whole set runs to 18,000 pages and 20 million words.

The difference between this and all previous alphabetical encyclopedias of dictionary type is the generous space allowed for explaining major subjects (such as the sciences and technologies) in long, thorough articles; the difference between this and all previous encyclopedias of circle-of-knowledge type is the alphabetical arrangement. Given its all-too-liberal quotations from literature, the *Encyclopédie* has something of the sourcebook about it too. It sold extremely well – a first edition of nearly 5,000 copies was a remarkable achievement for such a huge work – but it cost too much; it took up too much space; the scattering of illustrations and supplements made it difficult to use. Even the supplement soon began to go out of date, and the attempt to produce an improved and revised version of the whole encyclopedia led to the unmanageable and vastly complicated *Encyclopédie méthodique*, completed (or nearly completed) in 1832 in 124,210 pages. In a half-hearted attempt to bring related topics together this set of volumes was arranged in 88 subject areas – that is, 88 sections each running from A to Z, accompanied by 83 indexes. No overall index ever appeared. The *Encyclopédie méthodique* was a disaster and a dead end.

Luckily the original *Encyclopédie* had meanwhile caught the eye of an Edinburgh publisher, Colin Macfarquhar, who set his Scottish friends to work on an equivalent reference source in English, albeit on a more modest scale. The three fat volumes appeared between 1768 and 1771, and the chosen title shows immediately that Macfarquhar had the French model as well as Chambers's *Cyclopaedia* in mind: he called his new work *Encyclopaedia Britannica, or a dictionary of arts and sciences*.

Pliny's word *encyclopaedia* was clearly much too useful to lose sight of. In the sixteenth century, when reference books of the circle-of-knowledge type were briefly fashionable for the last time, a Latin example appeared in 1541 which was the first that actually claimed in its title to present the 'circle of knowledge' or *cyclopaedia*. That was a slight curtailment of the Greek word based on a variant text of Pliny's preface. The first self-proclaimed presentation of the 'full circle of knowledge' or *encyclopaedia* followed soon after in 1559. In 1728 Ephraim Chambers went for the briefer term once more. Diderot and his publishers preferred to name their work *Encyclopédie* 'the full circle of knowledge', a newly-coined French adaptation of Pliny's word. The next step was taken by Colin Macfarquhar when he created the Latin phrase *Encyclopaedia Britannica* as the title of his projected work. By this time the word *encyclopaedia* had given up its original sense: his title can't really be intended as 'the British full circle of knowledge', a not-very-meaningful concept. What had happened was that, thanks to the fame of the French *Encyclopédie*, the word 'encyclopedia' had begun to mean, as it still does today, 'a large-scale reference book in alphabetical order'. Macfarquhar's *Encyclopaedia Britannica* is, quite simply, 'the British encyclopedia'.

The *Britannica*'s first three-volume edition was followed by eight others,[4] gradually increasing in size. All of them retained the great feature that Diderot's work had suggested but (thanks to the separate illustrations and supplement) hadn't quite attained – a single alphabetical order, including both long and short articles. From the seventh edition onwards, in 1827, *Britannica* had indexes as well, but there was often no need to use them. The ninth edition (25 volumes; completed in 1889) and the eleventh edition (29 volumes; issued in 1910–1911) are classics of Scottish and American publishing. They were mammoth undertakings, much too big to revise rapidly. For this reason they were followed by reprints plus supplements which kept them on the market for even longer than they really deserved.

Reprints plus supplements were never quite good enough. Up-to-dateness remained the problem. And so, with the fourteenth edition, *Britannica* (now published in Chicago) took an astonishing leap of faith. From 1936 onwards there was to be a new printing every year, in each of which a selection of articles would be updated. But *Britannica* by this time ran to 25 volumes, each of 1,000 pages. To produce annual revisions of such a large reference set needed massive investment built on steady sales. There had to be a sustained marketing drive to sell the encyclopedia to a far broader market: hence the famous doorstep encyclopedia salesmen of the mid-twentieth century. But the new approach brought two tricky problems. First, although you might persuade libraries to buy a new edition every year or every few years (and many libraries did), it was harder to sell that idea to the home market. The answer to this was an idea borrowed from the competing *Encyclopedia Americana*: a series of annual *Year Books*, to which individual buyers as well as libraries were supposed to subscribe. Not many people ever bothered to use them, but they served in theory to keep any annual issue of the enyclopedia up to date. The second problem was slower to manifest itself: perhaps it was not even foreseen at the start. The more successfully the salesmen sold new *Britannicas*, the more the world was weighed down with old *Britannicas*. The more of them there were, the cheaper they became. One annual issue looked very much like another, and people soon discovered that a slightly used set of *Britannicas* was very nearly as good as a new set while costing a small fraction of the price. Sales initially held up well, but eventually, in the 1960s, they faltered. By the end of that decade it was clear that the only solution, from the marketing point of view, would be to build on the *Britannica* name and offer an edition that was really new and could be shown to be different.

The fifteenth edition in 30 volumes, published in 1974, demonstrated its newness by dropping the single alphabetical order. There were henceforth to be separate sequences of long, thorough articles and short, quick-reference articles, with very little cross-referencing between the two. An additional guide (to the long articles only) was to be found in the so-called 'Propaedia', a volume-length diagram of the circle of knowledge. This is a self-indulgence that several earlier editors of encyclopedias had also allowed themselves, though few readers thanked them for it. Annual revisions were abandoned but the *Year Books* continued. Amazingly, there was to be no index. The plan was fatally flawed. Ten years later, in 1984, this was tacitly acknowledged when a two-volume index was added to the set. Since that date *Britannica* has consisted of 32 volumes arranged in four sections, one of which is laid out systematically while each of the other three has an A–Z sequence. And from time to time the whole set is revised and reissued – but just how often this happens isn't easy for the casual enquirer to find out.

Strangely, therefore – and not by inexorable logic but for marketing reasons – *Britannica* with its three alphabetical sequences and its initial almost-useless diagram of the circle of knowledge has begun to work backwards towards the more complicated model of the *Encyclopédie*. This is not damning criticism. The *Encyclopédie* was a magnificent creation; the modern *Britannica* is pretty good too. This is a sign, though, that no printed encyclopedia can ever solve all the problems that we identified earlier. For *Britannica* in 1974, two steps towards logical arrangement and thorough explanation meant one step away from quick access and one step back from frequent updating.

Almost on cue, a new kind of solution began to emerge, one that didn't involve print.

The electronic encyclopedia burst on to the scene in two forms. At first the most practical seemed to be the CD-ROM. Remember *The New Grolier Electronic Encyclopedia*, which ran from 1985 to 2003? Remember *Compton's Family Encyclopedia*? Compton's had long been owned by *Britannica*, so this was *Britannica's* earliest venture into electronic publishing, and it ran from 1989 to 1998. Maybe you remember these, maybe you don't. But you certainly remember *Encarta*, which came along afterwards. *Encarta*, offspring of the all-powerful Microsoft, was dreamed up in the late 1980s as an answer to the *New Grolier*. Microsoft bought the electronic rights to *Funk & Wagnalls Encyclopedia* and afterwards to *Collier's Encyclopedia*. Microsoft was good at software and rich enough not to care whether *Encarta* on its own was profitable. The firm developed *Encarta* beautifully (while displaying 'casual disregard for quality work' in the estimate of Robert McHenry, editor-in-chief of the rival *Britannica*)[5] and began to distribute it in 1993. *Encarta* was sold cheap and bundled liberally. It swept the market.

So you may well not remember that *Encyclopedia Americana* (originally a clone of the *Conversations-Lexikon*, first published 1829) produced a CD-ROM version in 1995. What was really noteworthy was that when *Encyclopaedia Britannica* itself appeared in a CD-ROM version, in 1994, it would not fit comfortably on one disc: a big nuisance to any home user, but a clear sign to observant readers that it contained far more text, far more information, than *Encarta* at a very similar price.

The CD-ROMs were an approach to a solution, but they brought a new problem with them. They were distributed widely, and achieved this by setting very low prices, forced to do so by *Encarta*. *Britannica* on CD-ROM, briefly marketed at $1500, soon dropped to $200: by about 1999, if you knew where to ask, you could get *Britannica* free. Sales of printed encyclopedias plummeted.

Meanwhile – even before the first of the CD-ROMs – encyclopedias had been experimenting with an alternative electronic format. The first of them was the *American Academic Encyclopedia* (of which the *New Grolier* was an adaptation): experimentally this was available on the internet as early as 1980 (at a date when the internet was largely a resource for universities and scientific projects). Compuserve subscribers could access the *American Academic* from 1981, and Lexis/Nexis subscribers got a restricted version of the *Encyclopaedia Britannica* in the same year. It was the coming of the world wide web, from 1991 onwards, that encouraged livelier and more generally useful developments of this kind. *Encyclopaedia Britannica Online* arrived in 1994, in the same year as its first CD-ROM edition, though it wasn't offered at a price to attract home users until 1995; by that time *Encarta*, too, was online. The venerable *Encyclopedia Americana* appeared on the web in 1998. By about 2005 nearly all the people who might once have bought a printed encyclopedia could find it online. Printed sales fell further, and, as online access became simpler and quicker, sales of CD-ROMs gradually faltered in turn. Most of the modern encyclopedias charge a subscription for web access, but the higher the subscription, the more potential purchasers are inclined to look for alternative, free, sources of the information they need.

It's worth noting that after 2000, as disk storage became rapidly cheaper and optical character recognition improved, some of the greatest of the historic encyclopedias arrived on the web to join their modern competitors. The admired 1911 *Britannica*, the classic eleventh edition, went online in 2002. The eighteenth-century French *Encyclopédie* now has a well-crafted website. Vincent of Beauvais's thirteenth-century *Speculum Maius* is available too, hosted in the Netherlands; a more recent Latin encyclopedia, the 1698 *Lexicon Universale* of J. J. Hofmann, is hosted by a German university. Shen

Kuo's eleventh-century Chinese encyclopedia, *Mengxi bitan*, is available in full (if you read classical Chinese) through Project Gutenberg and at Wikisource. Even the enormous *Siku quanshu*, at 800 million characters the largest printed encyclopedia in the world, now exists in a searchable online version.

These are spectacular resources for scholars and historians. But for modern reference sources the online solution was in danger of being worse than the problem. Encyclopedias had become ever more widely accessible, not only to those who might formerly have bought them, but to those who might once have expected to find them in a library, and to millions who would never have thought of using a printed encyclopedia at all. They had driven one another down and down in price. Yes, it was possible to make existing text available at such prices, but it was never going to be profitable in these market conditions to produce a new encyclopedia or even a thoroughly revised one. So what would the future hold? Were the electronic encyclopedias destined henceforth to remain as limited as *Encarta* (paid for from Microsoft's surplus) or to become as outdated as the 1911 *Britannica*? Would people who were looking for full and up-to-date information be increasingly condemned to search engines and to sources of doubtful reliability? Or could there be another answer?

There was, as Douglas Adams had foreseen in the 1978 radio series *The Hitchhiker's Guide to the Galaxy* and in the books that followed it. The imagined *Guide*, which gave the title to his series, was an electronic encyclopedia. Not only that; not only did it compete successfully with the staid *Encyclopedia Galactica* although it 'has many omissions and contains much that is apocryphal, or at least wildly inaccurate'; the *Guide* also had an innovative editorial method. 'Most of the actual work got done by any passing stranger who happened to wander into the empty offices of an afternoon and saw something worth doing.'[6]

By the 1990s the word 'encyclopedia' was so closely associated with the kind of reference source we're talking about that no one would risk abandoning it. But computer people love to abbreviate. The first such project to be presented as potential fact was *Interpedia*, in 1993. The name (a portmanteau word, a mixture of 'internet' and 'encyclopedia') was invented by R. L. Samuell, but the idea was devised by Rick Gates, a pioneer of online reference, and Mike Salmon, one of those who still saw the whole internet as a potential encyclopedia.[7] *Interpedia* was... what exactly? The articles? The software that would index them? Eventually it was neither of these: it was never more than a project. And the same is true of its successor, *The Distributed Encyclopedia*. That 1997 idea still has a website, incidentally, but the page 'How to contribute' was clearly written in another universe, one in which the contributor must 'contact us, before you start writing'; then 'write your essay and bring it into an HTML-compliant form'; 'then 'find a computer that is connected to the internet and has a World Wide Web Server program running'; then 'mail us the headword and the URL of your essay... (don't worry if it's not your own account and you do not know the exact computer name or path, the owner of the account will help you certainly)'. What fun it would have been! *The Distributed Encyclopedia* ran to three articles, 'Linux', 'Sherry' and 'Sauna', all written by a software consultant and serial encyclopedia addict currently known on the German Wikipedia as Ulrich.fuchs.

A little closer to reality, at least briefly, was Nupedia, the last gasp of twentieth century encyclopedia-making. It matters here because of its ambitious parents and its remarkable offspring. It grew out of a conversation between Jimmy Wales, business graduate turned options trader, and Larry Sanger. Both were philosophy buffs and internet enthusiasts; Wales had set up a successful internet portal called Bomis. His real long-term ambition, though, was to create an online encyclopedia. He put Sanger to work on it. With Nupedia, launched from San Diego in March 2000, they claimed to be 'building the finest encyclopedia in the history of humankind' and also 'the world's largest encyclopedia'.[8] The name may simply suggest 'new encyclopedia'; it may also suggest 'GNU' and a link with the open content movement championed by Richard Stallman. Whatever its name meant, Nupedia invited experts to volunteer articles, which, once submitted, would go through an exacting peer-review and revision process. Two years later the site boasted 24 completed articles, and, yes, it would actually have become the world's largest encyclopedia if this rate of progress had been maintained for 5,000 years. That's assuming no other project overtook it meanwhile.

Just as the new century dawned, in a posting to the 2,000 or so eager members of the Nupedia mailing list, Sanger proposed 'to add a little feature to Nupedia'. This would be a supplementary site on which drafts and sketches for articles could be developed rapidly in a totally informal way. Once an article has been begun 'anyone else (yes, absolutely anyone else) can come along and make absolutely any changes to it that he wants to. The editing interface is very simple; anyone intelligent enough to write or edit a Nupedia article will be able to figure it out without any trouble. On the page I create, I can link to any other pages, and of course anyone can link to mine... Jimmy Wales thinks that many people might find the idea objectionable, but I think not,' Sanger added.[9]

The crucial added requirement was the software that would allow absolutely anyone to edit an existing page. This software was already in use – Sanger and Wales had just been introduced to it – notably at a discussion-and-resource site for software developers, WikiWikiWeb.[10] That site's strange name was a compound of 'web' and *wikiwiki*, a Hawaiian adverb meaning 'fast', adopted by the programmer Ward Cunningham (he recalled once having been told at Honolulu airport to catch the *wikiwiki* bus that circulates between the terminals). There are now thousands of wikis on the web, from specialised 'encyclopedias' on *Star Trek* to collaborative travel guides; there are many others that ordinary surfers never see, restricted to private networks operated by big organisations, such as *Intellipedia*, the CIA's non-public encyclopedia put together collaboratively by its staff and agents. At that time there was hardly any of this. There was WikiWikiWeb – a lively but quirky and very specialised site used only by computer buffs – and practically nothing else.

In spite of nagging doubts, Wales gave the go-ahead for a wiki supplement to Nupedia. On 10 January 2001, the same day on which Sanger had made his suggestion on the mailing list, The Wikipedia existed; on 15 January it was modestly launched. By 22 January there were 184 articles. Two months later Sanger was able to report, in an informal newsletter sent to the Nupedia mailing list, that there were already '2,953 (yes, 2,953) pages in Wikipedia.

Of these, 1,816 are relatively substantial articles. We started in January 2001, so we've made incredible progress – even we are surprised. Maybe you think that Wikipedia would end up being a rather low-quality product, since it's open to everyone. But perhaps it's the fact that it is open to everyone that makes a lot of these articles in fact not so bad,' he concluded modestly.[11]

The orotund style typical of very long encyclopedia articles was not much seen in those early days. On 15 March Cdani (an eager Wikipedian: *I'm from Andorra, a little country between Spain and France. I like to play chess and win you*) created the article **Military of Andorra**, which read, in total, *No military. Depends on Spain and France.* On 2 November Jimbo Wales (yes, it was he) created the article **Jimbo Wales**, which read, *The best place to learn about who am I is at my website www.jimmywales.com.*

But Sanger was right. There were also, already, some substantial articles, with an unexpected emphasis on philosophy and philosophers, a subject that (being Sanger's and Wales's area of special interest) was also one of the initial features of Nupedia.

Overall, Wales could pride himself on having taken rapid steps towards his long-term ambition. By Christmas 2001 he was the proprietor of a new, collaborative encyclopedia running to 20,000 pages and growing with ever-increasing speed. In November a heart-warming statistical digest had been circulated to users:

The number of people (unique IPs) that have edited Wikipedia on any given day of October ranged from 96 to 236... After the recently increased traffic from Google, it seems we can expect an average number of daily editors of about 170. We can expect this number to continue to climb, however, as the virtuous cycle of content–traffic–contributors–more content continues into the indefinite future. The number of unique visitors (editors or not) ranged from 3,112 to 7,983 in October... the post-October 28 average is shaping up to be something like 8,000. The latter is not expected to decline, because it is not due to press coverage, but instead to (we expect) stable and growing factors related to the amount of traffic Google sends us.[12]

Aside from the Google effect, the site had already earned good publicity, including a marvellously positive article by Steven Johnson in the *New York Times Magazine*. There were intermittent glitches but, most days, the wiki software made everything work – quickly, easily and very cheaply. Disk space and server load were minimal. It sometimes seemed that Wikipedia ran itself: the expanding army of volunteers didn't just write articles but also made links, carried out all kinds of housekeeping chores, and apparently enjoyed it. Douglas Adams's prediction that the founding editor of an electronic encyclopedia would, one day soon, 'explore the role of the editorial lunch-break' with the result that most of the work would be done by 'any passing stranger' who 'saw something worth doing', was well on the way to realisation.[13]

One tiny detail will have darkened the picture for Wales. Larry Sanger, though not sole creator, had got sole credit in the *New York Times Magazine*, and Sanger probably would not have objected too strongly to this if he had been asked about it in advance. 'I played a larger part than anyone in developing the formula', he insisted in September 2002.[14]

At this distance, his estimate can neither be confirmed nor denied. But had he ever felt like claiming that he was essential to Wikipedia's success, such a claim was soon to be tested. A dot.com bubble burst. Bomis Inc., Jimmy Wales's internet portal, ran short of money, and Sanger, just married, lost his salaried post in January 2002. 'We might earmark money to hire a fulltime editor again, although in the wikipedia system, this seems unnecessary,' Wales wrote soon afterwards, a remark that was echoed more publicly by Eloquence (then an observant Wikipedian of three months' standing, later to be Deputy Director of the Foundation). Sanger's 'frequent engagement in disputes was criticized by many other "Wikipedians" as too aggressive', Eloquence wrote on an IT news site; 'many felt that his authoritative tone was unnecessary and in contradiction to Wikipedia's goals. This may well be the right time to abandon the concept of "editorship" altogether.'[15] Sanger continued as a volunteer for a month, then resigned 'as editor-in-chief of Nupedia and [from] any position of authority I had with Wikipedia.' His resignation letter and later comments, addressed to those on the mailing lists, make clear his frustration that owing to the demands of Wikipedia he had allowed Nupedia to 'grow moribund'. The original project was 'currently "on hold" at best'. Although he dreamed of returning to the paid editorship if finance allowed, 'I'm not holding my breath'; but only in such a way, or by the appointment of some other volunteer editor, could Nupedia be revived. Turning to Wikipedia, Sanger in resigning expressed the 'hope that it can find its way forward without my involvement... Don't take my departure as an excuse to leave yourself,' he admonished the Wikipedians; his decision 'should not be taken as a reflection on Wikipedia... It still might succeed brilliantly.' A scintilla of doubt can be read between the lines here, because Sanger, however great his contribution to the birth of Wikipedia, was a Nupedia man at heart. He recognised, however, that it was Wikipedia that had truly engaged Jimmy Wales's enthusiasm. 'The continuing success of Wikipedia in my absence – which doesn't surprise me – makes it hard to justify my return as a paid lead/organizer,' Sanger wrote in July. 'It's a great thing Jimbo has made it his hobby and is supporting it as he always has. Nupedia is a different matter, of course. I'm still unemployed, by the way.'[16]

Why the difference? In hindsight Nupedia was an idea from the times when the internet was the preserve of academics and researchers. The 'philosophy PhD called Larry Sanger' saw as natural a site calling for volunteer contributions that was unashamedly elitist in its editorial principles and worked on the assumption that most of its volunteers would be PhDs writing on topics close to the subject of their doctorates.[17] Sanger hasn't given up this approach. He went on to animate encyclopedia sites run on similar lines, including the Encyclopedia of Earth and his current project, the oddly-named Citizendium. But the web was moving in another direction. The academic and research stuff is still up there, but so is the wholly personal, utterly non-academic, unashamedly commercial and certifiably insane stuff produced by everyone else. The academy doesn't rule (if it ever did). Even in the earliest years, and even among stalwarts of the Nupedia/ Wikipedia matrix, there were many who did not share Sanger's views. As early as October 2001, Jimmy Wales was ready to admit that he was one of them, describing the Wikipedia idea in one posting as *a separate project specifically for people like you (and me!) who are intimidated and bored (sorry,*

Nupedia!) with the tedium of the process of getting Nupedia articles written.[18] Then, in September 2002, in response to a comment from the academic but reasonable JHK about nitpicking among Nupedia's cliquish editors, the technician Brion Vibber (Wikipedia's sole employee) wrote: *Nupedia may well be wonderful, but I have zero interest in it. I first heard of it a few months before I got involved in Wikipedia; I went to the site... and got the distinct impression that I wasn't welcome unless I had a PhD*; and in reply to that brief reminiscence Wales himself chimed in.

Let me tell you my story :-), he began. He had completed the coursework, but not the dissertations, in two PhD programs in finance – specifically in option pricing theory – and had published an academic paper *in a real journal. This was not an important contribution to the literature,* Wales continued modestly, but it was a respectable enough publication for a graduate student. He then worked for a few years as a futures and options trader in Chicago. On Nupedia, logically enough, he volunteered to write a short biography of Robert Merton, founder of option pricing theory and winner of a Nobel prize. With adequate sources anyone ought to have been able to write such a biography; for Wales it ought to have been easy. And yet, when he sat down to write the article, he was overtaken by writer's block, an astonishing affliction for someone whose regular work involved writing emails and reports almost non-stop, eight hours a day, five days a week. *The fact is,* he admitted, *I was intimidated by the sheer snobbery and credentialism of Nupedia. And I had an inside track. The editor-in-chief worked for me. Everyone on the project knew who I was. I could expect to be given softball reviews and easy acceptance. Even so, I found the process just intimidating enough to find excuses not to write that simple article. – Jimbo*[19]

Since those were the views of the man who owned and paid for it, it can be no surprise that Nupedia eventually slipped to the bottom of the priority list. There was no relaunch. The site was shut down in September 2003.

But Wikipedia, Sanger's 'idea' that became Wales's 'hobby', went from strength to strength. One telegraphic paragraph of statistics and growth rates will show this well enough. Launched on 15 January 2001, in one week it had 184 articles; it passed 1,000 articles around 12 February 2001. Within two months it had 2,953 articles; in six months, 6,000; in nine months, nearly 13,000. Within a year, over 20,000 encyclopedia entries had been started, a rate of over 1,500 articles per month, and there were 350 registered users (and an unknown number who edited anonymously). On 30 August 2002, the article count reached 40,000; in 2003 it passed 100,000 articles, and in January 2004 it reached the 200,000 article milestone (it was about the football manager **Neil Warnock**, incidentally). The rate now began to increase, eventually approaching and even surpassing 100,000 per month. On 7 July 2004 article number 300,000 was begun; on 20 November 2004 number 400,000; on 18 March 2005 number 500,000 (this article was **Involuntary settlements in the Soviet Union**). The next milestone might have seemed nearly unattainable in Wikipedia's first year, but on 1 March 2006 Wikipedia passed the 1,000,000 article mark. First past the post was **Jordanhill railway station**, and I remember looking at it on that day. It's not a bad page. On 24 November 2006 Wikipedia reached 1,500,000 with the obscure **Kanab ambersnail**. Obscure but, by definition, notable; all species merit Wikipedia articles. The rate of increase is now perceptibly slowing but remains awesome at well over 1 article per minute, 1,700 articles per day or about 50,000 per month. Two million was reached on 9 September 2007 with **El Hormiguero**, an undoubtedly notable Spanish television series. On 12 August 2008 Wikipedia reached 2,500,000; on 20 March 2009 there were 2,800,000 articles. By the time this book appears three million will certainly have been attained.

Long ago the encyclopedia concept, along with the name, began to pass from language to language, and it went on doing so as book-knowledge spread across cultures and across the world.

There was a time (Pliny's time) when nearly everyone in the Mediterranean region who wanted to read an encyclopedic dictionary was able to read Greek, and nearly everyone who wanted to read the full-circle-of-knowledge could read Latin. The Roman Empire had a bilingual culture in which the small number of people who had the time and inclination for study were sure to be competent in those two languages. In medieval and Renaissance Europe,

Latin continued to rule. In and around China, from ancient to modern times, everyone who had the time and inclination to use an encyclopedia was able to read Chinese characters. And so, for nearly two millennia, Greek, Latin and Chinese apparently reached the potential market. Perhaps, if only the sketchiest equivalents of the great early encyclopedias are to be found in other historic languages – Arabic, Sanskrit and others – it is because readers and scholars in those languages did not feel the need for reference books of this type. Perhaps, up to the eighteenth century, those three languages were nearly enough. Let's remember that the French title of the great *Encyclopédie* was a newly invented word; until 1751 the concept had scarcely been expressed in French. English also had no word for it, and Greek and Latin titles – *Lexicon, Cyclopaedia, Encyclopaedia* – had to be used in English as names for the early encyclopedias. German, rather long-windedly, invented a new term made up of Greek and Latin elements, *Conversations-Lexikon*.

The modern English, French and German encyclopedias now exist in book form, on CD-ROM and online. Meanwhile in the nineteenth and twentieth centuries encyclopedias were begun in a surprising number of other languages, from Burmese to Swahili. Many of them were not only begun but triumphantly completed. But the smaller the number of speakers, the smaller the market for a big, expensive set of reference books and the greater the effort needed to keep it up to date. These smaller-language encyclopedias soon become tired, dated and dusty on library shelves. People are tempted to turn to the alternatives, the nearly-new *Britannicas* and their French and German equivalents. If this goes on happening a whole potential field of activity will be lost to minority languages and the day of their extinction will be brought closer... unless we can somehow add an extra element to our design for the perfect encyclopedia: it must be available in any language that potential readers want to use.

Jimmy Wales had foreseen this requirement and went to work on it just two months after Wikipedia was launched. On 16 March 2001 he announced to the mailing list: *I want to set up some alternative language wikipedias. French and German would be good, and Cdani has offered to not inflict his terrible English on us if we make a Catalan wikipedia. :-) I intend to setup the following domain names and wikis*; he names French, German,

Spanish and Japanese, with a caveat about web-accessible page names in Japanese script and concludes: *Anyhow, it seems like a useful thing to do this.*[20] Fifteen minutes later the German Wikipedia was in existence. Within two hours Clifford Adams, author of the UseModWiki software that Wikipedia was then using, reported that he was developing a translation facility for localising the interface (he also confirmed that wiki software was being used successfully elsewhere with Japanese text). And less than a day later there was a Catalan wikipedia too. By 3.41 on 17 March Cdani was hard at work developing brief articles: he worked systematically in alphabetical order from **ca:Àbac** ('abacus'), the oldest item in the Catalan database, towards **ca:Cafè**. Japanese appeared soon afterwards (but in Romaji at first, not Japanese script). The Catalan, German and Japanese Wikipedias were linked on the page **International Wikipedia** as early as 6 April 2001. *At the present time, I plan to create new wikis for each langauge only 'upon request' – but it only takes me 10 minutes to do it, so don't hesitate to request,* Wales promised anonymously on that page.

On 11 May another eight non-English wikipedias were enabled on the server. These eight, following after Catalan, Japanese and German, were Chinese, Esperanto, French, Hebrew, Italian, Portuguese, Russian and Spanish. The first French article, on the physicist **fr:Paul Héroult**, appeared on 19 May. Before the year's end all these languages were well underway and they had been joined by nine more: Afrikaans, Arabic, Basque, Danish, Dutch, Hungarian, Norwegian, Polish and Swedish, according to the 5 December 2001 revision of the same **International Wikipedia** page. The speed with which new languages were being accommodated demonstrates the extremely low storage demand, server load and maintenance costs of websites that run wiki software.

Some curious choices among the next six (Czech, Estonian, Frisian[!], Interlingua[!], Latin[!] and Slovene, all of them active by September 2002), go far to confirm that only one requirement for a new language wikipedia existed at that time: Jimmy Wales had to be persuaded that someone would start writing it, and he was easy to persuade. The Swedish and German Wikipedias at first relied heavily on one editor each (LinusTolke and StefanRybo). Admittedly linguistic knowledge wasn't all that widespread among early Wikipedians: the same StefanRybo asked a mailing list in July 2001 *Hi all! Why is there no Indian wikipedia? Mit freundlichen Gruessen*, admitting, when Wales set out to introduce him concisely to the linguistic maelstrom that is India, *You are right... I do not know what languages are spoken in india. I was just reading a world population statistics.*[21] Even Sanger, who knew a good deal more, was surprisingly complacent in claiming that the December 2001 round of enlargement covered *all the other major languages*.

Never mind that. The vision of a multilingual encyclopedia for a multilingual world remained, and this is worth emphasising, because the United States in general is not world-famous for encouraging the survival of minority languages. There are even people in the US who argue that English is enough for the world. Jimmy Wales and Larry Sanger are clearly not among them. Bomis handed on the torch to the Wikimedia Foundation on 20 June 2003, with Wales as the Foundation's first chairman, but Wikipedia's multilingual commitment continued. In the first nine months of 2004 the wikipedias doubled in total size, from 450,000 articles at the beginning of January to 1,000,000 in September. By that time 105 languages were represented, and the English Wikipedia accounted for less than half of the article total. The millionth, incidentally, is said to have been a Hebrew article that corresponds to the English **Flag of Kazakhstan**.

If I was right, previously, in my estimate that *Siku quanshu* contains 400 million words ('word' is a difficult concept in Chinese), and if the Wikimedia statisticians are right in their most recent calculations, the wikipedias overtook *Siku quanshu* around March 2005 and thus became, collectively, the largest encyclopedia the world has ever known.[22] In a TV interview during 2005 Jimmy Wales observed that according to Alexa.com Wikipedia was the fortieth busiest website in the world: 'if you compare us to the *New York Times*, the *Washington Post*, *USA Today*, we're larger than all of those, but, even more than that, we're larger than all of those combined.'[23]

By 2007 there were 250 different language wikipedias, with a total of 7,500,000 articles and 1.74 billion words. In April 2008 the 10 millionth article was created (in Hungarian, it is said). This means that between 2004 and 2008 the article pool, in all the wikipedias together, was growing at just over 200,000 per month. Nearly three-quarters of this figure is accounted for by articles that are not in English.

Some of the individual wikipedias are now themselves huge encyclopedias, bigger than anything previously available in those languages. German has always been the second largest, reaching 10,000 articles on 24 January 2003 and 900,000 on 4 May 2009, the day before I wrote this sentence. French keeps in step but never quite catches up: the French Wikipedia is likely to reach 800,000 articles on 6 May, the day after I write this. Anthere, a very early contributor and one of the first three admins of the French Wikipedia, succeeded Wales as president of the Wikimedia Foundation from 2005 to 2008 and was lionised in the French media (well, in one regional newspaper, anyway) as 'the ant who became queen of the encyclopedia'.[24]

The non-English wikipedias, however successful, all have fewer editors and fewer users than you would expect from the number of speakers of each language. There are at least three reasons for this: the problems of web access, the consequences of global multilingualism, and the simple fact that the English Wikipedia is the biggest and busiest. People who use the web are younger than average, more educated than average, more likely than most to be bilingual in English or, at least, good at English. They expect to use the web partly in English, and are likely to try English words in searches. They gravitate towards the big, ever-changing English Wikipedia.

The Chinese Wikipedia is far smaller than would be expected because web access is limited in China (and access to the Wikipedia site has been blocked there for long periods); also because many overseas Chinese can use English just as easily as Chinese; also because many find it easier to type in English. The wikipedias in Indian languages are relatively small, in spite of large numbers of speakers, because of the widespread use of English in India. The wikipedias in African languages are tiny because of difficulties of internet access and the common use of English and French in many African countries. The few wikipedias in native American languages are struggling for any audience at all because speakers are few and they expect to use either English or Spanish in education and writing. There are wikipedias in a surprising number of European minority languages; some are fairly successful, but many are very weak. An audience survey of the use of wikipedias in Spain showed 68 per cent using Spanish, 1.52 per cent using Catalan, 0.45 per cent Galician and 0.19 per cent Basque. The remainder – just under 30 per cent – covers users of English and all other wikipedias, including the minute number who look at the wikipedias in the minority local languages of Spain.[25] These figures can be compared with the percentages speaking each language as mother tongue: 73 per cent Spanish, 17 per cent Catalan, 8 per cent Galician and 2 per cent Basque. They were bad news for the editors of the apparently thriving Catalan Wikipedia, the third to be created, now growing at 50,000 articles per year and within sight of the milestone of 175,000; equally bad news for the Basque Wikipedia, which also began early, has shown steady growth and is well on the way to 40,000 articles.

All the minority language wikipedias have poor usage statistics by comparison with the really large ones. These statistics are indeed bad news, and not only because one likes one's work to be appreciated. The world of wikipedias is small but, as we shall see, extremely influential and well worth belonging to. Within this world there are league tables; there is pressure to develop every wikipedia, to copy material from one to another, to increase the number of edits, the number of 'hits' and 'pageviews', the number of articles, the length of articles, the number of illustrations – even though a reference source is not always better for being bigger and an article is often the worse for being longer; even though, as all 265 wikipedias grow to the size of the English one, the problems of serving the internal links, displaying the pictures, updating the inter-language links, in response to an ever-increasing volume of traffic, threaten to become unmanageable. The idea of sustainability has not yet reached the Wikipedia world.

The growth from about 20 languages in late 2002, to 250 by the end of 2006, was perhaps too rapid. It was followed by a period of, shall we say, reflection: a language subcommittee was set up (in September 2006), it developed a policy, and new proposals began to jump through the newly-devised hoops. Some were rapidly halted; hence although there are wikipedias in Anglo-Saxon, Gothic and Old Church Slavonic there is none in Ancient Greek because, about the time Ancient Greek was being proposed, the subcommittee quietly ruled out ancient languages. Bad luck.

Rules are for bureaucrats: the first rule of Wikipedia is Ignore All Rules. Still, when someone asks to be allowed to start a wikipedia in another language there has to be a way of deciding whether to say yes. Installing a new language requires a lot more than just ten minutes' work on the server. The MediaWiki software interface (mainly the messages presented to users) ought to be translated, because users of a reference website in one language with an interface partly in another may be unable to understand it fully and may conclude that the site is unprofessional. This translation can be done by volunteers (the same people who create the encyclopedia); volunteer editors will also be the ones who adjust articles and interwiki links in all the other wikipedias to insert the necessary information about the new one. But each language makes new demands on the programmers, and their time has to be paid for. It's necessary to judge whether the resources and effort put into each new language will be repaid by the eventual creation of a worthwhile encyclopedia.

At the very least, it was obvious by mid 2006 that a higher threshold for approval was needed and that (as Bèrto d'Sèra put it) *starting new language projects should be very much a predictable process based on objective criteria: nowadays it is not.*[26] Requests for wikipedias that must have appeared reasonable to someone in the old days look utterly unreasonable in hindsight. Take, if you will, the Siberian Wikipedia. Just as StefanRybo learned that there is no Indian language, so the Wikimedia Foundation learned that there is no Siberian language; but they learned it too late, after setting up the Siberian Wikipedia to be the plaything of a few Russian speakers with peculiar racial views.[27] Or take the Klingon Wikipedia, whose existence, as it soon became clear, would serve only to make Wikipedia look ridiculous, not only because no one really speaks Klingon (the same is true of Latin, Sanskrit, Classical Chinese and Simple English), not only because Klingon is an invented language (the same is true of Esperanto, Ido, Interlingua and Volapük), but because (quite unlike those others) it has no purpose in the real world: it is an incomplete language never intended to serve as anything but an element in a fictional universe. And in fact these two oddities, Klingon and Siberian, have now at last been expelled from the community of wikipedias, although the material written for them was not deleted; it can still be tracked down elsewhere on the web.[28]

Or take, if you prefer, the wikipedias in the languages of former central Yugoslavia. There was once, it was generally agreed, a Serbo-Croat language (written in two alternative scripts). Since the break-up of Yugoslavia it is just as widely agreed that there exist Serbian, Croatian and Bosnian languages, the differences between them now maximised where once they were minimised. In current political circumstances it is not really surprising that there should be three wikipedias, one each for Serbian, Croatian and Bosnian; nor is it surprising that all three are about the same size, because it is the easiest thing in the world to copy text among them. What is a little surprising is that there are in fact four wikipedias, because in addition to the expected three there is one in 'Serbo-Croatian' as well. It seemed superfluous to Andre Engels, who described it as *intended to be dead*, noted the spread of vandalism on it, and in February 2005 abruptly locked it with the message *that one can go to sr:, hr: or bs: instead*. After gentle protest it was reopened on 23 June of the same year. *There is still people who is not nationalist and believe in one language*, the protester refreshingly insisted.[29] Perhaps, had there only ever been one wikipedia in this language complex, its talk pages would have been filled to overflowing with inter-Slavic hatred; or perhaps the hatred would have exhausted itself and a single Serbo-Croat Wikipedia would by now have been bigger and better than all four of them. We won't know.

As the worldwide popularity of Wikipedia grew, it became fashionable to argue the case that any linguistic community 'deserves' a wikipedia. The language (whichever it may be) ought to continue to be used, and it ought to be saved from extinction; an internet community using the language will help to achieve these aims (which is perfectly true); therefore the Wikimedia Foundation ought to encourage the rescue mission by opening a wikipedia in the language. Enthusiasts can use this line of reasoning to propose new wikipedias even though they themselves cannot write the language concerned. An example currently under discussion is Manchu, an almost-extinct historic language of China. Viskonsas, stalwart of the wikipedia in

Samogitian (a little-known dialect of Lithuanian), who happened to have noticed the language subcommittee's Manchu discussion, chipped in with a very sensible question: *Can anybody out here speak this language?* The original proposer, Whlee, a perfume chemist and native French speaker who claims advanced knowledge of English, offered a reply: *As you can see i'm trying to learn Manchu language it is not easy but remain feasible.* Whlee, though a self-confessed beginner in Chinese, is a keen supporter of wikipedia proposals for minority languages of China and therefore a veteran of these discussions. Since no Manchu speaker was ever heard from, it was possibly unnecessary to add a further objection – that the Manchu script, which runs vertically, cannot at present be edited in the wiki system. *How will do you computerize this wiki?* asked Yes0song, regular contributor in English and Korean. *We will make a Main Page containing translitterated form*, Whlee suggested; but Yu Hai, who edits in English and Chinese, insisted that delay is called for in this case. *No, no romanlized article. Create it until it uses tradition Manchu script.*[30] As I write, the final decision has not yet been made.

The real issue has nothing to do with whether we (any of us) deserve a wikipedia: it is much simpler. A single enthusiast can ask for a wikipedia, but it needs more than one fluent writer to create it. Even in the case of international languages some virtual communities took a long time to gather around their wikipedias. The original group of Spanish contributors suddenly panicked in early 2002 at the possibility that Wikipedia would succumb to commercialism and would be vulnerable to censorship. Most of them broke away and founded the *Enciclopedia Libre*; after that the Spanish Wikipedia lay almost dead for a year or more, and the two competing online encyclopedias still exist. From time to time there is talk of reuniting them; it has not happened yet. As a result, the Spanish Wikipedia has never grown as rapidly as it might (though at 470,000 articles it is among the biggest, and seven times the size of the *Enciclopedia Libre*). The Russian Wikipedia is smaller than it might be for a very similar reason – the competing attraction of WikiZnanie, set up in 2003 with a slightly different philosophy. Again, both still exist. Among the other earliest wikis, the Hungarian one saw little activity, much of it vandalism, until it was relaunched in 2003; the Latin one suffered at first from an embarrassing lack of contributors who actually knew any Latin. Turning to languages beyond Europe, the Tibetan and Burmese Wikipedias are almost moribund at present: the mass of speakers in Tibet and Burma have no web access, while those who live elsewhere are likely to switch to a second language, such as English, when using a computer. The Hawaiian Wikipedia is equally weak: yes, many Hawaiians have computers, but very few Hawaiians speak Hawaiian. The Inuktitut and Cree Wikipedias have been of as much interest to vandals as to Inuktitut and Cree speakers: *there is no active community*, according to a close observer.

Proposals have continued to crowd in. 15 new languages have been approved by the subcommittee (or committee, as it now is); 66 proposals are in the waiting room, and some have been kicking their feet there for more than two years. The talk pages make depressing reading. Three issues recur in all of them. Does the community deserve a wikipedia? Yes, of course, it always does, and several people are sure to say so in the course of discussion. Does the necessary community of enthusiasts to write the wikipedia exist? Before the language subcommittee was set up there was no way of finding this out. Unfortunately there is still no way of finding out, because, although it is possible (and indeed compulsory) to set up a test wiki in advance, it'll be very hard to find, and few if any surfers are going to visit it. These two questions having been discussed inconclusively, the discussion will end ad hoc with a message from a committee member: *Currently x.xx% of the most used MediaWiki messages have been localised* [ie translated into the target language]. *Localisation of these messages is a requirement before your request is finally assessed... Thanks, GerardM.* The actual figure varies. For Gagauz it is 93.76 per cent; Gagauz is a Turkish dialect and the proposers surely copied the system messages from Turkish. For Manchu it is 0.00 per cent, because no one, certainly not Whlee, has ever tried to write software interface messages in Manchu and the necessary vocabulary does not exist. It would be like translating *Paradise Lost* into Klingon.[31]

Bèrto d'Sèra, already quoted above, wrote presciently on 4 March 2007: *if I wanted everyone upset against this* [Language] *Committee I'd do exactly what the Board* [of Trustees] *is doing. I'd have everything paralyzed, and let the Committee be the escape goat... Maybe for some people this is a very good reason for them to become real slow :)*[32] Since that date, and whether or not this was its hidden purpose, the language committee has succeeded in going *real slow*. It seems that very few of the remaining five or six thousand languages of the world will be favoured with a wikipedia.

In saying this I don't mean to criticise the Wikimedia Foundation's trustees: quite the contrary. The Foundation has to answer to its donors, who expect an ever-improving and ever-more-useful encyclopedia. While continuing to answer to this expectation, the Foundation is helping the speakers of 265 languages, whether used by a few hundred people or by a few hundred million, to keep those languages alive and active. 265 is a huge number. An encyclopedia that is actively growing in nearly all these languages is an unprecedented and matchless resource for the multilingual world in which we live, a resource that no one in the world would have dreamed of until, about ten years ago, Jimmy Wales dreamed of it.

Chapter 3
Why they hate it

The best feature of the site is that anyone can edit virtually anything contained on it. The worst feature of the site is that anyone can edit virtually anything contained on it.

    Ira Matetsky, 'Wikipedia, the Internet, and Diminished Privacy'

THE PRESS WAS at first bemused by Wikipedia. Its first airing in print may have been in the July 2001 edition of Australian *PC World* magazine, where it merited a feature article and the label of editor's choice for the month. Wikipedia was compared to Everything2, the previous month's choice; it was judged – already! – vulnerable to vandalism, but an 'interesting experiment' with 'some surprisingly accurate articles'.[33]

One of the earliest mentions in a general-audience newspaper was in *Wales on Sunday*. On 26 August 2001, under the title 'Knowledge at your fingertips', the paper's computer correspondent looked at reference sites: 'Both Encarta and Britannica are official publications with well-deserved reputations. But there are other options, such as the homemade encyclopaedias. One is Wikipedia... which uses clever software to build an encyclopaedia from scratch. Wiki is software installed on a web server that allows anyone to edit any of the pages. At the Wikipedia, anyone can write about any subject they know about. The idea is that over time, enough experts will offer their knowledge for free and build up the world's ultimate hand-built database of knowledge. The disadvantage is that it's still an ongoing project. So far about 8,000 articles have been written and the editors are aiming for 100,000.'[34] One might add that those 8,000 were fairly uneven in quality, and one might query what the writer meant by 'official' in this context; the result, anyway, was a modest boost for Wikipedia. A month later, on 20 September, Peter Meyers in the *New York Times* was equally positive and went into greater detail under the title 'Fact-Driven? Collegial? This Site Wants You'. Focusing on the still-novel interactive aspect of Wikipedia, he explains that '100 or so volunteers have been working since January to compile a free encyclopaedia...

Their work, which so far consists of some 10,000 entries ranging from Abba to zygote... suggests that the Web can be a fertile environment in which people work side by side.' Meyers comments:

'Wikipedians, as they call themselves, can not only contribute whatever they want but can also edit entries posted by other writers as they see fit. Anyone who visits the site is encouraged to participate by a note at the bottom of each page that says, "You can edit this page right now!" While that may sound like a recipe for authorial anarchy, the quest for communal knowledge seems to have prevailed so far over any attempt to pit individual opinions against one another. "It's kind of surprising that you could just open up a site and let people work," said Jimmy Wales, Wikipedia's co-founder... "There's kind of this real social pressure to not argue about things."'[35]

Mayers's points were soon being echoed by Steven Johnson in the *New York Times Magazine*'s special pre-Christmas issue 'The Year In Ideas'. Here, as already noted, Johnson gave credit not to Wales but to Sanger.

On the great majority of web pages, as Johnson explained, interaction was strictly one-way. But an intriguing new genre of sites 'called WikiWikiWebs' were truly interactive: users were able to write them as well as read them. 'If you don't like the perspective of the article you are perusing, you can go in and rephrase the concluding paragraph. If you stumble across a spelling mistake, you can fix it with a few quick keystrokes.' These sites, he continued, were like communal gardens of data, with some participants doing 'a lot of heavy planting' while others preferred to 'pull a weed here and there'. The most ambitious such project to date applied this governing principle to the creation of an encyclopedia, icon of human intelligence ever since the eighteenth century.

'The result,' Johnson announced, 'is the Wikipedia, created in early 2001 by a philosophy Ph.D. named Larry Sanger and billed as "a collaborative project to produce a complete encyclopedia from scratch."' Wikipedia had attracted more than a thousand new entries a month on everything from astronomy to the visual arts. With a total of 16,000 articles already, 'the Wikipedia' was large enough to be a source of generally reliable information, though admittedly stronger on 'Star Trek' studies than on the novels of Charles Dickens. It differed from conventional encyclopedias, however, in that each page was a work in progress. 'A visitor will draft a new entry, sometimes merely jotting down a few random data points, with a handful of links to other related entries; a few weeks later, another visitor might add a paragraph or two or a few more hyperlinks. Each entry has a revision history, like those featured in modern word processors, that lets you see at a glance any changes that have been made to the document.'[36]

Johnson is, forgivably, confused about WikiWikiWeb, which was actually not the name of the wiki software but of the first site to use the software. What 'modern word processor' he has in mind in the last sentence I don't know. In referring to 'the Wikipedia' Johnson is quite in step with early usage (only later did the definite article become unfashionable) and he is ahead of other commentators in noting that even at this very early stage of Wikipedia's growth individual editors were already distinguishable by their work patterns: some 'do a lot of heavy planting, while others prefer to pull a weed here and there'.

Looking back to the *Wales on Sunday* piece, it may seem strange that at a date when Wikipedia had only 8,000 articles, many of them sketchy and telegraphic, it was already being aligned with *Britannica*. Even in its infancy Wikipedia had set its sights on beating *Britannica*. Just two months after the launch, on 14 March 2001, in response to an item on dailynews.yahoo.com, Jimmy Wales wrote to the mailing list: *I think that Britannica's woes will only deepen. It's hard to compete against free volunteer projects like Nupedia and Wikipedia. Of course, we aren't really making a dent in them yet, but anything they do which presupposes that people will be willing to pay for their content will be disastrous for them in the "long" run – the 5–10 years it will take for Nupedia to be competitive with them, or the 1–2 years that Wikipedia will take.*[37] One to two years? That was real ambition. The same summer, on another list, Sanger reported that Britannica Online was becoming a pay site: it now offered only the first few words of each article, followed by an announcement: 'Need more? Full *Britannica* articles are available to subscribers and Free Trial participants. To view the complete article, register for 14 days free. To learn more about our premium service, click here.' Sanger commented: *I believe Jimbo said early on, and I believe I agreed, that Britannica simply couldn't maintain its business model with banner ads – they would either have to become open content (and therefore have a moral justification to ask for volunteers) or become a pay service. It seems they've chosen the latter route, which is great news for Wikipedia… In the space of a few years,* Sanger continued, Wikipedia would be bigger than *Britannica*.[38]

The idea of a contest with *Britannica* soon reappeared in a new perspective. At 15.02 GMT, on 11 September 2001, when Wikipedia had around 12,000 articles and some hundreds of registered users, it gained what was perhaps its first page of the breaking news type, when Pinkunicorn created **World Trade Center/Plane crash**. The initial text was: *At about 9:00 local time, a plane crashed into the World Trade Center. About 18 minutes later, another plane crashed into the other tower of the building.* In the next 90 minutes the page was edited 33 times. It was renamed: the other attacks had been linked in and it was now certain that terrorism was the cause. It was greatly expanded. Sub-pages were rapidly added. In October Sanger was still reiterating to the mailing list his view on the *Britannica* comparison: *Can you imagine what this project could be like in ten years, if we stay on track? It really could beat out Britannica in terms of quality,* but Clasqm replied from South Africa to insist that it was now time to look beyond.

Forget Britannica. This obsession with 'beating' an obsolete concept is something we need to get rid of fast. Instead, let's look at what is going on on WP right now. The people handling the 9-11 reporting are putting up pages for WTC victims. Think about that. In the past, to get your name into britannica you first needed to get famous (or infamous), to do something extraordinary. To get a page up on WP, all that is needed is for someone to think that you should be remembered. Hypothetically, we could have a page for every one of the six billion people on the planet. And one for every one of their ancestors yea unto the seventh generation. (At this point, Jimbo looks nervously at his hard disk capacity.) This is something new, and I don't think any of us can really predict where it will go. But there is no need to obsess about Britannica. It was a great product in its time, but moving an 18th century concept to the web does not move the concept itself into the 21st.[39]

Early newspaper comments on Wikipedia had been bemusedly admiring. In 2004 came the first signs that the press could turn antagonistic. *The Register*, a British online journal for journalists, set the new tone in a sideswipe at the **Buckminster Fuller** article in 'the world's most useless online text, the captive Wikipedia'.[40] Two weeks later, in response to two readers' letters, *The Register*'s Andrew Orlowski aimed a machine-gun at the 'children's encyclopedia... the encyclopedia that isn't an encyclopedia'. One of those readers had pointed out that in Alexa.com's web-hit statistics *The Register* was currently ranked 2,675; Wikipedia, at 621, was 'a few dozen times more useful than you'. Uncertain in his response whether to label the encyclopedia's editors 'wiki-fiddlers' or 'wiki-wankers', Orlowski gave a low estimate of their achievement so far. 'There's nothing wrong with Wikipedia that isn't summed up by the fiddlers' problematic war cry of "if you don't like it, fix it!" It's really rather like being urged to liven up a boring stranger's very poorly-attended party by showing up... There may be a good reason no one shows up... We wish them luck with the "emergent" project, and excuse us while we consult a real encyclopedia,' Orlowski concluded, adding an unsponsored link to the earnest and librarianly Resourceshelf.com. Around the same time the British *Times Higher Education Supplement* reminded its university and college readership that Wikipedia was no ordinary encyclopedia, though now claiming to be the largest reference source in the world (that claim was false, incidentally, but no journalists noticed; after all, the Wikipedia article on **Siku quanshu** did not yet exist). Entries could be written and edited by anyone, the *THES* observed: no credentials necessary. Fans of the site believed it to be refreshingly democratic and claimed that over time, accurate, comprehensive articles would materialise; but critics retorted that any particular page might be rubbish at the moment it was consulted. The *THES*'s parent newspaper, *The Times*, took up the report under the eye-catching title 'Your Reference May Be Rubbish'.[41]

That same year Nicholas Carr, a steady critic of excessive claims regarding the benefits of IT, gave a well-argued and damning report on Wikipedia in an online essay published on 3 October 2005. In the context of Web 2.0 (the interactive incarnation of the web) Wikipedia is, as Carr says, praised as 'a glorious manifestation of the age of participation' that allows us 'to pool our individual brains into a great collective mind'. He insists that the reality is more prosaic. Wikipedia is useful for a quick overview of a subject, but it is factually unreliable and shoddily written. He takes as examples the articles on **Bill Gates** and **Jane Fonda**. These are generously-chosen topics, because Wikipedia editors, given their usual skills and enthusiasms, ought to perform better than usual when writing on software magnates and on American actors. They do not. Here's the section of the Bill Gates biography that Carr quoted:

Gates married Melinda French on January 1, 1994. They have three children, Jennifer Katharine Gates (born April 26, 1996), Rory John Gates (born May 23, 1999) and Phoebe Adele Gates (born September 14, 2002).

In 1994, Gates acquired the Codex Leicester, a collection of writings by Leonardo da Vinci; as of 2003 it was on display at the Seattle Art Museum.

In 1997, Gates was the victim of a bizarre extortion plot by Chicago resident Adam Quinn Pletcher. Gates testified at the subsequent trial. Pletcher was convicted and sentenced in July 1998 to six years in prison. In February 1998 Gates was attacked by Noël Godin with a cream pie. In July 2005, he solicited the services of famed lawyer Hesham Foda.

According to Forbes, Gates contributed money to the 2004 presidential campaign of George W. Bush. According to the Center for Responsive Politics, Gates is cited as having contributed at least $33,335 to over 50 political campaigns during the 2004 election cycle.

'Excuse me for stating the obvious,' Carr writes, 'but this is garbage, an incoherent hodge-podge of dubious factoids (who the heck is "famed lawyer Hesham Foda"?) that adds up to something far less than the sum of its parts.' After quoting an even more embarrassing extract on the young Jane Fonda, he adds: 'At this point, it seems fair to ask exactly when the intelligence in "collective intelligence" will begin to manifest itself. When will the great Wikipedia get good? Or is "good" an old-fashioned concept that doesn't apply to emergent phenomena like communal on-line encyclopedias?'[42] Not every reader agreed, but Jimmy Wales did. He commented bluntly to the Wikipedia mailing list: *Bill Gates and Jane Fonda are nearly unreadable crap. Why? What can we do about it?*[43]

Soon after Carr's article, press attitudes were tested by two real, solid pieces of Wikipedia news.

'Sometimes the stupid-sounding ideas turn out to be the ones that take off,' began an editorial in *Nature*, the venerable scientific weekly, in December 2005. *Nature* had asked specialists to assess the main texts of 42 scientific articles in Wikipedia and Britannica Online without revealing to them which texts came from which source. The journal concluded that some of the early criticisms, though still commonly repeated in the press, appeared misguided. 'Wikipedia is now a huge reference source, with something approaching a million articles... It's true that many of its entries are confusing and badly structured; some of them are badly wrong, and sometimes the errors are deliberate'; yet, in a 'typical Wikipedia science article' the quantity of errors was 'not substantially more than in *Encyclopaedia Britannica*', although 'considering how Wikipedia articles are written, that result might seem surprising'. In an introductory editorial, 'Wiki's Wild World', *Nature* encouraged scientists to become Wikipedians.

'The idea is not to seek a replacement for established sources such as the *Encyclopaedia Britannica*, but to push forward the grand experiment that is Wikipedia, and to see how much it can improve. Select a topic close to your work and look it up on Wikipedia. If the entry contains errors or important omissions, dive in and help fix them... Imagine the pay-off: you could be one of the people who helped turn an apparently stupid idea into a free, high-quality global resource.'[44]

In the *Nature* survey (presented as journalism, incidentally, not as a peer-reviewed scientific paper) 'not substantially more' turned out to mean 162 errors in the selected Wikipedia texts versus 123 in *Britannica*. In reporting the survey most newspapers ignored the nuances and simply adopted the spin that *Nature* put on it, but Andrew Orlowski in *The Register* was less easily fooled. His headline 'Wikipedia science 31% more cronky than Britannica's' was followed by some well-selected quotations from the less-observant majority: '"Accuracy of Wikipedia matches *Britannica*, review shows," boasts CBC. "Wikipedia as accurate as *Britannica* on science," trumpets CNN's website. *Business Week*, which wants to be the house journal for Web 2.0 badgers, has no doubts: "A Vote of Confidence in Wikipedia," it shouts.'[45] Orlowski might have added that CNET's report was titled 'Study: Wikipedia as Accurate as Britannica.'[46] He easily demonstrated the weakness of these claims.

Orlowski's slashing piece was soon to be followed by a detailed critique by Nicholas Carr. Carr's first point, one that most of the press had failed to notice, was that *Nature* (a scientific journal, after all) had focused purely on topics related to science when selecting articles for the survey and had thus played to Wikipedia's strengths: 'Such topics... attract a narrower and more knowledgeable group of contributors.' The result of such a comparison, though interesting, could not be taken as valid across the whole range of subjects covered by the two encyclopedias. Carr then quoted from *Nature*'s supplementary notes, in which specialists' criticisms were listed. These showed that several reviewers had pointed to contrasts in article quality, one of the two (and it always seemed to be the Wikipedia article) being 'poorly structured and confusing', with 'undue prominence given to controversial scientific theories'. The published report had ignored all such remarks because they did not count as 'errors'. Finally, Carr observed, *Nature* had naively counted all errors as equal, but from the supplementary notes a strong impression emerged that Wikipedia's errors were more basic and substantial than *Britannica*'s. Carr's conclusion was quite fair and it was even more negative than Orlowski's: 'If you only look at scientific topics, if you ignore the structure and clarity of the writing, and if you treat all inaccuracies as equivalent, then you would still find that Wikipedia has about 32% more errors and omissions than *Encyclopedia Britannica*.'[47] But Orlowski's and Carr's were minority voices.

The publishers of *Britannica* reacted bitterly to the *Nature* survey and the majority press response. *Britannica*, they pointed out, had been dealt with much more cavalierly than Wikipedia in the selection of texts: there had been unfair cutting and patching; extracts from *Children's Britannica* and the *Year Books* had sometimes been used. Although *Nature* claimed glibly in its editorial not to be seeking 'a replacement for established sources' such as *Britannica*, this was small consolation when *Nature*'s reporting of its survey was bound to produce more pageviews and more editors for Wikipedia while sending fewer buyers to *Britannica*. The venerable encyclopedia needed to persuade potential customers that they were getting for their money something they could not get for free. But the press was now proclaiming that *Britannica*'s error quotient was very little lower than Wikipedia's, and commentators were assuming that the survey was scientific and the error measure adequate. *Britannica* issued a detailed report setting out the faults in the method and the flaws in the figures that had helped to produce these misleading conclusions.[48] It got some publicity – but not enough.

Wikipedians, meanwhile, were gratified by the general chorus of praise that followed the *Nature* report. They needed some good news. Just two weeks before *Nature* announced its survey, John Seigenthaler, a retired editor at the national daily *USA Today*, wrote an editorial for his old newspaper which began with the arresting words: 'This is a highly personal story about Internet character assassination. It could be your story.' It was, in fact, Seigenthaler's own story. Around 20 September 2005 someone had told him he needed to look at his Wikipedia biography. At that time Seigenthaler had heard of Wikipedia but didn't know that there was an article about him, **John Seigenthaler Sr.** It contained one fact about Seigenthaler, that he *was the assistant to Attorney General Robert Kennedy in the early 1960s*, followed by several falsehoods, of which the most striking and hurtful was the allegation that Seigenthaler was briefly thought to have been *involved in the Kennedy assassinations of both John, and his brother, Bobby. Nothing was ever proven.*

'I have no idea whose sick mind conceived the false, malicious "biography" that appeared under my name for 132 days on Wikipedia,' Seigenthaler wrote. 'It was mind-boggling when my son... phoned later to say he found the same scurrilous text on Reference.com and Answers.com... Executives of the three websites now have removed the false content about me. But they don't know, and can't find out, who wrote the toxic sentences. I phoned Jimmy Wales, Wikipedia's founder and asked, "Do you have any way to know who wrote that?" "No, we don't," he said. Representatives of the other two websites said their computers are programmed to copy data verbatim from Wikipedia, never checking whether it is false or factual.'[49]

The article had been created on 26 May by an anonymous user. Three days later it had been edited to correct the spelling of 'early'; the second editor did not notice, or did not question, the assassination claim. From then on, for four months, it simply stayed. Jimmy Wales's very recent claim in a television interview on the subject of Wikipedia vandalism, 'there have been academic studies showing that it's repaired within a median time of under five minutes,'[50] suddenly appeared highly misleading.

Seigenthaler wanted to get the false information removed and he wanted to 'unmask' his attacker. The first step was for a friend, Eric Newton, to replace the fantasy biography on Wikipedia with a correct one. This was done simply by pasting in Seigenthaler's official biography from the website of the Freedom Forum; and at this stage Wikipedia's luck, hitherto absent, returned. Chick Bowen, the first editor who encountered the new version of the article, on 24 September, might have taken it at face value but, in fact, correctly recognised that it was a copyright violation. At that point Bowen might have blithely reverted to the previous, scurrilous version but, in fact, he took on the task of making a new short article based on the good information that Newton had pasted in.

The two mirror sites, Reference.com and Answers.com, were much harder for Seigenthaler to deal with. Their pages could not be edited. They went on displaying the offensive text for some weeks, until the next Wikipedia download arrived.

The Wikipedia biography was now clean but the falsehoods were still in the history. On 5 October Seigenthaler phoned Jimmy Wales. Wales handed the problem to an admin, EssJay, who erased the earliest edits of the article from the database, removing both the scurrilous text and the copyright violation: for this reason Chick Bowen's rewrite now appears first in the article history. But Seigenthaler also wanted to know who wrote the false biography. Wales had no answer, and could only warn him, correctly as it turned out, that the internet provider would not be helpful. When Seigenthaler published his story, on 29 November, he was still in the dark on this point.

Not for long. Fortunately for his quest, he had included the IP address in the *USA Today* article. This was enough to allow journalists and internet sleuths to get to work.

The crucial discovery was made by Daniel Brandt, an indexer who had, like Seigenthaler, recently been annoyed by errors in his Wikipedia biography. This special interest in the subject impelled Brandt to investigate the Seigenthaler case, and he traced the IP address tentatively to a delivery company in Nashville, Tennessee. He telephoned the company but could find out nothing. Then he emailed, and the reply (remember the massive and impenetrable headers that we no longer see on emails?) carried the same IP address, confirming his discovery. Following up Brandt's information the *New York Times* also telephoned the company, and at that stage a worried employee, a certain Brian Chase, decided that the game was up. He composed an apology and hand-delivered it to Seigenthaler's office. His only reason for writing the fictitious biography, he explained, was to startle a colleague. It seems that after a conversation at work about the Seigenthaler family, Chase searched for John Seigenthaler on the internet, encountered his name as a Wikipedia *redlink*, clicked on it, and found to his surprise that he was free to begin an article on the subject. Knowing nothing about Seigenthaler except his work for Bobby Kennedy, he built a fictional biography on that basis.

Seigenthaler, a lifelong defender of free speech, took no legal action. Chase's joke had lasting consequences for Chase himself, however: he lost his job and became briefly notable enough to merit a Wikipedia biography of his own, **Brian Chase (Wikipedia hoaxer)**, which survived a deletion debate but was soon afterwards submerged in the article **Seigenthaler incident** on Jimmy Wales's personal instructions. *So am I to understand that Jimbo Wales' actions are unquestionable?* an editor queried. *I wouldn't personally say that*, another replied, *but I would say that edit warring with him is a superbly bad idea.*

'It started as a joke and ended up as a shot heard round the Internet, with the joker losing his job and Wikipedia, the online encyclopedia, suffering a blow to its credibility,' the *New York Times* reported on 11 December,[51] and the *New York Times* was right; the incident caused serious trouble not only for Chase but also for Wikipedia. Jimmy Wales reacted immediately and drastically, as he sometimes does. 'Mr Wales said that the Seigenthaler affair had prompted him to ban contributions from unregistered users,' *The Times* of London reported on 8 December, and many other papers said the same. This was merely an approach to the truth; Wales's ruling, though decisive, was not as draconian as all that. *The Register* was one of the few sources that got it right: the new rules would merely prevent anonymous users 'from creating articles... Anonymous edits to existing articles will still be permitted, and articles in the system that have been edited anonymously will remain. And accountability remains elusive: "editors" can still hide behind pseudonymous identities.'[52] The vast numbers of edits from unregistered users continued, and they still do; the encyclopedia would be much poorer without them.

Wales evidently saw at once that if this rule had been in force the Seigenthaler incident would have been prevented. 'Critics point out that registration takes only a few seconds,' *The Times* objected, but even the few seconds that it takes to get a Wikipedia account would have dampened the spark of mischief in a chance visitor to the site like Brian Chase. 'What we're hopeful to see is that by slowing [new article creation] down to 1,500 a day from several thousand, the people who are monitoring this will have more ability to improve the quality,' Wales was reported as saying. 'In many cases the types of things we see going on are impulse vandalism.'

If the newspapers were vague on Wikipedia's policy change, they were equally vague about who, exactly, were 'the people who are monitoring this': Wales's phrase didn't help them much. Wikipedia's 'body of knowledge comprises articles posted by members of the public on subjects as diverse as cupcakes and neurosurgery', *The Times* asserted in the same article, adding that there was 'a team of 600 volunteers who review facts.'[53] The reporter hadn't grasped that this 'team' was a mere ill-defined subset of the whole mass of editors, the ones who happen to spend some time reading and checking articles as well as writing them.

Wales was spot-on in his prediction that the policy change would reduce the number of new articles. December 2005 is precisely when the rate of increase of the English Wikipedia slowed, though whether this is really because a significant proportion of new articles had always been added anonymously and henceforth were not being added at all, or rather because it gradually becomes more difficult to find notable topics to add to the already vast corpus, remains to be discussed.

He was right, in any case, that fewer new articles, day by day, meant more opportunity for others to check, correct and, if necessary, delete them. But there was no room for complacency. A second reporter from *The Times*, equally unfamiliar with Wikipedia, thought that the new policy would 'prevent unregistered users dipping in and adding complete rubbish without any comeback',[54] but this prediction was belied (I think it's fair to say) by a third colleague, Rhys Blakely, who reported on 20 December that when he consulted it the article **Wikipedia** consisted of 'the one-line entry: "an encyclopaedia full of crap". Later, Wikipedia had posted on its own site this unflattering description: "Although it may seem factual, Wikipedia is largely a web of lies and falsehoods, and it is not to be trusted by any means... it is worthless."'[55] I set out to check Blakely's assertion, but I'm afraid I can only say that it's very probably true. I gave up after wading through hundreds of nonsensical and illiterate edits to that article in the few days before 20 December. Still another journalist at *The Times*, the columnist Rosemary Righter, tried creating a user account in 'this intellectual lunatic asylum' to see how easy it would be. She called herself Mickmouse. 'In the wacky world of Wikipedia,' she reported as a self-certified inmate, 'the missing bits are these: accountability, authority, scholarly credentials, accuracy and scrupulousness... to claim that this is an encyclopaedia (and, further, to declare its aim to be "*Britannica* or better" quality) is to hold learning in contempt.'[56] She made no edits, however. A surge of such accounts created by timewasters, and a longer-term increase in vandalism, nearly always rapidly reverted by Wikipedia's modest and heroic editors, were additional unwelcome consequences of the Seigenthaler incident. Like many British journalists, many US conservatives and libertarians had until that point known nothing about Wikipedia. Most of them now decided that they didn't like it. Vandalising prominent Wikipedia articles, a game regularly played by schoolchildren, briefly became fashionable among their parents. Months and years after the news had become stale the press continued to use the Seigenthaler story as a touchstone. Reference would always henceforth be made to Seigenthaler, and unreliability would be implied or asserted, when Wikipedia came up for discussion.

There was a strange coda to the Seigenthaler affair. At the end of the same month, on 28 December 2005, an article in the German Wikipedia, **de:Bertrand Meyer**, the biography of a French computer scientist and professor of informatics at Zurich, was edited three times within three minutes by an anonymous user. The first edit filled in Meyer's date of death as 1 January 2006 (three days in the future). The second and third edits moved this putative event into the recent past and added two sentences of text: *According to latest reports Bertrand Meyer died on 24 December 2005 at Zurich. On 23 December the examination results for his most recent class of students were announced. Links between this announcement and his death cannot as yet be confirmed.* The false information was still there on the morning of 3 January 2006, when it was noticed and reported on the German IT news website *Heise News-Ticker*: the hoaxer had 'probably used an Austrian dial-up connection'.[57] Within minutes the Wikipedia article was corrected and improved, again by an anonymous editor, but the cat was out of the bag and many news sites took up the story. Meyer, a Web 2.0 enthusiast, was philosophical on the subject. His next monthly blog was entitled 'Defense and Illustration of Wikipedia'. 'The system succumbed to one of its potential flaws, and quickly healed itself,' he concluded. 'This doesn't affect the big picture. Just like those about me, rumors about Wikipedia's downfall have been grossly exaggerated.'

His title, incidentally, was adapted from a famous 1549 literary manifesto by Joachim du Bellay. 'If you realize that the title of the present paper is a nod to a famous book but can't quite place it, a Google search will, at the time of writing, find it for you – in the *Britannica*,' Meyer teased in a footnote. 'Wikipedia just doesn't measure up for that particular example.'[58] Curiously enough, he was wrong: the French Wikipedia article about the book in question, **fr:Défense et illustration de la langue française**, was already a year old.

Two years later an incident that began in a strangely similar way ended very differently. On the French Wikipedia at 08.49 on 17 April 2008 the biography of a journalist and television personality, **fr:Philippe Manoeuvre**, was edited anonymously to include the statement that he died on the evening of the 18 April (one day in the future, that is). The edit was reverted (also anonymously) after 39 minutes, but the media news website C'est OFF got to hear of it, verified that Manoeuvre was still among the living, and published the item gleefully at 14.23: 'Wikipedia buries Philippe Manoeuvre and spreads false rumours'[59], making a juicier story of it by implying that the mistake was still on display; in fact, by that time, it was buried in the article history. Manoeuvre himself, a well-known figure and no stranger to controversy, was naturally disturbed to learn that his death had been anonymously 'predicted'. He had no way of knowing whether to take the announcement as a threat. He emailed Wikipedia. The reply assured him that the article was now being protected (so that only admins were able to edit it) and confirmed what he already knew from a news report at 20minutes.fr: the offending edit could only be traced to an IP address.[60] He took the matter to his local police station, where a case was opened against x.

Fortunately nothing happened to Manoeuvre on 18 April, but the wheels of justice slowly began to roll. *I've been summoned to the 17th Arrondissement police station this afternoon as a site moderator*, reported Céréales Killer on 5 May to his fellow admins on the French Wikipedia. *If they let me go again, I'll tell you all about it.*

Remember to get some pictures. We still need illustrations for 'Remand in custody' and 'Police brutality', said DocteurCosmos cheerfully; but Dauphiné was seriously worried: *How did they get hold of you? What do they mean by moderator? What has stuff like this got to do with us?*

To put your mind at rest, Céréales Killer eventually replied, *Philippe Manoeuvre knew my name because I originally dealt with his emails. We talked on the phone, we exchanged numbers, and that's how the officer in charge of the case invited me in. To show you there wasn't a problem, I'm out again! He just wanted to know how Wikipedia worked and how something like this could happen. I showed him the article history and he can take it from there. He wasn't sure how far he'd get.*

Whew! I was just about to wipe my hard disk and find a hotel in Geneva, said Dauphiné. Alain r commented: *That nasty edit was from a French IP address belonging to Neuf Telecom. So, if Ph. M. wants to press charges, the joker is fucked.*[61]

Alain r was right; and there was after all no justification for the suspicion, aired by certain other Wikipédiens, that a journalist had made the edit in order to create a new 'Wikipedia gets it wrong' story. *I had Philippe Manoeuvre on the phone earlier today*, Céréales Killer reported on 19 May, *telling me the latest news on the case against x. It's resulted in the arrest of a 21-year-old... arrival of the cops at 6 in the morning, confiscation of his laptop, the boy himself in custody... he thought he was safe behind his keyboard, and it took just a month for the law to get to him. Only one problem now: the lawyers don't know what to charge him with.*[62]

By the time Céréales Killer wrote this they had decided to charge the 21-year-old, known to us only as Ambroise, with nothing at all. During his three hours at the police station, Ambroise was able to prove (with the help of his laptop) that he had edited Wikipedia in good faith on the basis of an item he saw on the media news forum Mixbeat; realising later the same day that the story was false and there might be trouble, he went back to the forum and saved a copy of the page that had misled him.[63] This was very wise, because Mixbeat soon afterwards disappeared from the web. But why, then, on 17 April had Philippe Manoeuvre's date of death been given as 18 April? Although the news site Infos-du-net gets the credit for tracking Ambroise down soon after the police let him go, it was left to *PCInPact*, which interviewed him a day later, to remember to ask him this crucial question. 'That was just me,' he confessed. 'I got the date wrong. It was only 8 in the morning, after all. I had a hangover.'[64]

It was all 'a bit silly', to quote Ambroise's own summing up. The French press had by this time moved on from the Manoeuvre story. It had been categorised and is still remembered in France as one in a long list of incidents demonstrating Wikipedia's vulnerability to vandalism.

By the time Ambroise and his computer were exonerated, the first story on that list – the first media circus linking the French Wikipedia with vandalism – was already nine months old. It all began, as far as Wikipedia was concerned, with an article in the French left-wing daily *Libération* on 9

July 2007 entitled 'Wikipedia gets it wrong in every direction'.

The journalist, Frédérique Roussel, began this piece with a couple of examples of dubious information on the French Wikipedia. The first concerned a writer and professor of journalism, **fr:Pierre Assouline**, whose Wikipedia biography had contained the completely false claim that *in 2001 he won the French jeu de paume championship* (*jeu de paume* is the historic game of real tennis or court tennis). The second example was **fr:Tony Blair**: his French biography had asserted that he was a Catholic. The doubtful statements had survived for 'several weeks', Roussel claimed. The really surprising point came next: they had been inserted by Pierre Gourdain and four other postgraduate journalism students, all named in a footnote, under the direction of Pierre Assouline at the highly respected Paris *grande école* usually known by its nickname of 'Sciences Po'. Assouline, the article continued, had twice criticised Wikipedia in his blog, had debated the merits of the site with his students, and had decided to set them a project, as he put it, 'that no newspaper has yet undertaken: a group study, lasting several months. Take it apart and see how it works.'[65] Unfortunately in his preliminary research he didn't meet with the work of Alex Havalais, who had made a similar experiment two years earlier and added to his brief report of it the words: 'Please don't do this: vandalizing the site is not a good way to test it.'[66] Nor did Assouline encounter the page **fr:Wikipédia:Projets pédagogiques**, where he would have found plenty of encouragement, seasoned with a pertinent warning: *Do not encourage your students... to insert inappropriate content on existing pages... If your students vandalise Wikipedia, they may be blocked.*

What interested the first Wikipedia editors who happened to read Roussel's article was the matter of the statements inserted into Wikipedia – which aims to be a public encyclopedia, not a specimen for journalism students to 'take apart'. To the extent that they were intentionally false, the edits were by definition vandalism, and the article implied that its two examples were not the only ones. The priorities were, therefore, to confirm the source, to track down any surviving vandalism from that source, and, if possible, to make sure there wouldn't be any more.

Although not free from error, Roussel's article was useful as a starting point for research (just like a Wikipedia article, in fact). Initially David.Monniaux wrote to one of the students asking for a copy of their report.[67] Others meanwhile investigated the two edits that were mentioned. Both had been inserted anonymously from an IP address that was associated with repeated vandalism and that was traceable to Sciences Po. Both had been removed 13 days later (Roussel's 'several weeks' was mere journalism) by a named editor, Antigravity, who had made scarcely any other contributions. The history of the edits was fascinating. At **fr:Pierre Assouline** the anonymous contributor had inserted two details, the falsehood about *jeu de paume* and the correct information that Assouline was a professor at Sciences Po. An editor without close knowledge of the subject, once having recognised the *jeu de paume* detail as vandalism, would have played safe and reverted the whole edit. Instead of doing this, Antigravity had removed the false detail and left the correct one alone, a neat confirmation of this editor's closeness to the miscreant group.[68]

The Pierre Assouline biography was not of very wide interest so it isn't surprising that a false detail of this kind remained on it for a couple of weeks. **fr:Tony Blair**, by contrast, was of very wide interest; the article was constantly visited and was being watched by several editors. How could the claim of his Catholicism have survived so long? The answer is that it was plausible and had a certain validity: Blair was already known to be attracted to Catholicism, and if the claim had appeared seven months later it would have been verifiably true. The dubious detail was first inserted at 10.02 on 2 May 2007. It was removed seconds later by DocteurCosmos, with the comment *Vraiment?* At 10.14 it was inserted again. DocteurCosmos may have felt sufficiently uncertain on this second occasion to let the information stay until someone else came along to confirm or deny it.

No other edits had been corrected by Antigravity. No other vandalism had emanated from Sciences Po around the same date (except the creation of an article whose text consisted of the Spanish obscenity *me cago en tu puta madre*; for this, however, Pierre Gourdain and colleagues were probably not to blame). But the Sciences Po IP address had been responsible for various kinds of vandalism on Wikipedia ever since April 2006.[69] This new episode, organised by a professor and proudly reported to the press, was the last straw. The IP address was blocked, thus preventing edits of Wikipedia.

To this there were two responses from the *école*, very different in tone. The executive director of the School of Journalism, Agnès Chauveau, stated publicly that her students 'did not sabotage the encyclopedia', a not-quite-honest claim which is excused by her palpable embarrassment. As it happened, the *école*'s computer network had a single IP address. Thus, as a result of the actions of one of her professors, it was not just his research group, not just the School of Journalism, but the whole *école* that was prevented from editing Wikipedia. Assouline, given his views on Wikipedia, would probably have argued that this did not matter: Chauveau's complaint that Sciences Po was being 'punished' is cogent evidence that she at least disagreed with him.[70] More reasonable than Chauveau's response was an unsigned message that eventually appeared on the user talk page: *This IP address was blocked by Grondin on the grounds that some pages were vandalised. Maybe they were, but it's shared by five thousand students. You're preventing them from making contributions that could be good for Wikipedia. That's a pity, isn't it?* Less than a week later the block was lifted. Anonymous edits (and random vandalism) from Sciences Po have continued to this day.

The Sciences Po incident is important because it served to focus the anti-Wikipedia animosity that had previously been building up in the French blogosphere and to turn it into a campaign in the mainstream press.

In reality the story had begun with the publisher François Gèze who runs Éditions La Découverte. Sometime in late 2006 he wanted to verify a detail of the Dreyfus affair, a political scandal of the 1890s in which the false conviction of a Jewish army officer for treason exposed anti-Semitism and corruption in the French establishment. Apparently for no other reason than that it came at the top of the list in a Google search, he found himself looking at the Wikipedia article **fr:Affaire Dreyfus**. The first item in the bibliography was *Henri Dutrait-Crozon, « Précis de l'Affaire Dreyfus », 3ème édition, Paris 1938. Fundamental work to be consulted as a priority*. He was shocked, because this book is notorious, at least among specialists: Dutrait-Crozon was a pseudonym of two 'revisionist' right-wing authors whose aim was to show that Dreyfus, far from being an innocent, and indeed heroic, victim, was guilty as charged. Perhaps unfamiliar with Wikipedia until this moment, Gèze did not think of removing the reference or altering the comment, as I would probably have done, nor even of contacting Wikipedia, as Philippe Manoeuvre would probably have done. Gèze's action, quite typical in its way of a Parisian intellectual, was to contact the Human Rights League. This didn't get him very far. He then told Daniel Garcia, a literary journalist at *Livres Hebdo*, who related the story in his blog on 30 November 2006, beginning: 'Type 'Affaire Dreyfus' into Google. At the top of the list you will see (no! no! no!) yes, the Wikipedia article. Click on it. Scroll down to the bibliography....' After recounting Gèze's observation, Garcia added a further comment on what seemed to him to be hidden bias in the introductory sentence; this made him suspect (perhaps unfairly) that the whole article was tainted with right-wing views.[71]

Let's look at the Wikipedia side of it thus far. The Dutrait-Crozon book and the note about it had been added to the bibliography anonymously on 14 July 2006. The addition was not questioned, and this isn't really surprising. Superficially it looks OK – just like the kind of bibliographical addition that I often make to an article. Only a specialist would have known that there was something wrong; evidently no specialist was watching. It wasn't exactly vandalism. It's possible that the intention was honest, though the anonymity of the edit, and the assertive comment, suggest that the anonymous editor expected trouble. Anyway, from Wikipedia's point of view it counts as a very bad edit, because this particular book, being highly tendentious and quite outdated, did not deserve to be highlighted as a *fundamental work*; in fact it did not deserve its place at all in what was at that time only a sketchy bibliography on the subject.

Anyway, reference and comment both remained until, on the morning of 30 November 2006, an occasional contributor named Milpa, fresh from a reading of Garcia's blog, removed the sentence that he had disliked, removed the existing comment on the Dutrait-Crozon book and inserted in its place the words *ouvrage controversé* ('questionable work'). Milpa made a good start here, but modestly flagged the edit as minor. This was unlucky because it meant that others were not alerted to it. Milpa was also too shy to add a note on the talk page. It would have been useful to mention Garcia's blog, which no other Wikipedian appears to have read. But at this stage in a brief editorial career Milpa had never once edited a talk page.

Garcia's comments had also caught the eye of Pierre Assouline; this was why Assouline took up the issue in January in his own much more widely read blog. He saw the Wikipedia article in the state it had reached after Milpa's edits, but he didn't apparently look at the article history. Garcia's critique, he wrote: 'did not escape the vigilance of Wikipedia. Logically one might have thought that they would react to it by deleting the item from the bibliography. In fact, not only is it still in their bibliography, it's still first on the list, ahead of all the recent studies by real historians. It is only the comment that has been modified, and now reads *questionable* work. Understatement as a fine art...'

'In the eyes of Wikipedians at least,' Assouline summed up, 'this book remains the bible of the Dreyfus affair.' There's an important point to make here. In these sentences Assouline responds to Wikipedia as to a unitary organisation, indeed a potentially unfriendly and secretive organisation, with a unified set of responses and a decided opinion on history and bibliography. He supposes (it would seem) that this organisation, through its vigilance, had privately considered Garcia's criticism and decided to make the minimum possible change in reaction to it. I think this is a very odd perspective, but that's because mine is so different. I was already a Wikipedia editor at that time, and I already knew that Wikipedia never responds to anything as a unitary organisation and can never keep anything secret. No large randomly-selected group of Wikipedians would ever agree on any political, historical or bibliographical approach to any topic, still less would they agree to say nothing about it: rather they would discuss it openly, heatedly and endlessly. In this particular case the vigilant organisation imagined by Assouline was no other than Milpa (I picture Milpa as a foreign student in France, but this is only a guess) who, though knowing little of the Dreyfus affair, read Garcia's blog and was sufficiently stirred by the issue to make a minimal, rapid improvement to the page. Such was the opponent against whom Assouline scored his knockout.

But rehashing the story already told by Daniel Garcia had not been Assouline's main aim. He was shaping up for a look at Wikipedia as a whole, and from this section of his essay a rather more perceptive view emerges of the way that Wikipedia works. 'No question that the contents are rich, dense, seductive and sometimes surprising. But they aren't non-skid,' he begins. His real objection is to the principle embodied by Wikipedia that everyone is an encyclopedist, just as, in other modern contexts, everyone is a journalist, a photographer, a film-maker, a book critic or a food critic. 'On this site anyone can join in as soon as he feels he's an expert on something'; in contrast with *Britannica* and its French analogues, on Wikipedia the specialists are self-appointed and self-examined.[72] Now I'm sure that Milpa would not have claimed to be a specialist (let alone a *modérateur*, the term that Assouline chose when he re-told this story), but, aside from that, he was quite right. The anonymous inserter of the information had chosen to insert it, and had done so; Milpa had chosen to react to Garcia's criticism, and had done so; both were self-appointed. Equally self-appointed – and a very good appointment, too – was Van nuytts, who in response to Assouline's piece undertook a serious and much-needed revision of **fr:Affaire Dreyfus**.

Assouline's January essay was followed by another two months later, sparked by a review article in the Spanish press that happened to characterise the classic *Encyclopédie* as 'the eighteenth century Wikipedia'. 'Diderot didn't deserve that,' was Assouline's reaction,[73] and it was around this date that he decided to set his five students the project that caused all the trouble.

The Sciences Po affair supplied a new answer to a question that Pierre Assouline himself had formulated some years earlier. In one of his greatest books, *L'épuration des intellectuels*, he explores the actions of French intellectuals during the Second World War and the outcomes for them and for France when the war was over. A moral dilemma posed in this compelling text is 'Can one write without consequences?' Having asked the question, Assouline answers it, and I quote two sentences from his response.

The man of ideas, as one who in principle operates on the plane of intelligence, should take responsibility for what he writes at the very moment of creation. He should keep in mind, with every sentence, that there must never be a need in the future to deny his words, or to reproach himself for them, or to be ashamed of them – regardless of fashion, regardless of governments.'[74]

It was a pity, perhaps, that Pierre Gourdain and colleagues forgot these words. They set out to test Wikipedia by inserting statements that they afterwards intended to deny. Ironically, while proving nothing about Wikipedia that was not already well known, they did confirm that it was not possible to edit without consequences.

Two of the incidents surveyed above were, seen in retrospect, insignificant in themselves: one edit by Ambroise, erroneous but made in good faith; a couple of misleading edits by Gourdain and colleagues, one of which was truer than its authors realised. The mischievous edits about Meyer and Seigenthaler were more serious, and they were surely wounding to their subjects. But the real importance of all four incidents lay in the effect that they had on outside opinion concerning Wikipedia. Its advantages and disadvantages, reliability and lack of reliability, responsibility and irresponsibility, neutrality or political bias, were being weighed in the press with ever-increasing frequency. Of course they were, because more and more people were visiting, reading and editing Wikipedia; but the incessant references to errors, bias and vandalism began at times to amount to an anti-Wikipedia campaign. If there was indeed a campaign these incidents were its keynotes, its bullet points, its clichés. If there was indeed a campaign, heavyweight commentators such as Nicholas Carr and Pierre Assouline gave it intellectual backing and respectability.

As Wikipedia's notoriety grew – press attention in itself speeding the process – the feeling spread among some who didn't like it and didn't trust it that some kind of alternative, avoiding Wikipedia's faults, had to be created. In what must be seen as a back-handed compliment to the hated 'encyclopedia that anyone can edit', the various alternatives that sprang into existence around this time often use wiki software and sometimes look almost indistinguishable from Wikipedia. But, because their backers all agreed that one of Wikipedia's worst features was its openness to anonymous edits, most of them adopt the software option that permits only registered users to do any editing.

'Citizendium' is one of those portmanteau words, 'a citizens' compendium of everything'. A glance at its article 'Citizendium' reveals a claim followed by a disclaimer: 'We are creating the world's most trusted encyclopedia and knowledge base,' but 'this is a draft article, under development and not meant to be cited.' Citizendium is the youngest of Larry Sanger's virtual children, intended to be the success that Nupedia would have been if things had worked out right, an encyclopedia that collaborators can build 'under expert guidance' and at the same time take responsibility for their work by signing their real names. There aren't any pseudonyms on Citizendium. Well, hardly any. It was launched in March 2007 but languishes officially at the beta stage (or, as Wikipedians would put it, in the incubator); it contains about 11,000 articles, generally thorough and well-balanced, many of them selected from Wikipedia and only lightly edited. Only about 100 of them have surpassed draft status to be marked 'approved', and there may never be many more: the process looks as fearsome as it was for Nupedia. In spite of the ambition to cover everything, Citizendium 'will never have nearly as many articles about porn stars and sexual fetishes. We aim to be family-friendly.'[75]

Citizendium is run by nice and scholarly people and suffers very little vandalism, but its growth is painfully slow. Ed Poor, a computer programmer and polyencyclopedist who has edited Wikipedia ever since 2001 and has contributed to Conservapedia and Citizendium since their inception, heads his Citizendium talk page with a thought-provoking Churchill quotation: 'However beautiful the strategy, you should occasionally look at the results.' The French Wikipedia's David.Monniaux, in the course of an interview with *Le Figaro* in which his true mission was to defend the entirely different strategy of Wikipedia, predicted that there would be serious difficulties with Sanger's approach: 'Sanger wants to select experts by paper qualifications. These don't solve problems. Take Holocaust deniers: plenty of them have doctorates and university posts. If universities can't sort out their selection, I don't see how we could. And how would we avoid experts going off the rails? How would we arbitrate among them?'[76]

Conservapedia, 'the trustworthy encyclopedia', was launched in November 2006 by Andy Schlafly, a conservative lawyer who 'teaches one of the largest homeschool classes' in the United States. Its target audience includes students in similar homeschool classes and other Americans who share its views and go to bed early: 'editing, except by those with special rights, is usually turned off over-night (generally 1:00AM to 6:00AM) East Coast United States time. This is due to the high degree of vandalism at the hands of deceitful Liberals.'[77] In spite of the registration requirement, the site suffers frequent vandalism, enough to have made it necessary to lock articles on prominent politicians such as Dick Cheney. Conservapedia articles (over 30,000 of them, many very brief) are decidedly not neutral. They abjure racism but are pervasively pro-American and favour 'truth', or in other words conservative Republican politics and variants of Creationism. Initially the preferred variant was the Young Earth school according to which creation took place 6,000 years ago. More recently, it is said, the Old Earthers have begun to infiltrate.

The Conservapedia article on 'Abortion', one of those that is locked, has a three-sentence introduction: 'Abortion is the induced termination of a pregnancy. Abortion is a billion-dollar industry in the United States and Western Europe except for Ireland, Malta and Poland, where it is generally illegal. God warns in His word that a nation that sheds innocent blood will not prosper.' The last sentence was quietly moved up to this key position in April 2009 by a fervently Christian administrator. The lengthy talk page is studded with frustrated complaints that the article is mis-titled, since, beyond the first sentence, it is entirely devoted to opposing abortion and never describes the practice. The long article on 'Islam', largely based on a US government text, concludes with a list of 'prominent Muslims' in which a reader not familiar with US conservative discourse might be surprised to see the name of 'President Barack Hussein Obama (suspected)'; this detail links to a prominently-placed section of the biographical article on Obama containing 21 bullet points of evidence under the heading 'Obama is likely the first Muslim president'. The entry 'Kangaroo' offers two theories as to how the founding kangaroos, having alighted from the Ark, migrated to Australia.

Indeed, the lack of favour for Creationism on Wikipedia – making it out of bounds as a source on biological topics for some unlucky US schoolchildren – was one of the impulses for Conservapedia, as is suggested in its article 'Examples of Bias in Wikipedia': 'even though most Americans reject the theory of evolution, Wikipedia editors commenting on the topic are nearly

100% pro-evolution.' In the article as originally developed by Andy Schlafly the words 'most Americans' were followed by '(and probably most of the world)',[78] but this assertion was soon removed by a more fastidious editor with the comment: 'I think Conservapedia needs to be less sloppy than Wikipedia. Please don't say "and probably the world" if you can't back it up.' A similar impulse created the specialised CreationWiki, which boasts 4,000 articles in English and seven versions in other languages, but (as if to give the lie to Andy Schlafly) these other-language versions seem to have scarcely an active contributor among them.

It may well appear to an outside observer that Conservapedia is a window opening on to a lunatic fringe of US opinion. It's a wide fringe, though, and decidedly less lunatic than its European parallel, as evidenced in Metapedia, 'the alternative encyclopedia', which began in October 2006 in Swedish; if we include the affiliated site for Slavic languages, Wikislavia, there are or have been as many as 20 different language versions.[79] German, English and French Metapedias were launched in May 2007, riding the current wave of dissatisfaction with Wikipedia, but replicating on a small scale the infighting and edit wars that give Wikipedia a bad name. They all take a right-wing nationalist, and generally a neo-Nazi and anti-Semitic, standpoint. The Metapedias are forever short of users and short of articles; the 'Siberian' version, last refuge of the exiled Siberian Wikipedia, is likely to disappear any moment 'due to persistent vandalism and real lack of good editors', while Wikislavia (which recently claimed 100,000 Russian articles)[80] is having server trouble and the Swedish version has collapsed. The Google placement of surviving Metapedia versions is better than one would wish, and they look just like Wikipedia – so much like it, in fact, that the unwary might well be deceived were it not for the logo, on which the familiar unfinished globe of Wikipedia is replaced by the head of a supercilious curly-haired Aryan youth.

'I've been following the Wikipedia witchhunt against you,' said an editor on the French Metapedia, celebrating the appearance on that site of Jaczewski. 'Here you can work quite freely, without thought police or border guards. We're looking not to the mediocrity of quarrelsome democracy but the quality of the intellectual aristocracy'; then, a little later, 'I see the thought police have finally silenced you on Wikipedia. You're going to like it here. Freedom of expression reigns; well, almost!'

'It was hard for a right-winger to contribute anything on a site so fiercely protected by the antiracist militia,' Jaczewski replied.[81] Metapedia aims less to inform than to direct. At 'Holocaust' and linked pages the fact of the Holocaust is denied.

Articles on Metapedia, Wikislavia and Conservapedia, when compared with parallel Wikipedia entries, are generally one-sided, long on quotation and short on information; frequently they rely on single sources that share the site ideology.

'Reading these inbred cousins of Wikipedia is like stepping into a terrifying parallel universe,' writes David Wong on Cracked.com.[82] Inbreeding goes further. The sudden spate of anti-Wikipedia news in the press, in 2006 and 2007, led also to a spread of not-in-the-least-encyclopedic websites, or rather metawebsites, whose only raison d'être is to talk about Wikipedia. I won't explore these in depth; I'll cite them when they offer enlightenment on shenanigans that actually matter to the average user – yes, there will be some of those – and I'll roll them out here for reference. Classic Wikipedia storms (some better left in their teacups) are set out at Wikipedia Watch. Wikipedia Review is a forum populated by Wikipedia editors, whose attitudes range from fairly happy to extremely disgruntled. Like all forums you aren't involved in, the Review is penetratingly boring; which must be why I scan it, and, as you'll see, cite it. The insistently satirical Encyclopedia Dramatica offers revelations that are, at their best, livelier and less incoherent.

Then there's the material that Wikipedia has suddenly lost. Article history is, on rare occasions, filleted or, in Wikipedia jargon, oversighted. This is what EssJay did with the undesirable early version of the **John Seigenthaler** biography. Contemporary reports assert that the **de:Bertrand Meyer** article history was scrubbed on 3 January 2006, a minute after the false report of his death was removed. If I read the record correctly it has since been unscrubbed: the false information can once again be found in the history. Those who really want to know what's gone can occasionally find it. The site called Wikitruth set out in March 2006 to record information about untrustworthy decisions and oddly motivated deletions at Wikipedia. 'It's hard to tell someone who's devoting 40 hours a week to Wikipedia that it's going to fail. But it will,' said Wikitruth's main contributor.[83] Ironically it is Wikitruth that has faltered, though the site is still visible and some marginally important deleted Wikipedia articles survive on it. MyWikiBiz hosts (among other things) self-promoting articles, deleted from Wikipedia, about people and businesses; it takes an anti-Wikipedia stance. For the incorrigibly curious, other Wikipedia deletions survive in large number at Deletionpedia; for the less curious, some of the funniest are at BJAODN; one or two surprising cases are documented at Wikileaks.

Where Garcia and Assouline raised suspicions of right-wing politics and anti-Semitism in Wikipedia, United States commentators are much more inclined to see liberal and left-wing bias. Since anyone in the world can be a Wikipedia editor, all four of these tendencies exist among Wikipedia editors, along with every other imaginable tendency; and although *neutral point of view* (NPOV) is required of us, neutrality is more easily demanded than attained.

The historian Roy Rosenzweig observes that 'neutrality... is a "founding myth" for Wikipedia much as "objectivity"... is a "founding myth" for the historical profession.'[84] A 'lack of bias' policy was indeed imposed by Sanger and Wales on Nupedia in 2000; they were convinced (and they were probably right) that there would be no better way to limit the endless, fruitless debating that can sink any online collaboration. The policy was simply transferred to Wikipedia, where it was given the name of NPOV. After precisely a year of experience – and already uncertain of his own future with the project – Sanger in an online interview highlighted this policy as one of Wikipedia's strong points:

'The success of such an open project, staffed by such a large and diverse body of writers, is a puzzle [wrote Michael Singer]: how can so many people with so many different backgrounds collaborate with such little oversight? Project organizers say that it is partly because the participants can edit each others' contributions easily, and partly because the project has a strong "nonbias" policy; this keeps interaction relatively polite and productive. "If contributors took controversial stands, it would be virtually impossible for people of many different viewpoints to collaborate," says Sanger. "Because of the neutrality policy, we have partisans working together on the same articles. It's quite remarkable."'[85]

The aim wasn't necessarily to take one single 'unbiased' point of view throughout an article. With any truly controversial topic that would be impossible. 'Instead, Wikipedians say they want to describe disputes rather than to take sides in them, to characterize differing positions fairly,' Rosenzweig was to explain. 'The NPOV policy provides a shared basis of discourse among Wikipedians. On the discussion pages that accompany every Wikipedia article, the number one topic of debate is whether the article adheres to the NPOV.'[86] But it wasn't a perfect solution. Six weeks after Sanger's interview, Eloquence, in an essay that was sparked by Sanger's departure, wrote: 'It's easier to get a certain viewpoint into an article than to get it out. Disagreements often center on what is or is not "mainstream" opinion and what is or isn't a fact that does not need further explanation.'[87]

'Neutral point of view' is probably the most practical aim for a collaborative project like Wikipedia. Unfortunately, when neutrality is attained, blandness comes with it. In the case of hundreds of thousands of briefer articles, editors almost unconsciously borrow style as well as substance from their sources, so that as Wikipedia entries approach a definitive state they become 'largely indistinguishable stylistically from the... *Columbia Encyclopedia*'[88]; while in the case of big news stories, writes Jonathan Dee,

'Wikipedia functions like a massive, cooperative blog – except that where most blogs' function is to sieve news accounts through the filter of strong opinion, Wikipedia's goal is the opposite: it strives to filter all the opinion out of it.'[89]

And so, in this vast, studiedly neutral and sometimes rather doughy expanse of text, how can it be that Pierre Assouline and many others find right-wing bias where Andy Schlafly and many others find left-wing bias?

No institutional bias is imposed. No one bothers to discuss Jimmy Wales's political and philosophical views, although everything else about him that could possibly affect the present or future of Wikipedia is discussed endlessly:

this is because, whatever his views may be, there's no need to discuss them. They aren't relevant. Apart from fostering the development of exhaustive articles on Ayn Rand Thought, Wales's political and philosophical views don't affect Wikipedia's coverage. And although the Wikimedia Foundation's attitude is discussed when matters that might relate to libel or privacy laws arise, no one discusses the Foundation's attitude in the context of articles on left-wing or right-wing politics or religious or ethnic issues: this is because there's no need to discuss the Foundation's attitude. Beyond urging neutrality, it takes no interest in such topics. It doesn't try to influence their coverage. Any such attempts to influence coverage, by Wales or the Foundation, would be counter-productive in any case. Editors would argue vociferously and would refuse to go along with it. And these editors en masse accept the NPOV rule. So if there is 'systemic bias' in Wikipedia, it doesn't stem from Jimmy Wales, or the Wikimedia Foundation, or Wikipedia editors en masse.

Individually, however, it's hard for an editor (or anyone else) to distinguish correctly between 'my viewpoint' and 'a neutral viewpoint'. Whenever two editors take entrenched and opposed views on a disputed edit, each is sure to claim the NPOV.

Now although all imaginable views exist among editors, they aren't equally represented. Any census of userpages and talk pages would surely reveal that among active US editors there are more Democrats than Republicans; among active French editors, more Socialists than Sarkozians; among active British editors, more Liberal Democrats and Labour people than Conservatives. Simply because of their beliefs, lefties are somewhat more likely than political conservatives to give priority in their lives to a co-operative, non-profit-making endeavour that makes information widely and freely accessible. The userpage of the French admin Céréales Killer expresses this frankly: *Wikipedia is a perfect match for my views – views that some don't know and others don't approve. My ideals are left-leaning and libertarian, and that's why Wikipedia corresponds to my vision of the sharing of knowledge, the common ownership of grey matter, with no partisanship, for the good of all... I see Wikipedia as a great way to share knowledge in a completely disinterested way.* As a result, although there's no bias that all editors share, a noticeable majority favours liberalism over conservatism, and this majority, while promising and honestly aiming to be neutral, will tend to find neutrality somewhere left of centre. To this extent, Andy Schlafly is right, and this is why it's more difficult to start a 'Criticism of Barack Obama' article than it was to start a **Criticism of George W. Bush** article. Andy Schlafly's response to this observation was to found Conservapedia. It was a brave step, but some who share his political views didn't see it as the wisest step. Wikipedia still has a thousand times as many articles as Conservapedia, vastly greater prominence on Google, an enormously larger number of readers, an immense and growing influence. And so, for every conservative that fled to Conservapedia or, beyond it, to Metapedia, hundreds remain on Wikipedia, and sometimes contribute their own neutrality, a right-of-centre neutrality, to articles of political relevance.

But they get themselves noticed. Take one tiny example. When David.Monniaux, as already quoted, averred that *négationnistes* (Holocaust deniers) 'have doctorates and university posts and that universities can't sort out their selection', he certainly had in mind the public investigation in 2001, led by the Holocaust historian Henry Rousso, of a group of *négationnistes* at a Lyon university who had had the support of the university's president **fr:Gilles Guyot**. Now then: at the time when Jaczewski incurred opprobrium and blockage on the French Wikipedia for contentious editing (and retreated, as mentioned above, to Metapedia), one of the accusations was that during June 2008 Jaczewski, employing an alternate 'housekeeping' username, tidied up the biographical article on Gilles Guyot, and, among otherwise innocuous alterations, added to Henry Rousso's name the characterisation *left-wing historian*. Yes, it's typical of politically charged discourse to add such an adjective to a person whose opinions one wants the reader to dismiss (hence administrators on Conservapedia characterise mindless obscenities as 'Liberal vandalism'); it's also fairly common among Wikipedians to have more than one username, but the political sensitivity of this one-word addition by Jaczewski's alter ego led to searching investigations, to Jaczewski's confession of double identity, and to the Wikipedia arbitration committee. It was no use Jaczewski's arguing that, as a public backer of Ségolène Royal, Henry Rousso had incontrovertibly identified himself with the left; Jaczewski was wrong-footed, having been observed, on another occasion, boldly removing the characterisation *right-wing* from the name of a public supporter of Marine Le Pen.

As we see, right-wing editors are watched very carefully (especially on the French Wikipedia) and they are at continual risk of being blocked. *We're on our own against them all,* wrote another of Jaczewski's sympathisers. In these circumstances it's quite understandable that many small edits of a right-wing tendency are done anonymously, such as the insertion of the Dutrait-Crozon book into the bibliography at **fr:Affaire Dreyfus**. It's much safer that way. Others can, very easily, check what a known politically-motivated editor has done, and, if they are so inclined, revert any suspicious edits and begin a process that may result in blocking. But all pages can't be watched, or, at least, they can't be watched effectively all the time. There are too many of them.

That, finally, is why Assouline and Schlafly are both right. There is right-wing bias on Wikipedia, sporadic, often bitterly contested, but often anonymously inserted; and there is left-wing bias, the unconscious bias of a liberal majority.

Chapter 4
Why you use it

WIKIPEDIA MANAGED TO get itself indexed by Yahoo for the first time on 26 July 2001,[90] but Google had been listing it well before then, and even at that early date it was Google, not Yahoo, that mattered. 'Consulting the website logs, we noted a Google effect,' Larry Sanger afterwards recalled. 'Each time Google spidered the website, more pages would be indexed; the greater the number of pages indexed, the more people arrived at the project; the more people involved in the project, the more pages there were to index.'[91]

The 'Google effect' is often evoked in early discussions. *Google has been crawling through Wikipedia and including pages in their database rather slowly,* reports an April 2001 newsletter for Wikipedians. *For example, though the Wikipedia History of Levant page is the #1 item for the search 'history of Levant', the cached version is from way back on February 19 and the cached version of Ethical egoism is from March 2. Despite the delay, we have a slowly-growing source of traffic... 'if we build it, they will come' and in greater and greater numbers.*[92] An external link, labelled *This page was #1 on Google*, was proudly added to **History of Levant**. Sanger, the author of this news report, can be forgiven for indulging his egoism slightly in his Google search. He himself had written the Wikipedia article **Ethical egoism**, and it is comforting to see one's own work, however anonymous, riding high on a Google page.

Still in Wikipedia's first year of existence, on October 29 2001, new excitement was reported: *Yesterday, Wikipedia began receiving a substantially increased amount of traffic from Google.com, which will probably result in a permanent traffic increase of over 20% compared with the few weeks leading up to yesterday. We're not sure yet why this is happening. Google already was far and away the most important source of traffic for Wikipedia. If the increase is permanent, then in terms of new personnel and increased article production and editing, we can expect that this will have a long-term effect similar to that of a major news article or of a Slashdotting.*[93] A 'slashdotting', for those who don't know, was the immediate tidal-wave effect, already known to many website managers in this almost-prehistoric period, of having one's website mentioned in an article on the online IT news site Slashdot.org.

Almost from the beginning, then, Google has favoured Wikipedia. Why? Since the Google algorithm is a secret, we are in the dark, just as Sanger and Wales were in the dark in 2001. They could only offer a prayer of thanks or keep their fingers crossed. Whichever they did, the Google effect has continued; and, as they foresaw, it has been a cumulative effect. More pages meant more Google listings, which meant more visits, which meant more new editors, which meant more pages... The same high placing for Wikipedia is observed when Google is searched in other languages. Daniel Garcia's blog essay on the **fr:Affaire Dreyfus** received a comment from 'Michel', who wrote: 'One thing I always find strange is that the main search engines, like Google and Yahoo... systematically place Wikipedia pages at the top of their responses for nearly every enquiry – and the great majority of surfers do not look any further.'[94] Michel would be proud to know that his comment was read by Pierre Assouline, who in his own essay on the same subject wrote soon afterwards: 'Let's observe the "favour" (a euphemism, of course) enjoyed by Wikipedia in the indexing of search engines (Google, Yahoo etc.). Always on the first page, nearly always in prime position, and it's well known that a majority of readers does not look any further.'[95]

I'm reluctant to agree with Assouline if he meant by his word 'euphemism' to imply that there was a commercial or political motive behind Wikipedia's success on Google. If there had previously been a commercial motive, then Wikipedia would surely have lost Google favour in the course of 2008, because in that year the two sides were making their incompetent attempts to compete with one another – Google with its useless open encyclopedia *Knol*, Jimmy Wales's Wikia Inc. with its unadmired search engine Wikia Search – but no such effect occurred at that time and Wikipedia pages remained as well-placed as ever. Google is a commercial giant, but it can surely have no financial reason to favour Wikipedia, which is non-profit, takes no advertising and tries quite hard to exclude commercial links from its pages. Google could conceivably gain commercially from favouring Wikia Inc. (which houses little specialised wikis and is financed by advertising) but, as a matter of fact, Wikia sites don't show up especially well on Google. Google might gain from favouring some of the sites that mirror Wikipedia pages, like Answers.com, because many of these are financed by advertising too; but in fact Google nearly always places real Wikipedia pages just marginally ahead of their mirrors. This fact seems to suggest that it is some property of the pages themselves, not a property of the Wikimedia Foundation, that produces Wikipedia's high Google rating.

The factors usually identified are three. First, pages well-supplied with local links to other pages are favoured, because they ease the task of Google's web-crawling software. This helps to explain why Wikipedia did so well in its earliest years (because its pages are always liberally studded with easily-created internal links) and why the mirror sites and Conservapedia and Metapedia also do well: their internal format is identical. Second, pages that are the targets of links from other sites do well, because the web-crawling software is more likely to visit them. This criterion helps to explain why, in Google placement, Wikipedia pages remain ahead of the right-wing wikis and the Wikipedia mirrors: few other sites link to those, but many other sites link to Wikipedia. Third, pages that are visited are favoured, because links that some people found useful will make Google in turn appear more useful. The cumulative effect of all this on Wikipedia – making it simply grow and grow – justifies the observation of Nicholas Carr in an article in the *Guardian* in May 2007. Carr begins with some examples.

'Search at Google.com on evolution or Iraq or Aids or Gordon Brown, and the same site will appear at the top of the list of results: Wikipedia. Alter your search into one for John Keats or Muhammad Ali or Christianity or platypus or loneliness, and the same thing will happen. Pacific Ocean? Wikipedia. Catherine de Medici? Wikipedia. Human brain? Wikipedia. In fact, if you Google any person, place or thing today, you're almost guaranteed to find Wikipedia at or near the top of the list of recommended pages.'

Carr's real point was that although the total number of websites continued to increase, in another sense our web was shrinking: we were spending more time on fewer sites, and along with MySpace and Facebook, Google and Wikipedia were among the favoured few. Google was not only a beneficiary but a cause, Carr insisted. Google 'has had the effect of turning the web into a giant feedback loop. The more popular a site becomes, the more it comes to dominate search results, which ends up funnelling ever more links and traffic to it.' The effect observed and welcomed long before by Larry Sanger had become visible web-wide.[96]

But there could be more to it. I was wrong, perhaps, to dismiss Assouline's suspicion of a hidden motive for the Google favouritism. I am really reluctant to dismiss the observation of his predecessor, the semi-anonymous Michel, who, in late 2006, said simply that Google 'systematically place Wikipedia pages at the top of their responses'. We like to think that Google is random, giving us exactly what we deserve like Justice blindfolded, but, like Michel, in our heart of hearts we know that there's a system. Was there, after all, a moment when the system was weighted in favour of Wikipedia specifically? Nicholas Carr himself has provided some evidence for this. When in August 2006 he first surveyed a set of ten Wikipedia titles (some of which he was to name in his *Guardian* article, just quoted) to see how well they did in the Google placements, he found that they achieved somewhere between ninth place (**Genome**) and first place (**World War II** and **Israel**). 'I bet that most Wikipedia entries are continuing to move upward – and many will, like **World War II**, come to reach the top spot,' he wrote then.[97] How right he was. He did the survey again, on the same articles, in December 2007, and found that seven were in first place and none was lower than third (**Epilepsy**); his prediction had already come true. Carr regards Google's promotion of Wikipedia as 'inadvertent' and characterises his results as 'evidence of a fundamental failure of the Web as an information-delivery service'.[98]

So what is the system that Michel perceived, that Assouline suspected, and for which Carr has provided circumstantial evidence? I hesitate to believe everything that Assouline says about Wikipedia, or everything said about it by Andrew Orlowski of *The Register*, but among Orlowski's assertions on the subject that I believe deserve credit, this may very well be one. He explains Carr's results as follows. In late 2005 Google was fighting a losing battle against spam sites, which offer endless, meaningless content simply in order to be indexed and thus snare unwary surfers; and against blogs, which were multiplying far beyond reason. Google therefore took the conscious decision to favour Wikipedia because, though its faults are many, Wikipedia is the largest available source of serious text across all subject areas. Favouring Wikipedia was the simplest way to ensure that the average Google results page would look useful.[99]

Up to a point, it worked. And because favouring Wikipedia could only mean putting Wikipedia at the top of the results – and because (as Michel put it) 'the great majority of surfers do not look any further' or (as Assouline put it more classically) 'does not look any further' – you, as a member of that majority, are now fated to click on the Wikipedia link almost every time.

As I've explained, Google's web-crawling software follows links from other sites to Wikipedia. So do we all. If we're reading a news item online, and it contains a hyperlink to a site that offers more information, we may well click on it.

Since in 2001 and 2002 Wikipedia was a small and patchy encyclopedia, many of whose articles on important topics were mere stubs, it's a little surprising to see how quickly certain other sites began to link to it, but this is partly explained by the general rules that public websites tend to set themselves. If you run a free, non-commercial website you will avoid making links to sites that require payment, because most of your readers won't want to pay, will be angered at the waste of their time, and will trust you less in the future. If you run a commercial website that takes advertising, you will send readers to sites that expect payment only if those sites will pay you for the link or will send you readers in return. If you run a commercial website that charges a subscription you may well make links to other similar sites – but you don't have many readers to send there. And so, from 2001 onwards, on the pages of most of the big public sites, if you wanted to link to an encyclopedia you would prefer to avoid the current *Britannica* and *Encarta*. What other choice had you except Wikipedia or (if worst came to worst) the free-access *Britannica 1911*?

Of the many, many links from online news articles to Wikipedia, the earliest that's on record now (it may well not have been the first in reality) seems to be a London *Daily Telegraph* article of 17 August 2002, 'Japan and South Korea fall out over "sea with no name".'[100] The online version of this article has a marginal link to the Wikipedia entry **Sea of Japan** – and, incidentally, edit wars occur sporadically in the various language wikipedias over whether this sea should be called 'Sea of Japan', as the Japanese prefer, or 'Sea of the East', as the Koreans prefer. From that date onward the *Telegraph* began to link to Wikipedia more and more often. The next in date (12 October 2002) is a marginal link alongside the *Telegraph*'s news item 'Tebbit Will Stay, Says Tory Leader'[101] to the Wikipedia entry **Norman Tebbit**, a surprising choice because this plain-spoken British Conservative is much more popular among *Telegraph* readers than among Wikipedia editors. The entry as it existed at that date – the work of the veteran and still-active Wikipedian TwoOneTwo, though contributed anonymously – ended with a brisk estimate: [Tebbit] *is a extreme Eurosceptic and his outspoken views on race and immigration have brought him both support and opprobrium (he was nicknamed the 'Chingford skinhead').*

Such links show us that, whatever opinion about Wikipedia might be held by the newspaper's columnists and technology correspondents, staff working on the paper's website thought it useful enough. They don't, however, tell us – and this is also an interesting question – whether journalists were using Wikipedia for their research.

A set of pages headed **wp:Press coverage** helps to provide answers here, and a major contributor to these pages has been Fuzheado, professor of journalism (successively at Hong Kong and Columbia) and avid Wikipedian. One of the earliest frank acknowledgements of Wikipedia as a source in any major newspaper occurs in the 29 March 2003 issue of *The Age* (Melbourne), in which Simon Tsang, offering historical background to the invasion of Iraq, cites the Wikipedia entry **History of Iraq** and gives brief verbatim quotations: *the Mesopotamian plain was called the Fertile Crescent,* defined as *present-day Israel, Palestine, and Lebanon and parts of Jordan, Syria, Iraq and south-eastern Turkey.*[102] The second of Tsang's quotes is actually from **Fertile Crescent**, an as yet brief article begun by the longstanding Californian contributor Mav. **History of Iraq**, by contrast, was already in 2003 a very long piece by Wikipedia's standards at that time. It was also among the earliest, created in May 2001 by KoyaanisQatsi, who in the course of that first year improved many of the nascent articles about countries by judicious use of the public-domain *CIA World Factbook*.

On 28 May 2003 the *Sydney Morning Herald* was citing Wikipedia on the history of words, specifically the question of what **Weapon of mass destruction** used to mean before the Iraq War. This article already had Mav, Ed Poor and Eloquence among its contributors; it had most recently been extended by the mysterious Bon d'une cythare, who during 2003 was among several editors focusing on the general subject area of **Persuasive technology**.

In 2003 Wikipedia was still new and relatively small. Citations of Wikipedia embedded in journalistic text were extremely rare – and of great interest to contributors. *This is of course a great vote of confidence, but also brings with it a responsibility. Was French toast really called German toast before? Was the Mesopotamian plain really called the Fertile Crescent?* a compiler muses (there was no problem with the Fertile Crescent; we'll come back to the toast question).

By 2008, when Donna Shaw investigated the journalistic use of Wikipedia for *American Journalism Review*, Wikipedia was an enormous, ever-changing source of material, with thousands of active editors; yet citations of Wikipedia embedded in newspaper text were still relatively rare. Here are a couple of her examples.

'When the *Las Vegas Review-Journal* published a story in September about construction cranes, it noted that they were invented by ancient Greeks and powered by men and donkeys... Hubble Smith, the *Review-Journal* business reporter who wrote the crane story, says he was simply looking for background... when the Wikipedia entry popped up during a search. It was among the most interesting information he found, so he used it. But after his story went to the desk, a copy editor flagged it. "He said, 'Do you realize that Wikipedia is just made up of people who contribute all of this?'" Smith recalls. "I had never used it before."'

Smith was able to reassure the copy-editor, however. He had relied on a statement in the well-researched ancient history section of the Wikipedia article **Crane (machine)**. All credit, incidentally, to Gun Powder Ma, writer of this section, who really knows about the history of science and sometimes gets into spats with other Wikipedians because of a tendency to reject weakly documented claims of Chinese and Arab scientific priority. Gun Powder Ma had sourced this statement about cranes, and not just to any old source, but to a scholarly paper in the *Journal of Hellenic Studies*, a peer-reviewed ancient history journal. Short of acquiring and reading the original paper, which we'll accept that Smith and the copy-editor didn't have time to do, they handled this exactly right. They got the information from Wikipedia, decided it should be trusted, and credited Wikipedia for it. Citing the *Journal of Hellenic Studies* out of Gun Powder Ma's footnote would not only have been useless and boring for the *Review-Journal*'s readers: it would have been dishonest. If you're relying on Wikipedia (including its footnotes), cite Wikipedia.

In another of Shaw's examples the *Wall Street Journal* website cited Wikipedia as its source for information on 'turducken', a chicken cooked inside a duck cooked inside a turkey. The *Journal* admitted that some of its information was 'courtesy of Wikipedia's highly informative Turducken entry', and its reporter added: 'I'm not making this up. Although, I'll admit that somebody on Wikipedia might have.' Shaw discussed this example with Jimmy Wales, whose sensible comment was: 'Well, what other source would you use? *Britannica* doesn't cover this nonsense.' The **Turducken** article, to which ChildofMidnight (one among several contributors) has made more than 50 edits, is lip-smackingly good and fully deserves the *Wall Street Journal*'s tongue-in-cheek acknowledgement.[103]

Shaw notes that although some newspapers never admit the words 'according to Wikipedia', others do. The *Los Angeles Times* is one such: 'We're not going to exclude [Wikipedia] if it takes us somewhere,' an editor told her. 'If a reporter spots something in there and it makes them do an extra phone call,' then Wikipedia deserved credit – and it was credited, for example, in a 2007 *LA Times* story about **Greg Packer**, a professional 'man in the street' who has got himself interviewed more than a hundred times on topics ranging from Princess Diana's death to Jewish opinion on Pope John Paul II.

But the *LA Times*'s citation aroused an anti-Wikipedia claque. This time it was not the editorial staff of the paper that objected; nor was it *The Register* (in which a recent article by Cade Metz concluded with the perceptive words:

'When you consider that the world's newspapers are misguided enough to pull their info straight from Wikipedia, the two are closer than they might seem).'[104] It might well have been either, but this time it was the honestly-named forum Testycopyeditors.org. The news that the *LA Times* had cited Wikipedia sparked discussion under the heading 'No, no, a thousand times no', with comments including 'Shame on the Los Angeles Times' and 'I would just bet this entry was written by Packer himself, by golly.'[105] The last speaker would have been surprised, had he checked his facts, to find that the Greg Packer article had been gradually built up to that point by 15 named contributors and a roughly equal number of anonymous ones. These contributors had faced opposition from several talk page critics urging that Packer was not notable and therefore ineligible for Wikipedia. *If Paris Hilton is a notable person then this guy is notable too*, was the best approach to a reply.

From the debates among anti-Wikipedia journalists and copy-editors it's evident that the softest targets on the great big encyclopedia are the inaccuracies and out-of-date details. Daniel H. Pink, in a *Wired* story, had urged: 'Look up any topic you know something about and you'll probably find that the Wikipedia entry is, if not perfect, not bad.'[106] Paul Boutin, writing in *Slate*, retorted: 'Don't people use encyclopedias to look up stuff they don't know anything about? Even if a reference tool is 98 percent right, it's not useful if you don't know which 2 percent is wrong. The entry for *Slate*, for instance, claims that several freelance writers are "columnists on staff" and still lists Cyrus Krohn as publisher months after the Washington Post Co.'s Cliff Sloan took over.' Boutin will have reflected at this point (though he forgot to say so) that Wikipedia had brought him nearer his heart's desire than any general encyclopedia in history. Only on Wikipedia will there be an entry, albeit imperfect, on a pop culture topic such as *Slate*. Only on Wikipedia do the people at *Slate* have the power to update the entry themselves with instantaneous effect. But they have to want to do it, and, as Boutin continued, 'not everyone who uses a wiki wants to hit from both sides of the plate. The subset of enthusiastic writers and editors is orders of magnitude smaller than the group of passive readers who'll never get around to contributing anything... Wikipedia is a good first stop to get the basics in a hurry, especially for tech and pop culture topics that probably won't ever make it into *Britannica*.'[107] This final concession chimes with Jimmy Wales's view as quoted by Donna Shaw. Wales was not surprised that some journalists were testing Wikipedia cautiously. 'I think that people are sort of slowly learning how to use [it], and learning its strengths and its weaknesses... There are lots of sources that have weaknesses.' The best journalistic use of Wikipedia, Wales added, would be for background research rather than as a source to be quoted.[108]

So far, so negative. Journalists don't like Wikipedia, rarely use it (certainly not 'to settle a bar bet', Boutin insisted), and are forever telling their colleagues not to use it. But it's been suspected for a long time that this isn't the full story. Journalists often copy from Wikipedia and forget to acknowledge it. The earliest observed case of what seems to be wholesale borrowing is the article 'Left Alone', published on the *Guardian* website on 12 October 2003. This short and patchy sketch of 'the long and patchy history of attempts to unite the left' shares about two-thirds of its text with the then Wikipedia articles **Socialist Alliance** and **Scottish Labour Party**.[109] *Check the dates if this seems unlikely!* wrote Fuzheado after noting the case. Afterwards, perhaps doubting the validity of his observation, he deleted the note about it; I came across it only by chance.

The best demonstration that journalists are using Wikipedia as a source right now, and without checking further, and without giving it credit, was made in March 2009 by a final-year undergraduate at University College Dublin.[110] Shane Fitzgerald conducted a little experiment via the English Wikipedia. 'Reporters are relying on [the internet] more than ever,' he wrote afterwards in the *Irish Times*. 'I wanted to prove that this was indeed the case, and show the potential dangers that arise.' Early on 30 March, hearing the news of the death of **Maurice Jarre**, Fitzgerald decided to find the French composer's Wikipedia biography and add a 'quote' to it:

'*One could say my life itself has been one long soundtrack*, I wrote into the Wikipedia entry. *Music was my life, music brought me to life, and music is how I will be remembered long after I leave this life. When I die there will be a final waltz playing in my head and that only I can hear...* Neither Maurice Jarre, nor anyone else, has ever been on record as uttering these words. Social science experiments always have ethical issues, because you are in effect using people as guinea pigs. I did not wish to taint or distort anyone's reputation, so I purposely made the decision to put in a general, random quote that would not affect Jarre's stature.'

That night, in fact, the **Maurice Jarre** biography was very active. It was adjusted several times by Hektor and four other editors, between 21.47 and 23.39 on 29 March, to incorporate the fact of Jarre's death. Then, at 2.29 on 30 March, an anonymous user (evidently Shane Fitzgerald) added the above words in a new section headed 'Quotes'. Just two minutes later RayAYang added a flag to the article, immediately over this new material, noting prominently that it was unsourced. At 11.51 – nine hours after Fitzgerald had added his material – Cosprings removed it. This wasn't the end of it, however, because at 14.13 Fitzgerald returned to the entry and added the single quote above for a second time. This time it was deleted very rapidly. Fitzgerald, nothing if not persistent, added it a third time on the evening of 31 March. By that time it was 'supported' (in a feedback loop) by many other websites, and it remained for a whole day before its third and final deletion.

Incidentally, this was the last but not the only anonymous edit of Wikipedia from the Eircom.net IP address used by Fitzgerald. On 16 March some childish vandalism appeared at the head of the article **Guppy**. It was reverted after half an hour. On 17 March, at the head of the article on the Irish town of **Blessington**, appeared the line *blessington is the coolesat town ever their soccer team is the best(u12)!!!!!!* It survived just six minutes. Fitzgerald was practising, perhaps.

He had expected blogs and perhaps small newspapers to use his fictitious Jarre quotation, so he said. He was surprised to find that it appeared in major newspapers.[111] Others may be equally surprised to note that this happened in spite of the warning flag placed above his material two minutes after it appeared.

Oddly enough, the route by which it spread was exactly the same as in the earlier case of apparent journalistic borrowing from Wikipedia, six years previously. Again, it was the *Guardian*. The Jarre obituary in that paper was written by Patrick O'Connor and appeared on 31 March 2009. It opened with an extract from the Shane Fitzgerald quotation, one word omitted: 'My life has been one long soundtrack. Music was my life, music brought me to life,' and it closed with another extract: 'When I die there will be a final waltz playing in my head and that only I can hear,' this time not daring to adjust Fitzgerald's awkward grammar.

Among several other world newspapers The *Sydney Morning Herald* included the quote in its Jarre obituary, and credited the *Guardian* as a source. The fake quote has since been removed from the online text,[112] but Fitzgerald deserves a special accolade for having supplied the *SMH* with its headline, 'Life Was One Long Soundtrack', still visible on the page.[113] The full Fitzgerald quotation can even now be found credited to Jarre (I'm writing this on 31 May 2009) on Motion Picture Editors Guild and plenty of other news sites and blogs worldwide, but most of them are not directly dependent on Wikipedia; they are relaying, or abridging, the *Guardian* obituary.

On 3 April the *Guardian* itself inserted one of its many punctilious corrections (this one is now visible at the foot of the online version of the obituary): 'These quotes appear to have originated as a deliberate insertion in the composer's Wikipedia entry in the wake of his death on 28 March, and from there were duplicated on various internet sites.'[114] By clever choice of words the newspaper avoided admitting that Patrick O'Connor relied on Wikipedia and that most of those internet sites relied on the *Guardian*.

From the Wikipedia point of view Fitzgerald's experiments, like those of Pierre Gourdain and colleagues, were vandalism. All that can be said in Fitzgerald's favour is that his last experiment had some limited value. It was a timely reminder that 'there are lots of sources that have weaknesses', as Jimmy Wales had said, and that journalists use Wikipedia more often than they admit. It was a sign that flags such as *unsourced* and *citation needed* on a Wikipedia page are ignored even by users to whom it really matters (this, I would say, is because there are far too many such warnings). As a result, when an item of newsworthy misinformation is inserted in Wikipedia, we now know how quickly it can spread.

A good reason why journalists keep an eye on Wikipedia these days is that it may be first with the news. Let the detractors say that it can't be trusted. Tell them in return that all news media are inaccurate in their first reports of a big story, because rumours travel and no one ever has the full facts; tell them that if there are even rumours of a major incident, people want to know about it.

The exciting thing about Wikipedia is that potential sources are almost infinite and reporters are legion. Anyone in the world who has access to a computer can be a Wikipedia reporter. The death of **Andrea Dworkin**, feminist writer and activist, is a fine example. The news broke rather unobtrusively: a Wikipedia user account was created under the name of Stockma, and Stockma's first edit, at 1.58 GMT on 10 April 2005, was to insert a date of death (9 April) in the Andrea Dworkin biography. Four minutes later, an anonymous editor changed present to past tenses in the article where needed. So it rested, until at 5.23 a very occasional contributor, Lemuria, asked on the talk page: *What's the source on Dworkin's date of death? I haven't been able to find this on news sites.* Moink, a careful administrator, did some checking and reported: *I also am having trouble finding any evidence that she died.* At 11.59, therefore, Moink returned the article to its previous state (*reverting for now, until we have a reliable source for her death*). At 16.11, Viajero (an American living in Amsterdam) restored the information about Dworkin's death, adding on the talk page a reference to a message on a mailing list. Diderot (a Canadian living in Brussels) doubted this and reverted at 18.16, adding a reply to Viajero: *Third hand sources – Doug Henwood heard on Infoshop from someone forwarding a mail from no one knows who with a numbered e-mail address from comcast – and it's been a day and a half since the reported time of death and no media outlet at all has covered it, nor is there an announcement on Dworkin's website. I don't think she's dead.* Finally, however, Diderot's scepticism was proved false: *a new wikipedian*, perhaps Stockma, privately sent Moink copies of emails from Dworkin's colleagues reporting her death at first hand (these emails are now quoted in full on the talk page). Moink's next visit to the Andrea Dworkin page, at 22.41, was to restore the information about her death one last time.

All this time, nothing appeared in the press. At 2.07 on 11 April an anonymous editor added on the talk page: *I have it from sources within NYC now that Andrea, indeed, passed away yesterday morning. Unfathomable that Wikipedia is the first online source I could find for any discussion of her death.* Soon afterwards a couple of blogs picked up the story, one of which was Joegratz.net: 'Imagine an encyclopedia that had someone's death noted in their biography before the first major news outlet had even published an obituary. That's Wikipedia,' Gratz reflected.[115] Finally, at 17.22, Shmuel was able to close the case at **Talk:Andrea Dworkin**. *Any legitimate sources on her death yet?* a veteran and studiously anonymous contributor had demanded. *We had legitimate sources yesterday,* Shmuel retorted, *but the mainstream media has finally caught up,* and he added a link to a news item by Simon Jeffery in the *Guardian* which had appeared online seven minutes earlier. Having been a tiny bit critical of the *Guardian* above, I have to praise its straightforward honesty here. In a *Guardian* news blog piece on the following day under the title 'Wikipedia – first with the news' Jeffery recounted how the story broke, using the Wikipedia talk page as his main source:

'The news was circulating on feminist mailing lists shortly after Dworkin died in her sleep on Saturday, and from there it found its way to [Wikipedia] and some blogs. But a lack of corroboration from the press and certainty over the source – again gone over on the discussion page – meant the Wikipedia writers and some of their readers could not decide if it was true... it caused confusion here too, unused as we were to researching a news story and finding Wikipedia the sole supporting published source, breaking the news in its own quiet and understated manner.'[116]

So in the case of Andrea Dworkin's death the first Wikipedian got it right. The problem was: could the fact be verified?

We'll look later at the taste issue raised by the news of the death of **Tim Russert**, newsman at NBC. Enough to say here that he died at NBC's Washington headquarters; NBC itself did not report his death until his family had been informed, but the news meanwhile appeared in his Wikipedia biography. Other journalists, knowing only that he had collapsed, found that NBC had no further news for them but that Wikipedia had.

A very similar case occurred on the French Wikipedia, where the death of the 49-year-old sports journalist **fr:Thierry Gilardi** was reported well ahead of the newspapers. Gilardi died just after dinner. An anonymous edit reported his death at 20.25 GMT, an hour and a half before the news media relayed it; after which the page suddenly became busy, and some childish vandalism led EyOne to *semi-protect* it, locking it against anonymous edits for a week. Who got the news and put it on Wikipedia so quickly was never clear.

Caveant lectores. Sometimes the first Wikipedian gets it wrong; and unluckily the first Wikipedian very often doesn't care to cite a reference in a footnote (or doesn't know how). We recall that Ambroise's short-lived edit announcing **fr:Philippe Manoeuvre**'s death, an edit that was made in good faith but with no source cited, led to a police investigation. The excited discussion among Wikipédiens of the Manoeuvre incident was initiated by Anthere, with the words: *I'm always suspicious when journalists get to hear about an error that was only up for a few minutes. I wonder if there isn't a 'campaign' under way?*

Anthere wasn't being paranoid: she had in mind another little problem of a few days earlier, the premature announcement of the death of the aged Martinican author **Aimé Césaire**. *The Césaire business surely wasn't an attack on us*, Apollon reassured her. *There's no real similarity. The edit reporting his death was made after he was rushed to hospital.*[117]

In the Césaire case the error did not begin among Wikipedians. The first editor to report his death (T L Miles at 0.58 GMT on 11 April 2008 on the English Wikipedia) referred to an obituary in *African Global News*, 'Nécrologie: Aimé Césaire est mort'.[118] Miles continued to update and improve the page for an hour after that first edit. Twelve hours later, at 13.09, an anonymous contributor removed the death notice, adding the edit summary: *He's not dead yet: he's just in the hospital – no other serious information source reports his death for now.* Miles returned to the page soon afterwards and admitted ruefully: *The Senegalese papers pulled their death notices after I trundled off to bed, I can only assume put up on rumors.*

Césaire is not unknown in the English-speaking world but he is passionately interesting to French speakers: he is a major twentieth century French poet. And so, at 8.14 GMT, an anonymous editor copied the assertion of Césaire's death to **fr:Aimé Césaire**, the equivalent page on the French Wikipedia.

Another anonym removed it at 9.34 but it was reinserted two minutes later by WimDerNess, removed again, inserted a third time by Mehdi19 at 12.57, removed at 14.18, inserted a fourth time anonymously at 21.36 and removed by the same editor eight minutes later. Several further attempts to announce his death appeared on the page during 12 April, surviving between one minute and half an hour before being removed. Our old friend DocteurCosmos wisely imposed semi-protection on the page later that day. In fact Césaire was to die in hospital on 17 April.

Some of the later edits to the French page may well have been mischievous, because meanwhile, in the afternoon of 11 April, 20minutes.fr had published a poorly-researched article with the teasing headline 'Wikipedia buries Aimé Césaire too soon'. Of all the activity listed above, the reporter had noticed only Mehdi's edit and its subsequent revert.[119]

Mehdi, aware of having brought obloquy on the French Wikipedia, made immediate apologies at **fr:Discussion:Aimé Césaire**: *I am deeply sorry about the info I added to the article. I wasn't the first to do it, but never mind. I read on the English Wikipedia that Césaire had died; that's why I repeated it here, just as the others did earlier. It irritates me a bit that 20minutes.fr says I was the first to write this, but it was rubbish in any case and it's perfectly true that I wrote it.*

It's not so bad, said Pierre73 in consolation. *I'm already looking forward to the next mess-up on 20minutes.fr… Your information was sourced – cool – but it was wrong – shit. You can't always catch other people's mistakes. That's too bad, but it's a fact that speed and haste produce confusion around here.* Anguished discussion continued, fed by the uncomfortable fact (of which all were quietly aware) that Wikipedia had performed much worse than the somnolent 20minutes.fr ever noticed. Mehdi had forgotten to cite a source, other editors observed; in any case, another wiki would not have qualified as a source; yes, the English Wikipedia claim had been correctly sourced to one African newspaper, but surely the claim, if it were true, would have been taken up on other media as well; and in any case it is unwise ever to treat Wikipedia as a news source or blog rather than an encyclopedia; and look at the continual shenanigans at **fr:Nicolas Sarkozy**; and so on, and so on. *Why don't we ever announce the birth of a major personality?* asked Arcane17.

The reason for *African Global News*'s original mistake was never explained, but the likelihood is simply this: someone heard that the nonagenarian Césaire had been rushed to hospital and put two and two together. In all probability the same unlucky human tendency – to rush to judgement – led to one of the English Wikipedia's most notorious little slips.

On 20 January 2009, the day of Barack Obama's inauguration, the Wikipedia biography of **Ted Kennedy** became the focus of intense activity. An anonymous editor inserted at 19.44 the news that *Senator Kennedy collapsed during the Presidential Luncheon* on that day; another, a minute later, added the same information at another point in this long article, crediting the information to CNN but wrongly giving the date as 19 January. After other minor edits, at 19.50 a third anonymous edit added at a third point some additional news: *After attending Barack Obama's inauguration luncheon, Kennedy collapsed, and was taken out on a stretcher and later died.* The same edit included a date of death in the introductory sentence. A minute later, these two changes were reverted, also anonymously. At 19.59 a named account which had been used only for vandalism reinserted the claim that Kennedy had died; it was removed two minutes later, but almost immediately added again, perhaps in good faith, by a semi-literate anonym (*He passed away on January 20, 2009 at a lunchin after Barrak Obama was sworn in*) and reinforced by another confused editor, who reinstated elsewhere in the text the words *and died shortly after* but explained the edit with the words *There is no conformation of him dying.* The first claim of death had been removed again, but not the second, and the date of death still remained in the introductory sentence, at the moment of 20.03 when J.delanoy protected the article from further anonymous edits; the two remaining incorrect claims were deleted within the next two minutes by Rickyrab and the philosopher Sdornan.

Kennedy's Wikipedia page was not the only one affected. Senator Robert Byrd had left the luncheon early, and at 19.45 an anonymous edit inserted in his biography the claim that he had *collapsed*; between 19.52 and 19.56 four other editors inserted at different points in the article statements to the effect that he had *gone through some medical emergency*, and these claims were being removed, reinstated and tidied up for several minutes afterwards, with notes that NBC News, CNN, Allheadlinenews.com and WOWKTV were reporting the same incident. Then at 20.06 an anonym inserted 20

January 2009 as Byrd's date of death. The article was protected at 20.08. By 20.12 Cassandro and Joshmaul had removed all mentions of Byrd's death: *No one has said he's dead!* but it took until 20.56 for information about his putative collapse to be tidied and collected into an appropriate section headed 'Health Issues'.

Kennedy had indeed collapsed, but recovered; Byrd, apparently affected by Kennedy's plight, merely chose to leave the luncheon early. The *Washington Post*, in a magisterial response to the confusion on Wikipedia, showed considerable sophistication in documenting the issue. 'Kennedy, Byrd the Latest Victims of Wikipedia Errors', it proclaimed (admitting, lower down the page, that the *Post* itself in August 2008 had falsely reported the death of Democrat Senator Stephanie Tubbs Jones). Although it did not pick up the full complexity of edits on the Kennedy and Byrd pages between 19.44 and 20.12 on the day of Obama's inauguration, the *Post* had the main details right and its online version gives accurate links to Wikipedia page histories and user pages.[120]

Rickyrab, one of those who cleared up the little mess, tried to add a comment to the *Post*'s article. Finding comments 'disabled', he added it to his Wikipedia user page instead:

Hi, I'm Rickyrab. This sort of nonsense happens every time someone gets into a crisis or people get excited: people like to 'jump the gun' and say a President-Elect is President, someone badly hurt is dead, and so on and so forth. This leads to a lot of reversions, but it happens. At least reversions of vandalism tend to be prompt.

As Rickyrab demonstrated, and as Cory Doctorow had shown from his own experience (see his 2006 article 'Correcting the Record: Wikipedia vs *The Register*') when anything needs correcting or explaining Wikipedia is much more easily updated than a newspaper or news site. It faithfully reflects the state of informed knowledge: when something big is happening, people initially waver between doubt and certainty, between false rumour and true report. No wonder that lots of people, journalists included, are looking to Wikipedia for the latest information and even for just-breaking news. No wonder the journalists are frightened.

The earliest discussions of Wikipedia among academics, such as the fairly enthusiastic notice on the *Free Online Scholarship Newsletter* on 26 October 2001, said nothing about student use of this new resource, though there was already concern with the issue of reliability. 'Because all contributions can be revised or thoroughly rewritten by others... with no approval from anyone, there is no formal peer review in the traditional sense at all. But Wikipedia is not so much an experiment in scholarship without peer review as it is an experiment in communal peer review.'[121]

In late 2001 'an experiment' is exactly what Wikipedia was, and a student who found a Wikipedia page sufficiently full, coherent and convincing to serve as the complete answer to an assignment was a lucky student indeed. In 2007 Wikipedia looked very different – itself full, coherent and convincing in many topic areas – and it was in that year that the issue of student use of Wikipedia was in the news. The assignment with which faculties were faced was this: should Wikipedia be cited as a source of information?

It was only because universities have occasional panic attacks on the subject of plagiarism that this assignment appeared difficult. So it's necessary to put the plagiarism issue to rest. In the age of the internet, plagiarism – copying someone else's work without acknowledgement – is a much easier and quicker process than ever before. As a lazy student you can search the web for all kinds of approaches to a topic on which you are due to write something; you can sift these for relevance and style; having made your selection you can paste the most suitable text into your own document, edit it (if you feel the need), submit it, and sit back to wait for the plaudits. In the age of Google, however, plagiarism is also much easier to detect than ever before. As a suspicious professor you can take a striking phrase from a student essay and paste it into Google with double quotes around it; or you can submit the text to a plagiarism-finding program. Either way, you may come up with a close match for the whole essay, and in such a case you will invoke your university's disciplinary procedure and sit back to watch the results. At least one professor, known on the French Wikipedia as Loudon dodd, had found that plagiarism may identify itself more simply, or so he reported on a talk page. Presented with a strangely familiar essay, he realised that it had been copied and pasted from a Wikipedia article that he himself had written. *Incidentally, when I re-read it I noticed a mistake I'd made.*[122]

Plagiarists' sources may include original web pages of all kinds, as well as printed books. Wikipedia only comes into this because its factual articles are potential sources like the rest, and because they exist in ever-increasing numbers, steadily lengthening and improving. Copying a whole Wikipedia article, or any other web page, and presenting it as a student essay, is plagiarism. Copying any significant amount of text from a Wikipedia page, like copying from any other textual source, is also plagiarism unless the source is properly acknowledged, and professors and universities are often quite specific about what they consider proper acknowledgement to be.

Thus far, then, Wikipedia is no different from any other source. Wikipedia has developed a definition of *reliable source* and often issues reminders that Wikipedia itself is not a reliable source by this definition. From 2005, however, heavy negative press reporting threw extra doubt on Wikipedia's reliability and academic respectability. 'I never allow Wikipedia to be used in my courses,' said Isabelle Leloup of the University of Rouen. 'I tell my students carefully that it is in no way a scientific encyclopedia.'[123] 'To those of you who cited internet sites,' a US professor admonished his students, 'some are reliable, some are not. Screen carefully. You can use appropriate internet sources, but you must use at least 3 academic publications (books/ journal articles) to source/support your data. Please note that Wikipedia is not to be considered a reliable source: it is my understanding that anyone can put anything there, and it is not vetted for accuracy.' The advice is unexceptional, but the singling out of Wikipedia is evidence of the atmosphere of suspicion that surrounded the site. The issue was discussed more positively by the French National Institute of Educational Research, which in 2006 issued a careful critique of Wikipedia as a teaching aid.[124]

Older teachers tend towards conservatism, let's say, in their views about how students should go about their studies; and students tend to forgetfulness when it comes to citing every source from which they have copied a sentence or two. After a 2007 lecture at the University of Alberta about citation and plagiarism, in which Deborah Eerkes's main message had been the need to cite every source used, 'one person puts up his hand and says, "What about Wikipedia? Do we have to cite that?"' 'In a digital world where people regularly download songs from the Internet, share personal pictures on Facebook and update their whereabouts on Twitter,' the reporter of this story comments, 'it's apparent that today's students may have a different attitude toward the concept of information ownership.'[125] Wikipedia has become so very convenient. 'I tell them to write what they think, and they start copying from Wikipedia. They take it over word for word. They don't even bother to rearrange it,' one French schoolteacher complained. Another confirmed that Wikipedia had become the site of choice: 'The idea of opening a book never occurs to them,' Françoise Gonzales mourned, and when she raised objections she was told: '"Our parents use Wikipedia as well!"'[126]

So it comes about that while junior professors are editing Wikipedia in their own subject areas and steadily improving its range and depth, some of their students are forbidden to cite Wikipedia in their papers or even to use it at all.

Middlebury College in Vermont ruled against references to Wikipedia in February 2007 after several students in a history class repeated the same erroneous information in their essays: that the Jesuits supported the seventeenth-century Shimabara Rebellion in Japan. Unluckily for the students, their teacher, Neil Waters, was certain that the Jesuits had been in 'no position to aid a revolution'; the few Jesuits still in Japan at that period were in hiding. Waters soon realised that the students had all used Wikipedia. The article **Shimabara Rebellion** included a claim that *the rebels themselves were backed by the foreign power of the Jesuits and the Roman Catholic Church.*

The dubious statement had been inserted into the article very recently, on 5 November 2006, by a frequent anonymous contributor whose chief characteristics were enthusiasm for the byways of history, an obsession with Celts and Etruscans, and undeserved plausibility. It was removed on 29 January 2007 (after the students had submitted their papers) by another anonym, one connected with Vermont. This deletion, which was well-intentioned, was unfortunately made without any *edit summary*. As commonly happens with unexplained deletions, it was reverted on the assumption that it was vandalism.

Professors at Middlebury were already aware that students had been taught at school to use Wikipedia as a source, reported Noam Cohen in the *New York Times*, but the shared error in the Japanese history essays was the last straw.

'The Middlebury history department notified its students this month that Wikipedia could not be cited in papers or exams, and that students could not "point to Wikipedia or any similar source that may appear in the future to escape the consequences of errors"... Although [the] department has banned Wikipedia in citations, it has not banned its use. Don Wyatt, the chairman of the department, said a total ban on Wikipedia would have been impractical, not to mention close-minded, because Wikipedia is simply too handy to expect students never to consult it.'

Jimmy Wales, asked for his reaction to the Middlebury rule, was unruffled. 'Students shouldn't be citing encyclopedias. I would hope they wouldn't be citing *Encyclopaedia Britannica*, either.'[127] The immediate result on Wikipedia of Noam Cohen's report was that the erroneous words were once again removed from **Shimabara Rebellion** by the veteran Wikipedian Skysmith (the same whose reflex action, a month earlier, had been to reinstate them).

Students use Wikipedia, then. They use it all the time: they're bound to use it because it's at the top of their Google results and, unlike most of the other results, it will almost certainly give them some of the information they want. If they're reasonably lucky it'll give them other well-chosen links to pursue; if they're very lucky it'll give them a bibliography of articles and books to read (or at any rate to cite). A survey by the *Harvard Crimson*, the university's daily newspaper, revealed that one professor included nine Wikipedia articles on the reading list for his Jewish history class. He gave his reasons:

'Students know Wikipedia, and know where and how to find it. Therefore I hope there is a high likelihood that they will actually do the assignment. Wikipedia represents all that is great and all that is dangerous about the Internet. It is incredibly powerful and readily available, and yet can mislead the unwary and spread disinformation. One hopes that a good undergraduate education will enable students to assess what they are reading.'[128]

Will students cite Wikipedia? They'll use their judgment. Jimmy Wales is right: most of the time 'students shouldn't be citing encyclopedias', whether or not their teachers forbid them to do so. Most of the time they should be citing the sources they find with the help of encyclopedias. But if they want views probable or improbable, common opinions, common misconceptions, controversies, they may well quote Wikipedia and its talk pages. Why not?

Ever more often, students find themselves using Wikipedia because their teachers treat it as a teaching aid. It's surprisingly common for a class of students to be given the assignment of writing a series of new Wikipedia articles. One of the earliest university professors to use this approach was Andrew Lih, who in 2003 was teaching IT at Hong Kong University. He gave 80 students the task of adding to Wikipedia on a topic related to Hong Kong, as reported at CNN.com:

'Take Abbie Wong and Olivia Yuen for example, two Hong Kong university students who took their love of the local shoreline to Wikipedia. Wong posted a report on white dolphins, and Yuen offered a primer to Hong Kong's beaches. Just minutes after the articles hit the site, they were tweaked and polished by Wikipedia's cult-like following... Student Tony Yeung took a digital camera to Hong Kong's Victoria Peak and published a Wiki entry on the popular tourist lookout. "After that, I found that my careless mistake of my English was corrected!" Yeung says.'[129]

These three articles were all created on 14 July 2003. Abbie Wong found that in the following five days nearly 20 other users, including some fellow students, contributed to the **Chinese White Dolphin** article. Oeyuen's page on **Beaches of Hong Kong** also turned into a joint project: one notes among the rest an edit by Fuzheado – her professor in person – who carefully removed a small passage *directly lifted from other site*. Yeung's piece on **Victoria Peak** was pasted in by Fuzheado himself, and during the next two days Vicki Rosenzweig, an active and thoughtful Wikipedian, was among those who improved it from the other side of the world.

The historian Mills Kelly was another early proponent of Wikipedia as teaching aid, as he was to confess in an article headed 'Why I won't get hired at Middlebury':

'It seems to me that as educators we have an obligation to teach our students how to make appropriate use of the resources they are using and I'm not sure how a ban on citation will teach them anything worth knowing... I've required each student in my class to create or substantially edit one historical entry in Wikipedia... Then they must track what happens to their entry during the 14 weeks... Along the way we'll be discussing all the things that make us squeamish about Wikipedia – the constant ebb and flow of facts in the entries, the problems of vandalism, and so on... I'm willing to bet at least a few dollars that at the end of the semester my students will be much better consumers of digital historical content than those enrolled at Middlebury.'[130]

Noam Cohen discussed a third case in the *New York Times* report quoted above. In December 2005, a Columbia professor, Henry Smith, suggested to his graduate students a Japanese bibliography project to analyse resources such as libraries, reference books and newspapers and to describe them on Wikipedia.

With 16 contributors, including Smith himself, the project resulted in dozens of new articles including 13 on various Japanese dictionaries and encyclopedias. The students acknowledged that creating encyclopedia articles had taught them new writing skills, and that through Wikipedia they had encountered experts in the field. Cohen reported Smith's own conclusions: 'Most [students] were positive about the experience, especially the training in writing encyclopedia articles, which all of them came to realize is not an easy matter... Many also retained their initial ambivalence about Wikipedia.'[131]

The work of the Columbia seminar is easily tracked down on Wikipedia via its project page **wp:WikiProject Japanese Bibliography**; unusually, the real name of the student originally responsible for each article is listed, though *anyone, of course, is encouraged to edit any of the articles.*

Several additional examples of university projects were noted in an article on the *Wikipedia Signpost*; a great many more are now listed on the project pages in English and French. Others, without ever being publicised beyond university campuses, result in waves of new articles, better articles, or at least longer articles across the encyclopedia. But this isn't a simple thing to organise. The teacher has to understand Wikipedia thoroughly in advance. Once an article is created no one can prevent other editors getting to work on it, linking it where necessary, reshaping it, removing redundancy, adding references. If it's judged to be unsuitable to an encyclopedia, no one can prevent its deletion. Some teachers get things slightly wrong, as we'll see in a later chapter.

On a mailing list as long ago as August 2001 Larry Sanger was credited (by a disbeliever) with the view that Wikipedia had a self-healing quality, and he replied:

This isn't just my view. As far as I can tell, it is the view of most people who have been actively working on Wikipedia for more than a month or two – more importantly, it's common knowledge just how robust wikis are. You make it sound as if it were something that were a matter of serious dispute. Well... it isn't! Not at all! It's pretty much self-evident to old hands here that articles do tend constantly to be improved, repaired (when, as sometimes occurs, a disadvantageous edit is made), etc.[132]

The most obvious way to support this theory – which, since Sanger's departure, has been propounded by Jimmy Wales with equal conviction – is to watch what really happens when vandalism and 'disadvantageous edits' occur. Plenty of examples are supplied by articles discussed in this chapter and the last. The childish vandalism at **Guppy** and **Blessington** lasted half an hour or less. The false quotations attributed to **Maurice Jarre** were flagged with an *unsourced* warning two minutes after they were first inserted. The biographies of **Robert Byrd** and **Ted Kennedy** showed false information on these politicians' state of health intermittently over a period of just 20 minutes; similarly the biography of **fr:Philippe Manoeuvre**. But four factors tend to slow down the self-healing process. Because of these four factors, it's unwise to claim boldly that vandalism will be reverted within minutes. The most obvious vandalism nearly always is reverted very quickly, but that doesn't account for every case.

One factor is occasional poor communication among editors of this vast resource. **fr:Affaire Dreyfus** was not corrected when it could have been because the first editor, well-intentioned but hesitant, left no messages for others. At **Shimabara Rebellion** the dubious information was restored because the well-informed anonymous editor who had deleted it gave no edit summary. The vandalism by Keykingz13, mentioned in chapter one, lasted five days because the first editors who saw some of the evidence didn't investigate further. No one's perfect.

A second factor is the complicated layout of a typical long Wikipedia article. The announcement of the subject's death, for example, may call for changes to an infobox, an introductory sentence, and a passage concerning recent events or later life, and not only to those but also to verb forms elsewhere in the text. The urge to get the news right and to do it quickly leads to continual inconsistency, with different editors attempting to spread the information to those locations while others may at the same moment be trying to remove it. Over quite long periods a reader of **fr:Aimé Césaire** would not have known what conclusion to draw (as indeed the editors, collectively, did not know). For about 20 minutes the reader of the **Ted Kennedy** page would have been equally confused (as were the editors). Thus, even while self-healing is under way, Wikipedia may continue to broadcast false information intermittently and in a confused form.

A third factor that retards self-healing is the visibility of Wikipedia. Other sources now take up its information very rapidly. Those seeking to check dubious assertions can look to these other sources, find apparent confirmation, and reinforce the original error if that is what it was. Such feedback was already happening during the 20-minute Robert Byrd and Ted Kennedy uncertainties. This same factor probably delayed the removal of the false Maurice Jarre quotation the third time it was inserted; at that stage the *Guardian*, and sources depending on it, seemed to supply the confirmation that was needed.

The fourth factor is the difficulty of recognising malicious and wrong-headed edits in specialised subject areas. Only a well-informed reader would have seen the wrongness of the addition to **fr:Affaire Dreyfus**, and the same is true at **Shimabara Rebellion**. The case of **fr:Tony Blair** is similar. The addition asserting his Catholic faith was intended to be malicious, but there was something in it, after all, and simple uncertainty may well be the reason why DocteurCosmos reverted the edit on the first occasion but not on the second. Uncertainty as to the facts is also relevant in the cases of **de:Bertrand Meyer** and **fr:Pierre Assouline**. It did not seem impossible that Meyer had died or that Assouline was a former *jeu de paume* champion.

So much for self-healing, the matter of 'disadvantageous edits' (to use the term that Sanger chose) and their correction. But Wikipedia doesn't just self-heal. It also self-improves, and this process can be observed in the case of many articles used as examples above. Let's recall Jimmy Wales's comment in October 2005 after reading a Nicholas Carr article decrying the quality of Wikipedia. *Bill Gates and Jane Fonda are nearly unreadable crap*, Wales wrote. *What can we do about it?*[133] Dozens of Wikipedians were soon at work. Within a few days the **Bill Gates** biography had changed beyond recognition. **Jane Fonda** was the focus of intense activity from 16 to 23 October; by the latter date it had been largely rewritten. On the French Wikipedia Van nuytts, in response to Pierre Assouline's critique, began a serious and much-needed revision of **fr:Affaire Dreyfus**. The same editor keeps a close eye on it to this day and has been largely responsible for raising it to the coveted featured article status. As a long-term consequence of the Middlebury rule and Noam Cohen's reporting on *The New York Times*, the article **Shimabara Rebellion** was thoroughly reworked by Tadakuni, an admin and a specialist in Japanese military history, deservedly reaching good article status in October 2008. Back in 2004, soon after Dale Hoiberg, *Encyclopaedia Britannica* editor-in-chief, had observed to the *Guardian* that on Wikipedia 'the entry on Hurricane Frances is five times the length of that on Chinese art, and the entry on the British television show Coronation Street is twice as long as the article on Tony Blair'[134] the Blair entry was enlarged and improved throughout and, while **Chinese art** remained a brief overview, **History of Chinese art** was massively extended and transformed. Three months after Hoiberg's comment was published it was no longer valid.

Nature's comparison of 42 Wikipedia articles with their equivalents in *Britannica*, published on 14 December 2005, generated a great deal of favourable publicity for Wikipedia. It's not surprising that Wikipedians reacted immediately. A project was initiated to locate the defects identified by *Nature*'s anonymous reviewers and to correct them, with the (theoretical) result that Wikipedia would henceforth be as good as *Britannica*, or better, in every detail of those articles. It was not until 22 December that *Nature* published the full list of errors – a total of 162 items. Many articles had only one, or none at all, but some were more seriously astray: 19 faults in the biography of the chemist **Dmitry Mendeleev**, 11 in **Cambrian explosion**, nine in the biography of the physicist **Paul Dirac**, seven in each of **Acheulian industry**, **Neural network**, **Prion** and **Thyroid**. All these faults, as listed in the *Nature* document, are itemised on the Wikipedia project page.[135]

Most of the required corrections in the last three articles, along with those for Mendeleev, were made on the first possible day, 22 December. All of them had been completed by 24 January. The most difficult among them was the small matter of the relative order of Mendeleev's siblings. On this detail the project page reports: *Corrected Dec. 14, and further clarified on December 22. Even futher clarified, following a New York Times piece on the subject, on January 3. Factual correction to January 3 clarification on January 4.* The full story behind it is told in the footnote, quoted here as it appeared on 4 January 2006, soon afterwards deleted:

The number of Mendeleev's siblings is a matter of some historical dispute. When the Princeton historian of science Michael Gordin reviewed this article... for... Nature, he cited as one of Wikipedia's errors that 'They say Mendeleev is the 14th child. He is the 13th surviving child of 17 total. 14 is right out.' However in a New York Times article... it was noted that in Gordin's own 2004 biography of Mendeleev, he had the Russian chemist listed as the 14th child, and quoted Gordin's response to this as being: 'That's curious. I believe that is a typographical error in my book. Mendeleev was the final child, that is certain, and the number the reliable sources have is 13.[136]

The *New York Times* observed that *Britannica* described Mendeleev as the seventeenth child, and had done so ever since 1974. On such disputes encyclopedias are judged.

The brief and unsatisfying **Acheulian industry** article had been created in early 2004 by Lizard King, a business major interested in archaeology. It was now replaced with a much longer piece, complete with bibliography, freshly written by the archaeologist Adamsan: *rewritten article swapped in 24 December 2005*, the project page reports. The original **Cambrian explosion** article had been developed by Mav and others on the basis of Michael Jay Gould's 1989 book *Wonderful Life*. It was largely rewritten by the physics researcher Dragons flight on 15 December 2005, the day after the *Nature* article appeared. This left few remaining faults to correct. The Paul Dirac biography (begun by The Anome in the first year of Wikipedia's existence) was corrected throughout, as soon as the list of errors appeared, by Eb.hoop. So it was that the project page eventually listed the correction that had been applied to every fault; and on 30 January 2006 the *Wikipedia Signpost*, in an article by Michael Snow (founder of the *Signpost* and now chairman of the Foundation's Board of Trustees), reported that the work was done. Except that on Wikipedia nothing is ever completed:

As to Mendeleev, to cite one instance, Gordin's review called for more information about 'his role as an economic thinker, his work on the theory and practice of protectionist trade, his work on agriculture, etc.' The fact that Mendeleev worked in these fields is now mentioned, but without much explanation other than a laudatory quote from a Russian historian of science, so more could certainly be added.[137]

The additions to the Mendeleev biography outlined by Snow are still waiting to be made. It is frequently visited by schoolchildren (to judge by the heavy incidence of vandalism) but it isn't as yet one of Wikipedia's best.

In September 2001 the newly created Wikipedia, 'which one might consider intellectual anarchy extruded into encyclopedia form with a chat feature thrown in', was seen by Judy Heim, a commentator at *Technology Review*, as 'stemming a tide against charging for content on the Web'. She was writing under the title 'Free the Encyclopedias!' so this feature of the site was of special interest to her. Unlike the Wikipedians themselves, who were already talking of the day when they would overtake the rival encyclopedia, Heim judged that Wikipedia 'will probably never dethrone *Britannica*, whose 232-year reputation is based upon hiring world-renowned experts and exhaustively reviewing their articles with a staff of more than a hundred editors'. She went on to quote Tom Panelas, director of communications at *Britannica*: '"There are a lot of reference works on the Internet, but we don't concern ourselves about them too much."'[138]

By summer 2005 things looked different. Wikipedia had become the most popular reference site on the internet (according to Hitwise), relegating Dictionary.com to second place; *Britannica*, which continued not to be free, was nowhere visible among the leaders. That year, not very long before the *Nature* review appeared, Jimmy Wales gave an interview on C-SPAN (Cable-Satellite Public Affairs Network). The text, still available online, gives in the words of Wikipedia's founder some of the reasons why the site was gaining popularity and building trust. The questions begin to sound familiar: they crop up every time the site is discussed.

Brian Lamb asked Wales first whether the editing of political pages turns into a war between left and right. He answered by throwing doubt on the common assumption that Wikipedians fight over such articles along party lines. 'It turns out it's actually the party of the thoughtful and reasonable people and the party of the jerks. And those aren't left or right, they can come from all sides.' Within the community, he continued (using the term 'community' narrowly, I think, to exclude numerous comments from occasional contributors and anonyms), there had never been much controversy about the George W. Bush article, for example. It was edited a great deal, with frequent disputes over how to word things, but there was no fundamental question. It was taken for granted that the article should be comprehensive, factual and sourced. It should not be a one-sided political rant – on either side.

Did the anonymity of Wikipedia invite slander and libel? In general, no, said Wales. On any kind of website with broad participation – forums, mailing lists, blogs and comments on blogs – it was always possible that someone would write something unpleasant. 'It doesn't mean that we're perfect, of course, but the difference at Wikipedia is you have a community that's empowered to do something about it.'

As to vandalism, yes, there were vandals. 'Some people come in and they just think it's funny to post a disgusting picture or something... Well we revert that within a minute.' This invited Brian Lamb's interruption:

'Who is we?'

'Because there's the community, so there's...'

'You don't even know who does that?'

'Well, I can look it up,' Wales explained. Among the reasons why Wikipedia worked was that although contributors rarely used their real names, they had a consistent identity and this produced accountability. Editors gained reputations within the community for good work. It was possible to look at article histories and to see who was dealing with vandalism.

The next question was whether article protection was a serious limit on editorial freedom. 'We have to lock articles from time to time when they are under attack, but...'

'Who does that?'

'The administrators, the people, the community.' Editors could be elected as administrators; they could protect articles, block IP addresses, and temporarily or permanently block named users if they were causing trouble. The Bush and Kerry articles were protected for less than two per cent of 2004, Wales insisted, but *Time* reported that he had protected them for most of 2004. That gave the impression of a long period of protection which he personally had imposed, 'and that's really not accurate, it's the community that cares for it'.[140]

In 2007 the Wikipedia.org domain name (which means the encyclopedias themselves, excluding associated sites) ranked tenth busiest on the internet, counting not just reference sites but all sites. Readers of the article **Wikipedia** were warned that it would be difficult to rise above this position; yet in 2009 the site has climbed to a safe eighth or a risky seventh in the same ratings. French, German and other large Wikipedia versions are attaining similar ranking among sites in those languages; among French sites Wikipedia reached tenth place in 2007, ninth in 2008, and is still rising. Press articles about Wikipedia and press references to Wikipedia are multiplying. Google crawls Wikipedia more frequently than ever; as we shall see, there is now a risk that Google will even pick up ephemeral vandalism, as it did recently with the **Barack Obama** page. All these measures feed back into increasing use. As you read Google, Google reads you. Popularity builds on itself. Like it or not, in the future you will be using Wikipedia.

Chapter 5
Why we love it

THE LAUNCH OF Wikipedia, in the first month of the new century, was announced almost apologetically to the Nupedia mailing list. The result was overwhelmingly positive. Enthusiasm for an open encyclopedia, initially channelled towards Nupedia, had been frustrated by the creaky and elitist system for getting articles written, edited and approved: it took forever.

The Nupedians thereupon migrated – or rather, they started using Wikipedia as well, and soon found that they were using it all the time. They were Wikipedia's initial user base. They came largely from the academic, scientific and information technology communities, and many of these earliest editors naturally used their own names. Why not? They were professionals and they looked on the internet as a professional resource. They had been working on Nupedia, which required its authors to have academic accreditation. So here among the earliest users, alongside the founders Jimbo Wales and LMS, are academic historians such as MichaelTinkler and JHK.

Polymaths... are the backbone of Wikipedia, wrote the Anglo-Catholic ClaudineChionh from Melbourne on noting the arrival of science editor, former copy-editor and science-fiction reader Vicki Rosenzweig. Vicki was also welcomed by the Californian Mav, a biologist and expert on geographic information systems, still active on Wikipedia today, who avoids writing on biology and GIS *because that reminds me too much of work*. Mav began to write for Wikipedia on 1 January 2002. He is one of the many who seem to enjoy the housekeeping as much as the writing of good articles. He has done a lot of both, and has been a steward since 2004. People with computer skills, like Mav, have always been well represented: they find it just a little easier than others to grasp how pages are edited and how the encyclopedia is put together. Among the firstcomers in this category were SJK and Andre Engels, both still active, the latter now usually seen on the Dutch Wikipedia. Another early arrival in this category is Fuzheado, a professor of information science; another again is David.Monniaux, who teaches at the Ecole Polytechnique and was the admin on the French Wikipedia most closely involved with the Sciences Po incident. Aside from IT specialists, scientists generally are among the steadiest contributors: physicists such as Dragons flight; applied mathematicians such as Stevenj, professor at MIT, Wikipedia editor ever since February 2003 and still active today.

Expatriates, academic and other, are used to interacting online; perhaps it's not surprising that they count among frequent contributors to Wikipedia. I've already mentioned Viajero, an American in the Netherlands, and Diderot, a Canadian in Belgium. Diderot was proud of having chosen the best of all possible pseudonyms for an encyclopedist but admitted that he was really more of a lexicographer. As such, Diderot was the natural creator of **Bakers' queues**, a brief article explaining that Carlyle, in *The French Revolution*, used the phrase twice to condemn *the revolutionaries for their failure to meet basic public needs, and as synonym for the angry French public*. This article has a special distinction. It was put up for deletion as scarcely notable (*appears only in the work of one author, and only in respect of one event*) and since Diderot had by this time ceased contributing, there was no argument at all, merely a friendly discussion about where best to merge the material. Closing the debate, Keeper76 concluded: *Well, that's settled then. Go for it. Merge/redirect amongst yourselves.* But no one really cared to. Diderot's article survives untouched.

Remember the worry expressed by a certain Wikipedian, back in 2004, when noting that the site was already beginning to be cited in the press as an authority: *This is of course a great vote of confidence, but also brings with it a responsibility. Was French toast really called German toast before?* This particular issue was one that had naturally worried a lexicographer and foodie like Diderot, who in March 2004 wrote on the talk page of the article **Freedom fries** (an alternative term for French fries):

The article is fine except for this: 'Prior to World War I, Americans widely referred to French toast as German toast. This food, too, was briefly renamed "freedom toast."' I have not been able to find a well-documented source for either claim – just many dozens of webpages repeating the same unattributed source. The only documented use of 'German toast' known to me is the 1918 Fannie Farmer Cookbook, which does not qualify as an attestation of widespread use, since it uses strange names for other standard recipes as well. Besides, this etymology contradicts the claims made on the French toast entry. I can't find any reference to 'freedom toast' at all before the recent unpleasantness. I'm going to remove [the claim from the page **Freedom fries**] *and make the source explicit on the French toast page.*

Incidentally 'the recent unpleasantness', so politely evoked by Diderot, was the lack of enthusiasm on the part of the French government for an American-led invasion of Iraq. How to characterise this French standpoint: was it *extreme opposition*, as Kingturtle saw it? Was it *vociferous opposition*, as Stevenj, the applied math professor at MIT, preferred? Or were both expressions inappropriate? That was Anthere's view, and she tried to set out the French approach more explicitly; but that, too, wouldn't quite do. Such explanations belonged in the articles about the invasion of Iraq, not the page about freedom fries. Under the guidance of BigFatBuddha the single word *opposition* was restored and was seen to be all that was needed. Then Dante Alighieri wisely inserted the detail that, unlike the fries, French kissing and French poodles were never renamed. An anonym added French bulldogs to this list; Fuzheado took them out again.

Diderot's eyes, meanwhile, were fixed on an earlier period of history and on the claim that French toast had once been called German toast. This point had been added by the second editor of the page, Zanimum. Zanimum hadn't documented his claim; it was only half relevant anyway. Diderot removed it and then moved on to the article on **French toast**, where it also appeared and where it was relevant. The text that he was about to change had been written by Stevenj, evidently another foodie: *It has been alleged that French toast was referred to in the US as 'German toast' prior to World War I, but the term 'French toast' can be found in print in the US as early as 1871. The Oxford English Dictionary cites usages of 'French toast' in English as early as 1660...* For that first phrase, Diderot substituted: *Some people claim that this dish was called 'German toast' before World War I and was changed to 'French toast' in the US because of anti-German sentiment. A popular cookbook from 1918 does refer to it by that name*, and he cited *Fanny Farmer, The Boston Cooking-School Cook Book*. Like Diderot himself, the detail and citation have long since disappeared from Wikipedia. But Zanimum is still around, an administrator and a supporter of the as-yet-tiny Wikipedia in

Iñupiaq, the Alaskan variant of Inuit, which currently boasts 74 articles.

Most press reports don't penetrate very far into our Wikipedia world. Occasionally the editor who made some crucial move will be identified, more or less accurately, more or less appropriately. Rickyrab was named in the press as one who dealt with the Ted Kennedy incident; Mehdi19 was the unlucky one chosen for press attention out of the many who were confused about Aimé Césaire's state of health. But some long-serving Wikipedians have been interviewed and otherwise recognised in the world beyond Wikipedia, the world that's said to be real. An article by Daniel H. Pink on Wired.com got somewhat personally involved: he gave pencil sketches of six Wikipedians, and, attached to them, notes on what they did and why they did it. Among them was Danny, who came to Wikipedia because he Googled **Kryptonite**, stayed because he was intrigued by the edit button at the top of each page, and left (at least temporarily) in 2007 to work on an alternative model, Veropedia. Danny's first new article, in February 2002, was **Muckleshoot** (on a Native American people from Washington State); his last contribution to date, on 4 January 2009, was a proposed set of classically simple 'eliminations' to cure Wikipedia.

The doyen of Pink's list of Wikipedians was Carptrash, self-styled 'art historian without portfolio' who learned the ropes (with some difficulty, it has to be said) in June 2004 writing on the sculptor **Corrado Parducci**, a personal interest. Carptrash is still a very active Wikipedian, though he has *declared all my edits to be a diabolic mixture of opinion and original research*, which ought, of course, to eliminate them... 'I think of myself as a teacher,' he said to Pink over tea at his kitchen table.

'Right now, he's unemployed,' Pink reported. 'Which isn't to say he doesn't work. For about six hours each day, Kvaran reads and writes about American sculpture and public art and publishes his articles for an audience of millions around the world. Hundreds of books on sculptors, regional architecture, and art history are stacked floor to ceiling inside his trailer – along with 68 thick albums containing 20 years of photos he's taken on the American road. The outlet for his knowledge is at the other end of his dialup Internet connection: the daring but controversial Web site known as Wikipedia.'[141]

Also on Pink's list were Kingturtle, a Californian high school teacher with a special facility for lists and timelines, who began to contribute in 2003 and was among those trying to get the **Freedom fries** article right; and Raul654, yet another computer scientist, who is now a bureaucrat with various additional privileges, a keen analyst of Wikipedia and its future, and the organiser of the daily 'featured articles' spot on Wikipedia's main page. The last of Pink's interviewees was Ram-Man, one of the site's most prolific contributors, the creator (with automated assistance) of tens of thousands of articles about US cities and towns. Among those geographical articles Ram-Man created one for **Newton, Massachusetts** on 16 October 2002. It was cleverly done, almost untouched by human hand, full of verifiable statistics woven into businesslike and boring text. It was a good start, and next day Ortolan88 came along and began improving it. Attached to one of his edits is an edit summary: *The popular cookie, the fig newton is named after the city; other details (I live here).* As to Ortolan88, he had been a Wikipedian since late 2001. He still is, and he explained his fascination for the site in an interview with the online version of the *Boston Globe*: 'It's fun for me,' he said. 'It's an opportunity to continue to do a little bit of writing not constrained by anything but my mood.' But now to the youngest Wikipedian named by Pink:

'Wikipedia's articles on the British peerage system – clearheaded explanations of dukes, viscounts, and other titles of nobility – are largely the work of a user known as Lord Emsworth. A few of Emsworth's pieces on kings and queens of England have been honored as Wikipedia's "Featured Article of the Day." It turns out that Lord Emsworth claims to be a 16-year-old living in South Brunswick, New Jersey.'

Lord Emsworth, unlike other Wikipedians featured in Pink's article, was not sketched and not identified. He took his name from a memorable character in P. G. Wodehouse's 'Blandings Castle' series of novels, and between August 2003 and December 2006 he made an impressive number of edits of high quality, creating or significantly improving hundreds of articles in his favourite field. By that time he was an admin and he ranked highest by far at **wp:List of Wikipedians by featured article nominations** (as Raul654 took the trouble to inform him), with 57 successful nominations under his belt. At the end of 2006 Lord Emsworth added a message to his user page, *I am currently on an extended vacation, as I am busy with college.* Unluckily for Wikipedia, he has not been heard from since. And what is most astonishing is that he has not yet been overtaken in the featured article stakes, although, owing to his long inattention, some of those articles have meanwhile fallen from the state to which he helped to raise them, and Hurricanehink (who writes about hurricanes), having amassed 47 nominations by the end of May 2009, is quietly sneaking up on him.[142]

Turning to the French Wikipedia, David.Monniaux's interview with *Le Figaro* admittedly said little about him as administrator: it merely served to explain to a wider audience, not for the first time nor for the last, how the site works, what administrators do and how vandalism is reverted.[143] One Wikipédien whose work has caught the press's eye (though he was not widely named) is EyOne, the same, incidentally, who protected the **Thierry Gilardi** article. A business and economics student with a wide range of interests, EyOne's really newsworthy achievement is to have set up two statistical milestones. In March 2006 he created the article **fr:John Anglin**, which happened to be the 250,000th in the French Wikipedia. John Anglin, a bank robber, disappeared from Alcatraz with two comrades in 1962, is presumed drowned in San Francisco Bay, and is sufficiently notable to earn Wikipedia articles in six languages. Still assiduously editing, in December 2007 EyOne created the French Wikipedia's 600,000th article, **fr:Python birman** ('Burmese python'). The page has since been moved to the scientific name of this cuddly creature, *Python molurus.* Why edit Wikipedia? EyOne was asked, and he replied:

'Partly it's that I'm proud of making knowledge freely available to the greatest possible number; partly that I'm encouraging the survival of the French language, and enriching it, too, because one day the French Wikipedia is going to be a great resource. Wikipedia is a little of my time that I give to other people – and to myself as well, because, above all, contributing to it is a pleasure.'[144]

As part of their joint study of Wikipedia, eventually published under the title *La révolution Wikipédia*, Pierre Gourdain and colleagues studied the motivations of French Wikipedians. They cite the userpage of Céréales

Killer (from which I've already quoted) with views that are not unlike those of EyOne: *Wikipedia matches my vision of the sharing of knowledge... for the good of all.* They also interviewed a Wikipedia admin, and their choice fell on Esprit Fugace ('Fleeting Spirit'), then 23, now, two years later, possessor of a master's degree in physics and a teaching diploma. She met them at Le Guichet station on the outskirts of Paris and they plied her with apple juice. In return she was quite ready to say why the encyclopedia obsessed her. Esprit Fugace had reached admin status (one of 145 on the French Wikipedia at that date) after only six months' editing and with acclaim – 123 expressions of support, three of opposition. Her work brought her occasional rudeness from vandals and trolls, but also respect from the community of Wikipedians. 'On good days I can spend ten hours on the site, but when I'm studying it's only two or three each evening.' Wikipedia for her was somehow comparable in its addictiveness to an online role-playing game; it was relaxation after hard work; it was anything but a chore. More than any of this, it was a social network. Wikipedians interact with one another even if they never meet, she explained to her puzzled interlocutors: they soon develop a rounded picture of other editors from a few words on a user page, from glancing through the pages they have chosen to edit; they become friends.[145]

Here, then, is the first reason why we love Wikipedia. We love it because it's a virtual nation, or rather a virtual world. Jimmy Wales, in the interview just quoted, spoke of us as 'the people' and then corrected himself to 'the community'. No correction was needed. We, the people of this virtual world, can be as shy and anonymous as we like, and yet our work, good and bad, is listed and others can explore it. We may seldom speak to one another, yet our paths cross unforeseeably. In this book, although I avoid naming some of the vandals and their nemeses, I always name the major editors whose work I happen to mention, because these people really have contributed to the building of the greatest (well, the biggest) encyclopedia in history. Wikipedia doesn't write about itself, or not very much, but we know that inside the virtual world, behind the anonymous, public, encyclopedic face of Wikipedia, our labours are – virtually – recognised.

Towards the end of 2001 the announcements page drew the attention of Wikipedians to the site's new logo, *inspired by the old one, but with the text 'Wikipedia: The Free Encyclopedia' and a nifty new epigraph... 'Man is distinguished, not only by his reason, but by this singular passion from other animals, which is a lust of the mind, that by a perseverance of delight in the continued and indefatigable generation of knowledge, exceeds the short vehemence of any carnal pleasure.' In other words, Wikipedia is better than sex (and other carnal pleasures). We have this from the English philosopher Thomas Hobbes... The new logo was designed by The Cunctator.*[146] Behind Larry Sanger (LMS)'s chairmanlike prose a fierce dispute is hidden, one of Wikipedia's first. He liked the logo but he had a bitter quarrel with its creator.

Already in the second half of 2001 The Cunctator was a prolific contributor. His user page today carries the instruction: *To be a good Wikipedian, be respectful, overly combative, self-critical, vulnerable, hortatory, ambitious, and analytical. Above all, to be a good Wikipedian, edit and create entries,* and he follows his own advice, not excluding the *overly combative.* Among his early contributions were many pages about the 11 September 2001 attacks, the victims and the aftermath. Pinkunicorn, Swedish creator of the original **World Trade Center/Plane crash** page, wrote to him soon afterwards: *You're doing an absolutely amazing job on the September 11, 2001 terrorist attack pages,* and Sanger agreed: *We might disagree on other stuff, but I have to say your continuing work on the 9/11 pages and the aftermath... is really great.* Those pages are now the backbone of the separate 9/11 wiki at Sep11memories.org.

Apart from writing encyclopedia pages, The Cunctator loved to discuss Wikipedia and its policies. He spoke for anarchy (or at least an absence of hierarchy), eventualism (Wikipedia will get there in the end; his pseudonym means 'the delayer') and inclusionism (the wikiphilosophy whose motto could be 'let there be more articles'). He was, for a while, a fierce critic of Jimmy Wales, but that was smoothed over. His natural opponent turned out to be Sanger, who took a pivotally opposite view both on anarchy (he was against it) and on inclusionism (Sanger had deletionist tendencies). Sanger soon put his opinion into effect by deleting some of The Cunctator's newly created pages. *I do reserve the right to permanently delete things,* he insisted, *particularly when they have little merit and when they are posted by people whose main motive is evidently to undermine my authority and therefore, as far as I'm concerned, damage the project.* He proposed a scenario: if he entered into discussion of such deletions, these same unhelpful people would take up huge amounts of his time in discussion *and will never simply say, 'Larry, you win; we realize that this decision is up to you, and we'll have to respect it.' Then, in order to preserve my time and sanity, I have to act like an autocrat.*[147]

In early November 2001 Sanger tried to broaden this argument by appealing, in non-anarchic tones, for community backing:

I need to be granted fairly broad authority by the community – by you, dear reader – if I am going to do my job effectively. Until fairly recently, I was granted such authority by Wikipedians. I was indeed not infrequently called to justify decisions I made, but not constantly and nearly always respectfully and helpfully. This place in the community did not make me an all-powerful editor who must be obeyed on pain of ousting; but it did make me a leader. That's what I want, again. This is my job.

On a talk page his added comments were even more peremptory: *When push comes to shove, if a decision must be made and there's a serious controversy, and I'm partaking of it, sorry, but I'm going to get my way. And you'll be expected to hold your tongue after that.* SJK, a user who joined in summer 2001 (and is still active in 2009), created a page in the new discussion workspace **m:The Role of Larry Sanger in Wikipedia**, quoted those two statements by Sanger, and asked: *Am I the only person who detects a change in LMS's view of his own position? Am I the only person who fears this is a change for the worse?*

Others didn't immediately know how to respond. Some surely feared a collapse of the project in which they had invested many hours of time and effort. The Australian Robert Merkel suspected that Sanger and Wales *have decided that arguments that don't end when LMS puts his foot down like they used to are interfering with where they want the project to go.* Merkel was prepared to trust Sanger, he announced. Not surprisingly, The Cunctator was among those who disagreed:

I think it's a little sad that he feels he has to regulate the direction of Wikipedia so strongly; I'd rather he spent more time encouraging what he felt was the correct direction, than discouraging what he felt was the wrong direction... It means that he can't fully harness the energy of volunteers. What's so great about the Wikipedia system is that it doesn't have to resort to censorship... but that's what Larry feels he has to resort to now.

Like the Wikipedians, Wales took this dispute very seriously. Criticising the 'culture of conflict', he argued that Wikipedians needed to build Wikipedia, not to talk about it. In his next words, however, there may be an echo of the understanding he had previously reached with The Cunctator. On the point at issue, Sanger didn't have Wales's unqualified backing: *Just speaking off the top of my head, I think that total deletions seldom make sense. They should be reserved primarily for pages that are just completely mistaken (typos, unlikely misspellings), or for pages that are nothing more than insults.*[148] He decreed that page deletions should be explained and the explanation should be archived.

Soon afterwards The Cunctator opened hostilities with Sanger on a new front. Foreseeing that Wikipedia and its servers could at some point be overwhelmed by a sudden flood of new users, Sanger had proposed 'The Wikipedia Militia', a team of volunteers to keep things running in any emergency. Many disliked the military metaphor. 'The Wikipedia Guard' was even worse (Wales intervened personally to rule that name out). *You can't pick and choose who you have visiting and editing the site. If you are automatically going to look down upon newbies, or give them a negative connotation right away, then you might as well leave the site now, because that is just pathetic,* an opponent argued on the talk page, and Sanger replied:

Leave the site I started? Why would I want to do that? :-)... I should have added... that we love and need new contributors, and that none of this should be construed as in any way criticizing someone just because he or she is new to the project. If we criticize anyone, it should be because they're writing bad articles, acting trollishly, or otherwise acting in a decidedly noncontributory fashion.

The Cunctator was certainly the target of the last sentence, and the undercover sniping had Wikipedians on edge again. *I agree that it's important, but does* [this] *belong on the main wikipedia site?* Robert Merkel demanded of

Sanger; but too late. The Cunctator was already shaping up for the challenge: *You start deputizing groups of people to do necessary and difficult tasks, fast-forward two/three years, and you have pernicious cabals.*

Turning to the Militia or Guard, The Cunctator dismissed it as *a mediocre idea, poorly presented, which will encourage the type of communal behavior which usually leads to the stanching of creativity and communication. The characterization of high traffic as an 'invasion', a 'major disaster', 'war', etc. that 'old hands' have to combat is detrimental.* Wikipedia shouldn't need a defence force: by its very nature it was robust and indestructible. He would have reacted in the same way whoever had proposed the idea, The Cunctator insisted. He didn't believe that Sanger was trying to be a dictator or autocrat. *The only difference is that his ideas are official policy once they're written.*

In response, Sanger undertook a difficult balancing act, attempting to show that he wasn't authoritative at all and – at the same time – that The Cunctator was an isolated troublemaker who had been *constantly trying to undermine what little legitimate authority I claim.* Sanger continued:

The Wikipedia Guard... seems to have gotten quite a bit of popular support – which is totally unsurprising to me, because I know the Wikipedia community!... You're constantly harping on as if I were trying to be a dictator or an autocrat... I am a paid project organizer. I think it's my job to formulate Wikipedia policy, finding consensus when I can, and presenting things fairly.

A few days later Sanger tried another name: *What do you all think of 'The Wikipedia Welcoming Committee'? I think that is much better all around,* he hazarded. And someone now unidentifiable squashed him with: *Committees are even worse. At least militias get bayonets. The only thing good about committees is if there's a free buffet, and even then usually the cheese danishes are stale.*

We enjoy finding these old arguments on forgotten talk pages. Partly because they explain why Wikipedia is the way it is – and that matters to you as well as to us. Looking back at Jimmy Wales's intervention between Sanger and The Cunctator and his ruling that page deletions should be explained and the explanation archived, we realise that this is the exact precedent for what is done now: if a new page is nothing but vandalism, or a mispelling, or totally unsuited to an encyclopedia, it can be deleted on sight by any admin. But if it's arguably out of scope or insufficiently 'notable', any editor may propose to delete or merge it, and there'll be a discussion, which someone will, after a few days, conclude, announcing a consensus one way or the other. If there's no consensus, the article survives by default. This practice, for which The Cunctator can claim credit, means that although the more unprepossessing pages are deleted, their shadows – the deletion discussions – live on.

We enjoy it partly because in these discussions we're watching the doings of Wikipedians long ago when the world was young. In these two debates we not only see The Cunctator, SJK and other current editors cutting their teeth: we also see Wales watching from Mount Olympus as Sanger talks himself into bitter personal disputes with 'the community'. It was very shortly after this that Bomis found it could no longer afford Sanger's salary.

And we also enjoy it because it reminds us of an eternal truth. In the Wikipedia world we can talk things over, and over, and over. And this is the second reason why we love Wikipedia:

The talk page of any truly high-quality article [wrote Michael Snow, perhaps quite seriously] *should be longer than the article itself, from the extensive discussion about what material to include, how to ensure that all important aspects are covered, verification of the contents, negotiation about how to appropriately represent different points of view, building of consensus over disputed points, etc. In all likelihood, there would be enough discussion that we'd already have archived it a time or two. Perhaps we should make this a requirement for featured article status.*[149]

In fact this never has been made a requirement (I think Michael Snow had his tongue in his cheek) but even if we set aside debates about policy, practice and the Wikipedia Militia, it's a fact that debates about article content can go on at mind-numbing length. In a study of Wikipedia's historical articles Roy Rosenzweig talks of 'the literally hundreds of pages devoted to an entry on the **Armenian Genocide** that still carries a warning that the neutrality of this article is disputed'.[150] Rosenzweig could have chosen any number of other examples, from the world-shaking to the ridiculous. This is the feature of Wikipedia that inspired Raul654 to enunciate 'Raul's Laws of Wikipedia' number 5. *Over time, contentious articles will grow from edit-war inspiring to eventually reach a compromise that is agreed upon by all the* *editors who have not departed in exasperation. This equilibrium will inevitably be disturbed by new users who accuse the article of being absurdly one sided and who attempt to rewrite the entire article. This is the cyclical nature of controversial articles.*[151] It was this feature, too, that saw off some of the early academics who had originally transferred from Nupedia. Some still remain, but many dropped out in the early years. In an article on Slashdot in 2005 Larry Sanger misleadingly implied both that the numbers of disaffected were greater than they really were, and that the exodus largely happened soon after his own departure. Still, he probably got the reasons exactly right. Some of those academics did not 'suffer fools gladly'. They found themselves getting involved in disputes with users whose approach was far from academic. In certain cases they attempted, at first, to deal with these interlocutors patiently and reasonably; in certain cases they unleashed their *odium philologicum* at the start. Whatever patience and reason had been available eventually ran out, either as a result of many small and frustrating interactions with a succession of eager and naive non-experts, or after one or two long-running, painful disputes. Persistent and difficult contributors 'drive away many better, more valuable contributors'.[152]

To take one early example, H. Jonat, whose personal experience evidently stretched back to Germany in 1945, wrote articles in bad English on the former German east and its former German population: one such article was on **Siebenbürgen** (the territory known in English as Transylvania). JHK, who certainly did not 'suffer fools gladly', reacted to Jonat's early draft with slashing edits and hot-tempered messages in October 2001, aiming to demonstrate that *there is more to the story than your constant attempts to prove that anywhere Germans lived belongs ipso facto to Germany... My only vested interest was in replacing the disjointed crank cant that you put up there with something actually informative.* H. Jonat's views, and the increasingly impatient responses of JHK and several others, can still be found in the debris of pages such as the long-deleted **Silent ethnic cleansing** (a term which Paul Drye thought, with justice, to be *one of those wonderful code phrases so beloved by political extremists... Serbian nationalists, Nazi apologists, and extremists on both sides in Northern Ireland*). Jonat disputed this dismissal of the term, citing *the millions of people killed due to the Potsdam agreement* *and the allies at that time going along with communist brutality.*[153] There was also, once upon a time, a page **German names of places taken by Poland**. In the version of its introductory paragraphs that now survives, each sentence by H. Jonat is followed by a note *(this is untrue)*;[154] it soon becomes clear that the annotator is right and H. Jonat is wrong in each case, but the really sad fact is that what took other contributors some effort to verify was known all along to H. Jonat.

And so at the end of summer 2002 JHK left Wikipedia. On 4 September she gave some reasons on her user page:

Every time I come back, it's the same old stuff, the same old tired people trying to push their agenda. Folks, it's been a blast, but I'm too tired to play anymore... I enjoyed being here because I felt I was part of a community with a common goal... Because the wikipedia is open to all comers, experts are not really welcome except by the few who are both open to constructive criticism and secure in their own abilities. As the wikipedia has grown, I have seen more and more people without those qualities take their places among us... at present there is no real mechanism for dealing with people who consistently contribute badly written articles or behave in an anti-social manner.

On the previous day she had explained at greater length in a posting on the Wikipedia mailing list which ends:

'The two things that have driven me off on "breaks" in the past (and most likely the future) are the lack of respect for my hard-earned knowledge and a general lack of communal cooperation from a very few (but for some reason, interested in history) people who make me think: my time is too valuable for this – I spend way more time fighting to make other people's articles passable than writing new stuff.'

For some, JHK's departure was the last straw. On the same day on which she wrote this, discussion of H. Jonat broke out on the mailing list. It is interesting to see how this most painful of the early editorial conflicts was handled – as eventually many of them are – by banning or blocking. Jonat herself had belatedly been invited to join the list. Reading a history of criticisms of herself was bound to be disheartening, but she was strong in her own defence, claiming to see and know a lot more about things than JHK could 'read in her school books. Her books tell onesided stories, war propaganda, but not the full truth.' H. Jonat, in her own view, saw the complete picture. To which Stephen Gilbert replied: 'Your actions contradict your words. When I read your contributions, all I see is a one-sided perspective that is hostile to the views of others.' Jimmy Wales then tried to limit discussion to Jonat's interaction with other editors: 'We aren't here to debate German history, the Holocaust, Poland, etc. So let's not do that ... We are here to discuss with [H. Jonat] the problems people are having with her biased writing.' Wales's current view, he added, was that she needed to 'straighten up' or go away; but she had been kind enough to come before a very hostile court of opinion, 'so we should be kind enough to listen.'[155] All credit to him for trying. H. Jonat was banned from Wikipedia for three months on 9 September 2002, and her username did not return, though an anonymous contributor whose style is, let's say, hard to distinguish from hers continued to make frequent edits until disappearing in February 2004.

In the old days the debates on talk pages were matched by unending edit wars in the articles themselves, tit-for-tat edits in which a change made by one editor is reverted by another, and reverted, and reverted, and reverted; and I'm not saying it doesn't still happen. The classic case concerned one of those 'German names of places taken by Poland', the article on **Gdańsk**. The earliest still-recorded edit to this page, in January 2002, included H. Jonat's change from *Gdansk is a city in Poland* to *Gdansk is currently a city in Poland* – an edit that was reverted one week later by David Parker with the blunt edit summary: *Revanchist bias removed*. Soon afterwards, in a thorough rewrite, the first sentence was altered to *Gdansk or Danzig is a city in Prussia, since 1945 in Poland* by the none-too-mysterious anonymous contributor just mentioned. Parker reverted again, summarising: *Tedious chauvinistic claptrap replaced*. But the real Gdańsk wars began in October 2003. They initially focused on whether the introduction should start with the words *Gdańsk (Danzig) is a city on the Baltic coast* or whether the first mention of the name Danzig should be postponed from the first to the second line. The dispute spread like fire in the grass across the hundreds of other pages on which Gdańsk is mentioned. Almost unbelievably, it was not resolved until March 2005, after a fairly unusual process (for Wikipedia): a real vote, still visible at **Talk:Gdansk/Vote**. Editors laboriously voted on which name should be used in referring to each of six periods of the city's history, and which name in biographies, and how to define the special circumstances in which both names should be given. 'It took two years of back and forth to reach this point,' writes David Runciman; 'a traditional encyclopedia editor could have settled it in ten minutes', and it is partly because of the endless heart-searching discussions of such issues on the English Wikipedia that I enjoy the Latin Wikipedia even more. Nationalists currently don't care much about Latin placenames.

A few other examples will show what sort of questions are up for debate in a real Wikipedia duel. **Nicolaus Copernicus**: *Was he Polish, German or Prussian?* **Raven Riley**: *Is this porn star Italian? Native American? Puerto Rican? Cypriot? Does she have Indian blood? Who cares? She's hot and she gets naked, but make sure that, when you change it, you don't even think about citing any source; please feel free to insult whoever put in the previous ethnicity.* **Gasoline**: *See the talk page for a debate about the total number of English speakers in the world (and whether Americans should be considered an important part of it),* for *claims that UK-wikipedians are set to re-establish the British empire by moving pages to British spellings* and *counter-claims that Americans who want 'gasoline' are being their usual nationalistic/culturally-imperialistic selves.* There was even a move to divide the article into American and British versions. Yes, and can there legitimately be a different American pronunciation of 'Rowling' (as in **J. K. Rowling**)? Is it or is it not correct to say, under **Victoria of the United Kingdom**, that the 'reference style' is 'Her Majesty'? Some think it's high time to replace this with 'Her Late Majesty'; but if we change it can we still allow the 'direct style' to read 'Your Majesty'? And is the **European robin** also commonly known as the **English robin**, or not? And, last but not least, what about **Jimmy Wales**: do you personally think he founded Wikipedia or co-founded it?[156]

Yes, edit warring happens – I won't say that it's the fourth reason we love Wikipedia, but I will say that some of us do rather too much of it. It does the encyclopedia not the slightest good. Admitting that the **University of Sydney**'s Latin name is widely given in the University's own materials as *Universitas Sidneiensis*, is it true that the University of Sydney has a Latin name? Enochlau, who fought for three months to exclude these two Latin words from the article about the university not because they were false, not because they were irrelevant, but because he could find rules allowing him to exclude them, is my type specimen of an edit warrior (but then, as a Latinist, I might be biased). At least there is now a recommended maximum so that our pleasurable indulgence doesn't grow into an addiction. In 2004 the three-revert rule was introduced: *A contributor who reverts the same page, in whole or in part, more than three times in 24 hours, except in certain circumstances, may be blocked from editing.* 'Three changes per 24 hours in a work of reference might seem absurdly fluid by traditional standards,' Runciman comments, 'but for Wikipedia this was a draconian measure, adopted with deep reluctance by some.'[157] We often breach it (it's amazingly easy to forget how many times you have reverted since breakfast), and we are often blocked for our transgressions.

We love Wikipedia because it lets us write about whatever we want. It's 'excellent for Klingon, BSD Unix, and Ayn Rand', said Andrew Orlowski,[158] probably the nicest thing he's ever said about Wikipedia. A Wikipedian boasted: 'Wikipedia kicks Britannica's ass when it comes to online mmp games, trading card games, Tolkieana and Star Wars factoids!'[159] Like the *Hitchhiker's Guide to the Galaxy*'s lengthy entries on drinking, added Paul Boutin, 'Wikipedia mirrors the interests of its writers rather than its readers.' Can we agree with that? Isn't it more likely that the writers and readers think alike, especially since the two sets overlap? Anyway, as Boutin specifies, 'You'll find more on Slashdot than the *New Yorker*. The entry for Cory Doctorow is three times as long as the one for E. L. Doctorow. Film buffs have yet to post a page on *Through a Glass Darkly*; they're too busy tweaking the seven-part entry on *Tron*.'[160] To update Boutin, a disambiguation page now lists 15 potential topics called **Through a Glass Darkly**, five of which (including the Ingmar Bergman film) already have Wikipedia pages. Internet journalist Cory Doctorow still has a longer page than novelist E. L. Doctorow, but six of the latter's novels now have pages of their own. Otherwise, all these observations are still perfectly fair. 'Relying on volunteers and eschewing strong editorial control leads to widely varying article lengths in Wikipedia,' wrote Roy Rosenzweig. He continues:

'It devotes 3,500 words to the science fiction writer Isaac Asimov, more than it gives to President Woodrow Wilson (3,200) but fewer than it devotes to the conspiracy theorist and perennial presidential candidate Lyndon LaRouche (5,400); American National Biography Online provides a more proportionate (from a conventional historical perspective) coverage of 1,900 words for Asimov and 7,800 for Wilson. (It ignores the still-living LaRouche.) Of course, American National Biography Online also betrays the biases of its editors in its word allocations...'

But Wikipedia's different: we have all the space we want. It's true, as Rosenzweig says, that Wikipedians 'are more likely to be English-speaking, males, and denizens of the Internet' and that vast swathes of Wikipedia reflect those people's typical obsessions; but while some of us are starting pages on every professional footballer and on each Pokémon character – and on many, many topics more obscure and sectional than those – historians have been gradually writing about every imaginable ancient and medieval personality; botanists and zoologists are adding numberless articles on species; every galaxy, every star, every asteroid, every man-made satellite has its page. For the great majority of these topics Wikipedia is the only available encyclopedic source. Every wine appellation will soon have a bland, hypnopedic entry... and why shouldn't the site's hospitality extend to every wine producer?[161] As argued lengthily on the wine project page, perhaps that's going a bit too far. And every restaurant? When visiting **Mzoli's** on the outskirts of Cape Town, Jimmy Wales himself, in a moment of weakness, decided that any restaurant qualified, and he started the page himself. There was considerable debate, which Wales won – not by arguing (he never really seems to argue) but by being the leader of a community that loves to get its teeth into such challenges. **Mzoli's** was a weak little stub at first; now, having survived its delete discussion (which got a lot of amused media coverage), **Mzoli's** extends to seven paragraphs and 18 footnoted references to press reports; it has earned good article laurels.[162]

Mzoli's is notable, but perhaps not quite as notable as the article says. The bias in Wikipedia articles, Rosenzweig went on to observe, 'favors the subject at hand,' and he goes on to quote the honest admission of this defect, formulated by Jengod in 2004, still visible at **wp:Why Wikipedia is not so great**. *Articles tend to be whatever-centric. People point out whatever is exceptional about their home province, tiny town or bizarre hobby, without noting frankly that their home province is completely unremarkable, their tiny town is not really all that special or that their bizarre hobby is, in fact, bizarre.*[163]

David Runciman noted a similar problem about **Ayn Rand** and her **Objectivism**, object of Jimmy Wales's enthusiasm. Runciman had decided on a test of Wikipedia's vaunted neutral point-of-view policy: he would look up Ayn Rand on Wales and Sanger's encyclopedia to find out what she was all about. 'It's hard to express in mere words just how dispiriting an experience it is trying to find out about objectivism on Wikipedia. This isn't because the entries seem biased or uncritical. It is just that they are so introverted, boring and just long.' The entry on Ayn Rand herself was more than 8,000 words in length and covered her views on everything from economics to homosexuality in dull and technical detail. There were (and of course still are) separate lengthy entries on objectivist metaphysics, epistemology, politics and ethics, as well as entries on all her books, including the novels *The Fountainhead* and *Atlas Shrugged*. There were entries on every character in these novels, there were plot summaries, there were even entries on individual chapters. 'All of it reads as though it has been worked over far too much,' Runciman added, 'and like any form of writing that is overcooked it alienates the reader by appearing to be closed off in its own private world of obsession and anxiety.'

He compared this exhausting Wikipedia coverage with the entry on Rand in the 1993 *Columbia Encyclopedia*, in which she gets four lines and a couple of references: 'By allocating her 70 words, the Columbia editors give some indication of what they think she's worth: on the same page she gets more space than the French architect Joseph Jacques Ramée (1764–1842) and the Swiss novelist Charles Ferdinand Ramuz (1878–1947), but fewer words than... the Scottish chemist Sir William Ramsay (1852–1916).'[164] And he's right to criticise the dispiriting length of some otherwise good Wikipedia articles. It's a problem that will always be there, because we can write about whatever we want; but featured article rules and project evaluations currently make it more of a problem than it needs to be.

There are exceptions to our freedom to write. One exception is that Wikipedia doesn't let us write about Wikipedia. The **Mzoli's** article doesn't say anything about the media circus surrounding its own existence and the burning question of whether Wales's pet article would be deleted.

Although we know that Wikipedia avoids this kind of self-reference, we test the thing from time to time, just to make sure. The **Andrew Orlowski** entry itself is a test of the rule, with a whole section about his criticisms of Wikipedia, currently requiring *cleanup*, freely supplied with links to Orlowski's articles, and keyed to a soul-searching section on the talk page. *Every time Orlowski stamps out another 'witty' diatribe against Wikipedia,* demands Antaeus Feldspar, *do we need to link it here? Do we do this for any other human ~~shitstain~~ gadfly with a bug up his butt?* Was Anastrophe right or wrong to suggest, after reading Antaeus's view of Orlowski, that he had better not edit the article any more?

Anyway, at least the article **Wikifiddler** has been deleted. That would be self-reference.

We love Wikipedia because we enjoy testing the limits of **wp:NOT**, or, to be more explicit, **wp:What Wikipedia is not**.

The first principle on this long-established policy page is *wiki is not paper*. There are no size limits, Sanger insisted back in 2001 in an essay subtitled 'Wikipedia Unbound' (and Wales commented: *I agree with this one completely*):

I see no reason at all why Wikipedia shouldn't grow into something beyond what could ever possibly be put on paper... Why shouldn't there be a page for every Simpsons character, and even a table listing every episode, all neatly crosslinked and introduced by a shorter central page...? Why shouldn't every episode name in the list link to a separate page for each of those episodes, with links to reviews and trivia? Why shouldn't each of the 100+ poker games I describe have its own page with rules, strategy, and opinions? Hard disks are cheap.[165]

Not being paper is good, and Sanger's project for the **Simpsons** department of Wikipedia is, needless to say, now a reality. But somehow, after that good beginning, the continuing negativity of these often-cited principles seems almost to taint the atmosphere. *Wikipedia is not a dictionary:* articles must offer something more than a definition... but how much more exactly? *Wikipedia is not a soapbox... Wikipedia is not a mirror of source material... Wikipedia is not a directory of everything that exists or has existed,* nor is it *an indiscriminate collection of information...* except that every encyclopedia is an indiscriminate collection of information, Wikipedia more indiscriminate than most. *Wikipedia is not a crystal ball...* And, a principle so often invoked that it has its own page, **wp:Wikipedia is not for things made up one day**, *such as a new ball game invented in the park, a new word or phrase invented in the playground, a new language, or a new drinking game invented at a particularly memorable party.*

Wikipedia is not a recipe book, though, like a typical recipe book, it does say some unreliable things about food. Among those involved in the wise decision that Wikipedia would not in future be a recipe book was the Californian chemist Gentgeen. I notice that the first of his 21,000 edits, on 5 October 2003, was to the article **Highland Park Single Malt**. Before Gentgeen's work it read, in total, *Highland Park is the Northernmost distillery in Scotland.* He helpfully added links: *Highland Park is the Northernmost <u>distillery</u> in <u>Scotland</u>.* It is a much longer article now, but not in all ways better.

The policy against recipes was agreed in early 2004 and willing hands began to move the recipes that had thus far lodged in Wikipedia to their new home at Wikibooks. To one of these willing hands, Karen Johnson, Gentgeen wrote on 23 February 2004: *Karen, keep on doing what you're doing. Some, maybe all dishes, have encyclopedic value, but their recipes do not. The wikipedia article on Apple pie should tell what an apple pie is, where it was developed, why it's culturally significant, and then link to the recipe at wikibooks. Keep on transwikiing stuff to wikibooks, and thank you.* Gentgeen was happy, as we see, but Anthere was not. In those early years she was protective about French culture on Wikipedia, and she chipped in to object to Karen's work:

For any important dish, an article must be kept (a stub if you wish) and a link to the recipee preserved. Now, I have the feeling this has been done for many dishes, though not for several french dishes. I do not say it was done on purpose against french food; however, I would not be surprised that if those moving the recipee are able to recognise which british or american dish is famous and relevant to the description of a certain way of life, this may not be the case for french cooking. If so, I would hope that you will accept my own expertise on the matter, when I tell you that not preserving recipee links for Coq au Vin or Crêpe, or plain deleting Ratatouille is bad; and that these articles are important to our folklore.

By October 2004, perhaps as a result of such disputes, Karen Johnson had had enough of Wikipedia. She disappeared soon after giving her opinion in favour of deleting the article 'List of pornstars and sex symbols who innovated in science', one of a series created by the enthusiastic 141. *An inane and meaningless list,* said Karen Johnson. It did not take much deleting: it listed only two actors, one of them being Hedy Lamarr (she and her husband pioneered frequency hopping spread spectrum radio communication).

Aside from their inanity, 141's lists contravened the policy that Wikipedia is not a collection of lists of loosely associated topics. 'Actually there is rather a lot of this' (as the *Hitchhiker's Guide to the Galaxy* says about sex) but the fact that the rule exists is handy whenever someone wants to get others to agree to deleting some of it. 'List of heterosexuals' was deleted some time in 2003, and 'List of people who have not committed suicide' in 2004 (I suppose they might have become rather long lists); 'List of female basketball players' was deleted in March 2008, but if you really want it it can still be found at Deletionpedia.

On Wikipedia we don't say any more, as we once quietly did, 'Could it go in *Britannica*? If not, then not in Wikipedia either.' That no longer works, because articles about suburban railway stations and characters in second-rate computer games could never go in *Britannica*. These days we go back to first principles. Everything followed for Descartes from 'I think, therefore I am.' In just the same way, every kind of decision about what can go into Wikipedia follows from the rules set out under 'What Wikipedia is not'.

The fifth reason why we love Wikipedia is that in this virtual world we're all equal, from professors, like Stevenj, by way of late-middle-aged polymaths, like Carptrash, to unexpectedly learned schoolkids, like Lord Emsworth; so equal that it really doesn't matter whether we have described ourselves accurately on our user pages. That's why it ought not to have mattered whether EssJay, who became an editor in February 2005, had described himself accurately.

'Essjay' is the spelled-out form of my initials... I get a lot of requests for personal information about me; however, in these days of internet stalking, anonymity has become more and more important. Here are some details I'm willing to share. Alias: Justin Stewart. I am male, past 30 but not yet 40, gay and in a long-term relationship with my partner, Robbie, an attorney. We live in the Northeastern United States. I teach theology at a university in the eastern United States. My area of expertise is Roman Catholicism.[166]

The same user page had until recently claimed four university degrees rounded off with the elite Doctorate in Canon Law. EssJay was our equal, but *primus inter pares*: he was an editor, admin and bureaucrat of astonishing energy. His talk page by late 2006 was stuffed with the thanks and praises of other Wikipedians whom he had helped to get out of a hole. In July 2006 he was canonised, when the *New Yorker* ran a long article on Wikipedia with an admiring profile of EssJay,

'who holds a Ph.D. in theology and a degree in canon law and has written or contributed to sixteen thousand entries. A tenured professor of religion at a private university, Essjay made his first edit in February, 2005. Initially, he contributed to articles in his field – on the penitential rite, transubstantiation, the papal tiara. Soon he was spending fourteen hours a day on the site, though he was careful to keep his online life a secret from his colleagues and friends (to his knowledge, he has never met another Wikipedian).... Essjay is serving a second term as chair of the mediation committee. He is also an admin, a bureaucrat, and a checkuser, which means that he is one of fourteen Wikipedians authorized to trace I.P. addresses in cases of suspected abuse.

He often takes his laptop to class, so that he can be available to Wikipedians while giving a quiz... Wales recently established an "oversight" function, by which some admins (Essjay among them) can purge text from the system, so that even the history page bears no record of its ever having been there.'[167]

We have seen EssJay's hand on the oversight button: he was the trusted admin deputed by Jimmy Wales to clean up the history of the **John Seigenthaler** page. EssJay was so good, all round, that the people over at Wikipedia Review were beginning to wonder whether he was a committee; and Daniel Brandt, in August 2006, ruminated that 'it's possible that he has made up all of his biographical details. He's too busy on Wikipedia to be a full-time professor.'[168]

If EssJay had as yet met no Wikipedians in real life, he was soon to do so. In early January 2007 he took the salaried post of Community Manager for Wikia, the money-making arm of Jimmy Wales's wiki-empire. At Wikia EssJay created another user page for himself, and now the biography was different: *My name is Ryan Jordan... I'm a 24 year old guy from Kentucky; I grew up in Kentucky, and studied philosophy and religion at... the University of Kentucky and University of Louisville... Before coming to Wikia, I was an account manager with a Fortune 20 company, where I worked on a ten person team that managed roughly $500,000,000 in annual sales. Prior to that I was a paralegal for five years...'[169] If EssJay was this one person, Daniel Brandt and everyone else could now see that he wasn't the other person as well. There had perhaps been time for uncompleted studies at two universities; there most certainly hadn't been time for two doctorates and a tenured professorship.[170] The poor old *New Yorker*, famed for its fact checking, had to admit (reluctantly, after a long silence, in the 5 March 2007 issue) that here were some facts it hadn't bothered to check:

'He was willing to describe his work as a Wikipedia administrator but would not identify himself other than by confirming the biographical details that appeared on his user page. At the time of publication, neither we nor Wikipedia knew Essjay's real name. Essjay's entire Wikipedia life was conducted with only a user name; anonymity is common for Wikipedia administrators and contributors, and he says that he feared personal retribution from those he had ruled against online... Jimmy Wales, the co-founder of Wikia and of Wikipedia, said of Essjay's invented persona, "I regard it as a pseudonym and I don't really have a problem with it."[171]

The reason for EssJay's new biography was quite simple. It was as a real person that he had applied for the post at Wikia; starting work there seemed like the ideal moment to unite his previous Wikipedia identity with this real person. But internet pseudonyms are strange things. People know that EssJay (and Raul654 and Zanimum and all the others) are pseudonyms, and, as such, a proper and convenient means of distancing their real-life owners from their interactions online; and yet, if the owners of the pseudonyms attach biographical details to them, people expect those details to be very near the truth.

In retrospect, EssJay made just two errors. His second error was to allow his false biography to be repeated as if true in the *New Yorker*. Yet what else could he have done? At that time he didn't want to emerge as a real person; but then, soon afterwards, he took the post at Wikia, and the subsequent revelation looked to observers like one more of those disastrous Wikipedia mistakes.

EssJay's first and fatal error was to make his pseudonymous identity more weighty and academic than his real persona. In general, people on Wikipedia don't do this (so far as we know!). It isn't worth it, because academic qualifications don't net you a lot of credit in the Wikipedia world. They don't count for nothing, however, and it's easy to understand the temptation, in one who could very well have achieved a doctorate, to claim that his Wikipedia persona already had a couple of them. Having awarded them to himself, he had unwarily used them to pull rank in some discussions. Words that he wrote at **Talk:Imprimatur** (*this is a text I often require for my students, and I would hang my own Ph.D. on it's credibility*) were among those that now came back to haunt him, and looked to observers like one more demonstration that Wikipedia couldn't be trusted.

Jimmy Wales as potential employer 'didn't have a problem' with the differences between EssJay's original biography and the truth. Many of the Wikipedians who had interacted with EssJay admired his work so much that they didn't have problems either, once he had made his excuses. It was the use that EssJay made of his imaginary qualifications that rankled, not only with those editors who had shown respect for them, but eventually also with Jimmy Wales. The unwelcome press attention soon began to rankle too. Wales suddenly found that he had a problem after all, asked EssJay to resign the post at Wikia, and hastily issued the general threat that *contributors to the site who claim certain credentials will soon have to prove they really have them.* Anthere, who now chaired the Wikimedia Foundation, disagreed: *I think what matters is the quality of the content, which we can improve by enforcing policies such as 'cite your source', not the quality of credentials showed by an editor.*[172]

One more case of Wikipedian identity momentarily hit the headlines in 2009. Oddly enough, the story involved another meteoric rise to prominence, that of Sam Blacketer, and another meandering discussion on Wikipedia Review. Blacketer, a new user in December 2006, had made 1,000 edits in his first ten days and, astonishingly, had been elected to Wikipedia's august Arbitration Committee (known to insiders as ArbCom) less than a year later. But who was he? His real identity wasn't on record. The Committee's discussions take place on the web, and its members don't necessarily ever meet, yet they are trusted with confidential information about other Wikipedians.

By clever observation of patterns of Wikipedia editing, and with the help of serendipity, Tarantino on 22 May 2009 announced that he had pinned Sam Blacketer down. He didn't reveal what he'd found,[173] but Blacketer realised that the game was up: on 23 May he identified himself privately to the Committee and resigned, adding to his very brief message the admission: *Before joining the committee I had used the account Fys for editing which should have been disclosed.* To those who recognised the name, as long-serving Wikipedians did, this sentence was loaded with meaning. Fys (the word means 'knowledge' in Manx) wasn't the beginning of the story. The username Fys was newly adopted on 7 October 2006 by a Wikipedian whose previous name had been Dbiv.

During a three-year spate of contributions to Wikipedia, beginning in March 2004, Dbiv clocked up 14,706 edits. From the beginning of his term as a Wikipedian it was evident that he was interested in UK politics. He made many undoubted improvements to biographies and current affairs articles related to Britain. Even when he got into disputes he was often proved right by posterity – as when he boldly commandeered the page title **The Sun** for a certain British newspaper, the phrase having formerly served on Wikipedia as a mere redirect to *the ball of hydrogen and helium most every living human being sees every day* (as Marskell put it during a brief battle over this issue). Marskell was on a loser, and the move by Dbiv was ultimately successful.

Dbiv sometimes signed his talk page comments as 'David' and it soon became clear what his real name was. At that stage he seems not to have wanted to conceal it. In fact he also created the username DavidBoothroyd but used it only in order to argue openly that the Wikipedia article about himself, **David Boothroyd**, wasn't notable and ought to be deleted.[174] David Boothroyd is a Labour councillor on Westminster City Council and the author of *Politico's Guide to the History of British Political Parties*.

In January 2005, by consensus, Dbiv became an admin. He *reluctantly* applied for election to ArbCom in January 2006 and nearly made it. But Dbiv was often in trouble for edit warring and incivility. Prominent in the archives is his war with Irishpunktom over the article on **Peter Tatchell**, left-wing politician and gay activist. Dbiv was blocked three times while an admin, and on one occasion he boldly unblocked himself, giving the explanation: *Yes, I know I am not supposed to do this. Justification 1: Block was wrongly applied. Justification 2: I have a major edit which I am not going to lose come what may.* This was one of numerous incidents that eventually led to the revocation of Dbiv's admin status in August 2006 *for abuse of protection, unblocking, and rollback powers, as well as poor judgment shown in edit warring.* He was blocked three more times during September.

There were no doubt several motives for the name change from Dbiv to Fys, but one was surely the loss of adminship and the wish to put this rollercoaster history behind him. Another, if I'm interpreting the record correctly, was that the Dbiv account had recently been used for vandalism, perhaps by someone who had briefly commandeered Dbiv's computer or had learned his password. Anyway, on 7 October 2006 Dbiv became Fys. Dbiv still exists (it's only on Wikipedia and in *Doctor Who* that this kind of thing is possible) but has made no further contributions. On Dbiv's current user page appears only the information: *I have laid down this title and do go by another.*

Regardless of the loss of adminship and any associated irritations, Fys contributed busily, ceasing to do so only in November 2007. Fys, like Dbiv, was a combative editor, particularly rude on occasion: to a certain *twit* and *idiot* (I borrow Fys's own words from edit summaries); and to another who was admonished: *try not to be an idiot in future*; and to a third who mistook the name of a certain Cambridge college and was told: *don't fucking mis-spell it, you idiot.* And so, for a period of eleven months, Fys was continuing to edit and occasionally to insult; he was blocked no fewer than seven times, on the last occasion by Viridae for *gross incivility, personal attacks – continuing despite repeated warnings.* And simultaneously Sam Blacketer was hard at work (he had first appeared in December 2006) building up the squeaky-clean record on which he was soon to gain election to ArbCom. Strangest of all, the editing paths of Fys and Sam Blacketer crossed on nearly 500 pages. To take one example, the article **Caroline Cox, Baroness Cox**, begun by Irishpunktom in March 2006, was afterwards expanded and watched successively by Dbiv, Fys and Sam Blacketer, who took over the patrol in August 2007.

Once elected, Sam Blacketer said goodbye to Fys and was an excellent and hard-working arbitrator from the beginning (practically no one has disagreed with this). He ought to have told the Committee his history at the start, no doubt, and he ought not to have involved himself in numerous cases about editors and admins who had previously had disputes with Dbiv/Fys, although, since there's no sign that he held grudges, his improper involvement probably did not change the outcomes in these cases. He certainly showed no animosity towards Viridae, or towards the so-called *twit*.[175]

When the story broke, Cade Metz on *The Register* was perhaps the first outsider to notice that Sam Blacketer had recently made an edit to the biography of **David Cameron**, leader of the Conservatives (in opposition to the Labour party of which David Boothroyd/Dbiv/Fys/Blacketer is a member). A previous editor unsympathetic to the Conservatives had inserted, as the leading image on that page, an unflattering picture that showed Cameron making a silly face against a background that gave the strong impression of a halo around his head. Sam Blacketer had reverted this edit, restoring the normal picture that showed Cameron in more human guise. Metz didn't notice, or at any rate failed to say, that Blacketer's revert was in Cameron's favour. Instead Metz quoted Blacketer's amused edit summary: *Revert choice of picture to one not carrying saintly overtones.* This allowed readers to infer that Blacketer – now known to be Boothroyd – had inserted an image less favourable to Cameron and had thus been using a pseudonym to make anti-Conservative changes to the page.[176] It laid a trap for journalists who read *The Register* uncritically. James Tozer of the *Daily Mail*, a fiercely Conservative paper, was perhaps among those misled:

'A Labour councillor has been exposed for changing David Cameron's entry in the online encyclopedia Wikipedia. David Boothroyd used a false name as he made regular alterations to the Tory leader's page. Now he has been forced to resign from his position on the website's arbitration committee, whose members settle disputes over just such changes.'[177]

Sam Blacketer had in fact been defending the Cameron page against vandalism and politically motivated edits, as he still does; but there was no story in that. Uneasy with neutrality, Tozer took refuge in innuendo: 'Although the alterations were not inaccurate or overtly critical, many were unfavourable... it is another blow for the hugely popular website, which has tried to stamp out malicious tampering.' Sam Blacketer is still, as I write this, hard at work on Wikipedia. On the **David Cameron** page he recently repaired vandalism in a direct quotation. The words that the speaker concerned had actually used, *a truly remarkable young man*, had been nefariously altered to *a truly remarkable creep*. If Sam Blacketer's revert of this edit wasn't neutral, what is?

It's generally thought to be a good feature of Wikipedia usernames that after a chequered history under one name it's possible to abandon it and start again under a new name with a clean slate. Many have done so. The uncomfortable feature in the Sam Blacketer case was that the two identities, with rather different patterns of behaviour, overlapped.

So EssJay is no longer a Wikipedian and Sam Blacketer has resigned from his elected position on ArbCom. Apart from them we're still all equal. We can all still say whatever we like about ourselves. We can all have as many identities as we need, just as long as we don't use them to contribute two voices to the same discussion.

We're equal wherever we learned our English and even if we haven't yet learned much of it. From the beginning the English Wikipedia attracted contributors from all over the web-enabled world. Among the English speakers Australians, New Zealanders, Indians, Scots, English, Canadians and all manner of others jostle with those who are US citizens, those whose affiliation is only revealed by their obsessive interchanging of American and British spellings, and those who don't identify themselves geographically at all. And beside these there are great numbers for whom English is not a mother tongue. For some of us, even if fluency is not a problem, grammatical English doesn't come naturally. *A good thing is that these persons are participating in making English version of Wikipedia, don't you agree*, XJam wrote to MichaelTinkler in March 2002. XJam is Slovene, incidentally. *I wonder how many non-English wikipedians are there? And their participation in its English part is not forbidden, right? Of course I am trusting you in making things look English.* MichaelTinkler has contributed only sporadically in the last seven years, but XJam is still an active Wikipedian (*since I am participating here, I must say, my interests have grown to very high altitudes almost from a nowhere-land*), an administrator and assiduous contributor. He is now a bureaucrat on the Slovene Wikipedia, on which he has made 75,000 edits – but the first of these was in July 2003, meaning that, for the first 15 months of the Slovene Wikipedia's existence, he preferred to spend his time entirely on the English one.

We're equal on Wikipedia whether we arrived yesterday or have been on-site since 2001, and whether we have made 50,000 edits or only five. But what about the results of our work, the encyclopedia pages to which Google leads our readers: which types of Wikipedians made the greatest contribution to them? Jimmy Wales used to say that there was a popular misconception about the site: 'thousands and thousands of individual users each adding a little bit of content and out of this emerges a coherent body of work'. He used to argue that the truth was rather different: Wikipedia was actually written by 'a community, a dedicated group of a few hundred volunteers'.

'I know all of them and they all know each other... It's much like any traditional organization... For me this is really important [he would add] because I spend a lot of time listening to those four or five hundred and if... those people were just a bunch of people talking... maybe I can just safely ignore them when setting policy and think about the million people writing a sentence each.'[178]

Wales confirmed his own view with a statistical survey, counting who made the most edits. He rather 'expected to find 80% of the work being done by 20% of the users, and was surprised that the pattern was actually much tighter: 50% of all edits were made by 0.7% of users (524 people), and an astonishing 73% were made by 2% of users (1400 people)'.

Aaron Swartz, a member of the audience at a lecture in which Wales set out these statistics, wasn't convinced, and ran a study of his own. He took the **Alan Alda** article, which when first created by an anonymous editor on 4 April 2001 consisted of two sentences: *Alan Alda is a male actor most famous for his role of Hawkeye Pierce in the television series MASH. Or [In?] recent work, he plays sensitive male characters in drama movies.* By the time Swartz was writing, **Alan Alda** had become 'a pretty standard Wikipedia page' with two pictures, a few links and lots and lots of text. First off, Swartz went through the history of nearly 400 edits, one by one. The changes he saw fell into three groups. Just five were vandalism, each followed very soon afterwards by a revert. The vast majority were small changes: corrections of typos, formatting, links, categories and so on 'making the article a little nicer but not adding much in the way of substance'. A much smaller number were 'genuine additions': new information added to the page. When it came to responsibility for these genuine additions Swartz's observation totally contradicted Wales. Almost every time he saw a substantive edit, he found that the editor was not an active user of the site. 'They generally had made less than 50 edits (typically around 10), usually on related pages. Most never even bothered to create an account.' So he followed up with a computer program that analysed each edit to the **Alan Alda** article, counting how many letters from that edit remained in the current version of the page – a method that Wales had considered but hadn't as yet tried out. Swartz found that if you counted edits, as Wales did, you would deduce that the biggest contributors to the article (seven of the top ten) were registered users, the fourth largest contributor having made over 7,000 Wikipedia edits in total, and the seventh 25,000. You would conclude that most Wikipedia content is written by busy, habitual editors. But by counting what survived into the final version of the article you would get a dramatically different result: only two out of the top ten contributors were registered users, while six out of the top ten had made fewer than 25 edits to Wikipedia. Contributor number nine, in terms of the number of characters contributed to the eventual version of the article, was an anonym who had edited **Alan Alda** just once and had never made any other Wikipedia edit. Swartz ran the program on other articles with similar results. Most of the **Anaconda** article, it turned out, had been contributed by a user who had only made 100 edits to Wikipedia. The largest number of edits to **Anaconda** were made by a user who had contributed no text at all to the final article – all those edits were 'deleting things and moving things around'. Swartz summed up his findings as follows:

'An outsider makes one edit to add a chunk of information, then insiders make several edits tweaking and reformatting it. In addition, insiders rack up thousands of edits doing things like changing the name of a category across the entire site... As a result, insiders account for the vast majority of the edits. But it's the outsiders who provide nearly all of the content... Everyone has a bunch of obscure things that, for one reason or another, they've come to know well. So they share them, clicking the edit link and adding a paragraph or two to Wikipedia. At the same time, a small number of people have become particularly involved in Wikipedia itself, learning its policies and special syntax, and spending their time tweaking the contributions of everybody else.'[179]

I'm not about to say that Swartz's study isn't valid. It's always referred to, alongside earlier statements by Sanger and Wales about the Wikipedia 'community', by anyone trying to analyse how Wikipedia articles get written. But Swartz made one slip, and it's one that's more obvious to a Wikipedian less familiar with busy areas (such as articles in English about popular TV actors) than with the fairly peaceful backwaters (such as the Latin Wikipedia). When you've been watching one of those fairly peaceful backwaters for a couple of years you begin to see beyond the anonymity. Just look again at the telltale words: 'they generally had made less than 50 edits (typically around 10), usually on related pages. Most never even bothered to create an account'. How does Swartz know that they 'never even bothered to create an account'? Didn't I say above that we 'can be as shy and anonymous as we like'? Some Wikipedians are very shy indeed. I can list right now half a dozen contributors to the Latin Wikipedia who have accounts but who often edit anonymously, and this mental list of mine includes three prolific creators of new content. Five of these six, when editing anonymously, appear at a different IP address each day, because that's the way home connections usually work. I can only recognise them by their style and interests. If I didn't I would have to say, just like Swartz, that they generally make fewer than 50 edits in total, 'typically around 10, usually on related pages' and during a single visit – that's exactly how it looks – but, because I recognise them, I don't say that at all. I can list another half-dozen who (so far as I know) have never created an account and hardly ever appear on talk pages but, again, edit from a different IP address each day and can only be recognised by their style and interests. This second list of mine would include five prolific creators of new content. I'm prompted to guess that if Swartz's research were taken further, several **Anaconda** enthusiasts and even several **Alan Alda** enthusiasts would resolve into a couple of timid, semi-anonymous, hard-working Wikipedians.

This nuances Swartz's observation: it doesn't invalidate it. The 500 Wikipedians most familiar to Jimmy Wales are not the ones who often contribute anonymously and avoid the talk pages; so, as Wales would probably now agree, he really is less familiar with the main creators of new Wikipedia content than he used to think.

Swartz's analysis quoted above is followed by these words, in which he makes an imprudent leap beyond his data:

'Other encyclopedias work similarly, just on a much smaller scale: a large group of people write articles on topics they know well, while a small staff formats them into a single work. This second group is clearly very important – it's thanks to them encyclopedias have a consistent look and tone – but it's a severe exaggeration to say that they wrote the encyclopedia. One imagines the people running *Britannica* worry more about their contributors than their formatters. And Wikipedia should too. Even if all the formatters quit the project tomorrow, Wikipedia would still be immensely valuable. For the most part, people read Wikipedia because it has the information they need, not because it has a consistent look. It certainly wouldn't be as nice without one, but the people who (like me) care about such things would probably step up to take the place of those who had left. The formatters aid the contributors, not the other way around.'[180]

Actually, other encyclopedias don't work like that. It's true that the biggest ones draw on large groups of specialised contributors, but the extent to which these experts are drawn on shouldn't be exaggerated. Even in the most academic of encyclopedias a great many workaday articles – a big proportion of the total content – are filled in by editorial staff, who also spend their time knocking the long externally-written articles into encyclopedic shape. The people running *Britannica* have waved their door-to-door salesmen goodbye; right now they're trimming their list of experts and inviting content from volunteers; but sacking their core editorial staff is the last thing they'll do before filing for bankruptcy.

It's true of Wikipedia too. If all the 'formatters' – the people who spend a lot of time doing editorial things – left Wikipedia, and if Swartz turned out not to be as good a substitute for them as he thinks, Wikipedia would be immensely less valuable than it is now. Imagine for a moment that Google's encyclopedia plan has borne fruit; imagine yourself lost in a vast, uncontrolled, unnavigable *Knol*... Yes, that's why you have to hope that we go on loving Wikipedia.

Chapter 6
Chaos and beyond; or
Why we love it, version 2.5

Internet cruelty is easy. We do not have to look at the people we hurt.
    David Shankbone, 'Nobody's Safe In Cyberspace'

LET'S NOT DENY the obvious. When the New Zealand minister of commerce, Richard W Worth, made some minor edits to the page about himself that tended in his favour, he was doing something that lots of people do. The two unusual features are that he was open about it – he edited under his own name – and his edits diverged only slightly from neutrality. When Bactoid recommended a ban if Worth persisted, it probably didn't occur to him that fairness would have dictated a ban on Jimmy Wales for the same offence. The article **Jimmy Wales** was not only begun by Jimbo Wales, as noted above. He has also edited it at least 18 times since. He has even, in a half-hearted way, edit-warred on the page, repeatedly deleting phrases that characterised Larry Sanger as co-founder of the site. On the subject of Bomis, his internet portal, he changed *Bomis Babes softcore pornography section* to a less in-your-face phraseology, *Bomis Babes adult content section*. These interventions didn't escape the keen eyes of the press, and Wales was asked for a comment by *The Times*. He confessed:

The real question here is the ethics of editing your own biog, which I would discourage. But it is very hard to resist... It raises a lot of questions about whether you can be unbiased about yourself and whether it's possible to distance yourself from the story. I wish I hadn't done it. It's in poor taste.'[181]

We love Wikipedia because we love talking about ourselves. But we have to say this quietly, because we aren't really supposed to do it. In Wikipedia terms, it's hard to take a neutral point of view about yourself. In May 2005 **Joshua Gardner** tried to pass himself off as the Duke of Cleveland to youngsters at Stillwater Area High School in Minnesota. To back up his claim he took the username Earlofscooby, edited the article **Duke of**

Cleveland to add to the list the identity he was currently claiming, *the Earl of Windsor's nephew, Caspian James Crichton-Stuart IV*, and twice tried to create a biography under that name (both attempts were rapidly deleted). The edit to **Duke of Cleveland** was reverted after 12 minutes by Mackensen; it was inserted twice more anonymously and rapidly reverted each time. Some months afterwards these archived edits served as the 'first clue' in student newspaper investigators' quest to unmask Gardner, a former sex offender.[182]

Alan Mcilwraith is another who failed to take a neutral point of view about himself. In a page created anonymously in early October 2005 and afterwards edited under the name MilitaryPro he described himself as a Parachute Regiment veteran with NATO service and a KBE. He also added himself to the **List of honorary British Knights**. That edit was reverted two hours later: Necrothesp's edit summary noted that *Google has never heard of him – pretty good for someone supposedly knighted this year*. The Mcilwraith page was deleted in late October, re-created and speedy deleted twice more; on the last occasion Katefan0 *deleted and salted* it to prevent recreation. The Wikipedia article was merely a memory when Mcilwraith, who had also managed to pass himself off in a British magazine and the world beyond as a war hero, was exposed as a hoaxer by the Scottish *Daily Record*.[183] He was in fact an unmilitary call-centre worker from Glasgow. This dubious notability perhaps justifies the factual biography which now exists on Wikipedia.

There's to be no autobiography, then. But what if there's a page about you on Wikipedia and you see an error or vandalism on it? You should correct it, making your identity clear; but anything that's a matter of interpretation, and anything that others are likely to dispute, it's better not to touch. Raise it on the talk page and get agreement how best to fix it. The worst thing to do is to edit yourself anonymously. If the subject of an article is open about identity, several potential lines of criticism are stymied.

Admittedly it doesn't solve all problems. **Stephen Schwartz (journalist)**, who became a Muslim in 1997 and writes from a conservative angle in the US press, was dissatisfied with the neutrality of his Wikipedia biography. He began to edit it, under the name SulejmanSchwartz, and in January 2006, still dissatisfied, is said to have made legal threats against Chalst (academic Wikipedian since August 2004, *a copy-editor and former logician*) and against Chalst's university and Wikipedia. Briefly, Schwartz had Jimmy Wales worried; but all that remains to be seen is a series of long talk pages and a closely-watched article which Schwartz continues to edit.[184] Schwartz arouses extremely strong feelings, as shown by the discussion that took place on 15 January 2006, at the moment when Wales cut down the existing, weakly-sourced article to stub length:

Since the article is in dispute, it will be wise to add back information only when it is very very carefully sourced to mainstream reliable sources. If you don't have a source, don't add it back. Period. Jimbo Wales

Here here. We should apply this noble standard to all of our articles, not just those that are in dispute! Can't sleep, clown will eat me

This is being worked on. See wp:Verifiability/temp. Jacoplane

But I think things do change when we have a strong objection from the subject of an article. In such cases, we should be extra vigilant. Ordinarily, mundane facts not in controversy probably don't need a specific reference... Jimbo Wales

Well given we have the man himself at hand (see above) can I mention the fact that he is a former Leftist from a traditionally Left-wing family with a Jewish Father and a Christian Mother who has now become a Muslim? Do I need a source for that too? Lao Wai

Yes, of course you need a source for that. I've personally never heard of the man before, and so as a reader of an encyclopedia, I want to know where the facts come from... Jimbo Wales

In general, if the subject of an article appears on the talk page and politely proposes changes, the response will be polite. If Richard Worth had put in an appearance on his article's talk page he would have had a fair hearing. Even Jimmy Wales gets a fair hearing (yes, he has some Wikipedians on his side).

Cory Doctorow, science fiction author, demonstrated how it might work when he reacted to anonymous edits in September 2004 to the page **Cory Doctorow**. The anonym began by claiming that Doctorow's later books *have not achieved the same critical or commercial success despite massive publicity and free downloads* and that to his championing of copyright reform *the response from Doctorow's fans has been somewhat restrained*. After this testing of the waters, further edits made much fiercer criticisms than these. Alerted to these comments, Doctorow's response, on 10 November, was to edit the page anonymously and vigorously, asserting that the copyright experiment was working better than ever, and adding some more information that a neutral observer probably wouldn't have thought of. Immediately afterwards, realising that it was better not to be anonymous, he created the account Doctorow, completed his rewrite and kept on watching. The result was an edit war between Doctorow and the anonym and a tense discussion on the talk page, resolved after ten days by another anonymous editor who rewrote the whole piece neutrally. Doctorow called this unknown peacemaker 'a Wikipedia moderator' (strange how people trust that word) in his essay about the dispute, which concludes positively:

'That's what it was like when someone maligned me on Wikipedia: within five minutes of discovering it, I was able to correct it, and subsequently I had a public discussion with the guy, hammering out a consensus. The record of our discussion is kept by Wikipedia, so others can see how the entry got the way it is.'[185]

Comments regularly appear on the talk page about the extent to which Doctorow has edited the article, but the point is just as regularly made that he did it openly and was prepared to talk it through.

Increasingly writers, artists and other media people who depend on audience recognition to go on earning an income need to be on Wikipedia. Increasingly they recognise this and take steps to ensure it. 'Even in France,' wrote Pierre Assouline (as if France is somehow less subject to such temptations), 'certain specialists in self-promotion – artists and others – are clever enough to write for themselves, or have someone write for them, a long and favourable article out of proportion to their importance.'[186] How very true that is. I have to confess that I've edited the **Andrew Dalby** biography (to add references and to correct a name in the text: 'Gonzalo Pizarro', not a personal friend); and although I didn't create the page, I have to admit that I wasn't unaware of its creation; and all this happened even though I'm in France. My case is not so very different, after all, from that of **Marshall Poe**. His biography, by his own confession, was created by MarshallPoe himself, historian and journalist, though at that moment he was working in anonymous mode. Alai, a good Wikihousekeeper (*current fixations: eliminating reducing trying to keep vaguely in touch with the oversized stub categories... expunge all incidences of recieve from the 'pedia...*) marked the Poe article for deletion on 13 September 2005 with the comment: *no real evidence of notability beyond the proverbial average college professor (though I'd be happy to be proved wrong on that)*. Five editors rose to this challenge, and the article survived – decision reached on 23 September – which was just as well, because Poe's friendly investigation of Wikipedia was about to appear at that moment in *Atlantic Monthly*. Having quoted Alai's dismissive estimate in his prologue, he was able to add an epilogue:

'Bear in mind that I knew none of these people, and they had, as far as I know, no interest other than truth in doing all of this work. Yet they didn't stop with verifying my claims and approving my article. They also searched the Web for material they could use to expand my one-line biography. After they were done, the Marshall Poe entry was two paragraphs long and included a good bibliography. Now that's wiki magic.'[187]

What writers, artists and musicians need in order to keep their biographies on Wikipedia is a minimum level of demonstrable notability – often interpreted as two independent reviews in mainstream print media, a fairly easy target to aim at. Notability has to be not just demonstrable but actually demonstrated in the article. Many new biographies in these areas get deleted simply because unpractised editors can't grasp that the references or links to independent sources, proving the subject's notability, have to be right there in the article, verifiable by others. That's why **Marshall Poe** was nearly deleted when it was a one-liner. And that's how other editors saved it: they took on the job, as they did with **Mzoli's** and as they do with thousands of other cases, and showed from independent sources that the topic was notable although the original author hadn't managed to show this.

There's a problem with this simple notability rule. It applies equally to the wikipedias in the other 264 languages; theoretically, if you meet the qualification for one biography, you qualify for 265 of them. Some self-publicists, not content with a biography in the languages in which they write, have found that it's not too difficult to spread themselves across the others. If you can manage, with friends' help, to draft a one-line article in some foreign language, never forgetting the references and links, the editors in that language may fail to find arguments for deleting you. Even if you don't bother with the translation – even if you put an English version of the article on that other Wikipedia – some gullible editor may come along and translate it for you. It all helps with Google hits and it all helps with publicity. This is why the moderately obscure German physicist **Hagen Kleinert** (editing as Kleinert) has extended himself to 21 wikipedias, the moderately obscure Italian philosopher **Luciano Floridi** (editing as Floridi) has a biography on 35 wikipedias, while Wikipedia biographies of the most successful of these cross-wiki adventurers, the personable Austrian translator **Klaus Ebner** (editing as Klaus Ebner and distinguished with difficulty from Litteralittera) can be found in no fewer than 67 languages, all the way from Bengali to Yoruba. It's tempting. An unknown Spanish writer of comics, **Arthur Balder** (editing as Julila), briefly increased his international sales via a well-timed cross-wiki campaign that reached 61 languages and paid off in Googlability.

It's tempting. But it's a really bad idea. There's no good reason why you shouldn't get into the Haitian Creole Wikipedia before Goethe and Beethoven get into it (Kleinert and Ebner have both achieved this) but there's also no good reason why you should. What's more, there are cross-wiki observers who make a point of urging that such multiple pages be deleted; when they get their way your foreign-language efforts will have been a waste of time (your own and others'). The result will be one or two remaining pages about you in languages that few people read, no page about you in your own language, a listing in the Latin Wikipedia's spam catalogue **la:Vicipaedia:Propaganda**, and lasting unpopularity among Wikipedians; and none of this will help your long-term sales.

By contrast with these spammers, there have been a few notable cases in which the subjects of biographies in Wikipedia have wanted their biographies deleted, the best-known being Daniel Brandt, mentioned earlier in connection with the John Seigenthaler and EssJay incidents, and Seth Finkelstein, who writes about internet and privacy issues. Because of Wikipedia's aim to be a general encyclopedia covering all notable topics, historical and current, the only handy argument for deleting the biography of a person about whom adequate information exists is that the person is not notable. In Daniel Brandt's case, it fell to SlimVirgin to fulfil his request by making a case for deleting the page:

Okay, a clear and detailed, albeit repetitive, case. (1) He is of very marginal notability. It may not appear that way to us, because we talk about him a lot, but that's an internal Wikipedia thing. Outside in the real world, he's not known, and he's not a public figure... (2) Because of the fuss surrounding it, the article has attracted a lot of... immature and unprofessional editing... and I don't see that changing any time soon. (3) The article has caused a lot of trouble, and it isn't worth it... (4) The subject says... he wants it deleted, and I believe that bios of borderline notable living persons should be deleted on request. I hope this is a clear and detailed enough case.

That hope wasn't fulfilled. A long discussion followed (*think of how many good articles could be written with the energy that has gone into this debate*, said IronGargoyle) but it ended the way Daniel Brandt and SlimVirgin wanted. Finkelstein argued the same case for himself, fluently and without loss of temper:[188]

If some troll edits my biography to read e.g. 'He was thought to have been involved in the assassination of John F. Kennedy, but never indicted' (example deliberately chosen, but you can use your imagination), that affects me. I bear the cost of any reputational damage done. Wikipedia has no cost, except in the extraordinarily rare situation where the person who gets hit has enough power to make a fuss, generating bad publicity for Wikipedia. Otherwise, nobody home. This is deeply problematic. Seth Finkelstein

The same person can put up a web page in a vast number of places on the World Wide Web saying the same thing. That people can publish things about other people that damage their reputation has no bearing upon whether people warrant biographical articles in an encyclopaedia. Uncle G

Wikipedia is different from putting a page up on the web, because Wikipedia strips out attribution, and worse, adds an unwarranted air of authority. Or are you saying that Wikipedia articles are... in general trusted no more than a crazy ranter's website? Wikipedia's poor troll control has a lot of bearing as to whether it should contain biographical articles on people who can be hurt by them. Seth Finkelstein[189]

This is a really difficult issue for Wikipedia housekeeping. If the biography of someone interesting isn't there (either because it never was, or because it's been deleted), some Wikipedian will very soon try to create it. If it was deleted because of a straight decision that it was not notable, the next creator may well succeed in showing that the topic is notable after all, and all will be for the best in the best of all possible 'pedias. But if it was deleted because an unenthusiastic subject requested self-deletion, the only result of re-creating the article will be to make the subject still more unenthusiastic. We have a way of avoiding this – we delete and salt the page, obstructing any attempt to re-create it – but the result is a running sore, because future Wikipedians will not understand the obstruction and there will be no way of explaining it without a renewed discussion of the unenthusiastic subject.

During the first years of Wikipedia, when blogging was in its infancy, online news sites were few and limited, and little personal information was broadcast on the web, it seemed reasonable to some to make a point of insisting that their names be kept off Wikipedia, as they might insist on not appearing in a telephone directory or in Who's Who. There were people who were active in some public or intellectual sphere and yet were invisible on the internet, if that was the way they happened to want it.

Those days are long gone. It has now become unwise (I would say) to demand that your biography be removed from Wikipedia. Instead, accept Uncle G's reminder about all the other places on the web where references to you, and even purported biographies, now seem to be appearing without your approval; admit the validity of Seth Finkelstein's rejoinder that Wikipedia is different from those other places because it *strips out attribution and... adds an unwarranted air of authority*; and finally, with Cory Doctorow, consider that Wikipedia may be a little bit better than those other places because, if you need to, you can assume that air of authority and correct your Wikipedia biography yourself.

Some teachers and students – some others too – love Wikipedia because they can treat each page, whether existing or not yet created, as a clean sheet on which to write or copy whatever they fancy.

Here I'm not talking about Wikipedia projects that take account of how a Wikipedia page needs to be written. These projects demand a leader already familiar with Wikipedia; they demand an evaluation procedure allowing for the fact that once a student has created a page, it necessarily becomes a work of collaboration. And, as we've seen, it can be done. No, I'm talking about the pages that suddenly, before a Wikipedia-watcher's eyes, turn from familiar to alien shape because a teacher, student or other kind editor has deleted what was there before and pasted in something completely different. There are many such cases: these examples just happened to be on my *watchlist*.

I first saw it happen with a page on a medieval personality, **Agnes of France (Byzantine empress)**. It was a small, weak page which I was thinking of improving. Suddenly, all at once, it changed: an anonymous editor had inserted a new text, much longer and considerably more exciting, but with no links. I and another editor set to work reducing this new text to Wikipedia style, but I became suspicious: hadn't I seen these bold speculations before? Yes, I had. The text had been lifted, whole, from the website Roman-emperors.org, which consists of a copyrighted series of biographies by named authors. To our frustration, our work on the text was wasted: it had to be deleted forthwith. Wikipedia does not plagiarise, though many other sites plagiarise Wikipedia. I reverted to the old version and gradually completed a rewrite.

I next saw it happen with the page entitled **Symposium (Plato)**, on one of Plato's best-known works. Again, it was an unsatisfactory page. I had recently revised one section that was relevant to work I had done in the world beyond Wikipedia, but I had no appetite to improve the rest. I'm no Platonist. Suddenly, in October 2006, the whole article changed. A named user, Brenda Maverick, who described herself as *a writer, and a professor of philosophy and religion*, had replaced it with a long and readable essay that *focused on the sensual and sensational at the expense of giving a good account of the dialogue* (to quote Akhilleus on the talk page) and opened with a *misleading, weirdly sexually fixated characterization*, in the words of Tempest67, who got a username specifically in order to protest about the new slant and unexpected phraseology: *After Alcibiades' mock eulogy to Socrates,* *who is ugly as a satyr but godlike within, the three men play a little grab-ass on the couch.* Brenda defended her work as *a summary outline that highlights the entertaining elements of the dialog. Plato was a masterful wit. Why do we want a summary that dulls him down?* She added similar texts, always with strong sexual overtones, to **Satire**, **Diogenes of Sinope** and elsewhere, and fought opponents vigorously until January 2007, when (*I'm sorry, but I haven't slept in a few days*) her involvement suddenly tailed off. At **Symposium (Plato)** the consensus was against her: the new texts didn't answer the questions that people ask an encyclopedia.

And then I heard of a third case, different again. Between 8 and 11 December 2008, edits traceable to a school in Atherton, California had replaced about 15 articles with completely new text. Most of this was done from an anonymous IP address,[190] but some of it was by a new named editor, Pickles4u, whose user page betrays, let's say, a lack of appreciation for the collaborative spirit of Wikipedia:

Hey I'm pretty much the coolest person ever and probably either the top or second best contributor to the wikipedia website. Though your contributions and edits are considered, usually my work is way better than yours. I would appreciate you not bothering me all you anal editors. Thank you.

The articles were on minor ancient and medieval personalities, who might have been selected almost at random out of a biographical dictionary apparently without considering whether Wikipedia's existing articles were good, bad or indifferent. Whatever links, whatever bibliography and footnotes the pages already had were deleted when the new text was pasted in.

The big problem for Wikipedia when this happens is that if the existing page is very weak, editors are tempted to retain the new material. As Pliny would have said, no edit is so bad that some good cannot be got out of it; but getting the good out of it takes a lot longer than reverting it. In the case of the Atherton essays, Singinglemon, with scant concern for the bruised sensibilities of Pickles4u, restored sense and proportion to **Euclid of Megara**. I dealt with the problem of **Duris of Samos** (a poor article, based on the 1911 *Britannica*, had been replaced by a much longer one that was far worse) by writing a third version, fully annotated and (I claim) better than anything that was there before. A teacher in Atherton is in my debt for this. I commented on a talk page: *In some other cases – e.g. Festus (historian) – what we had before was so terrible that anything would be an improvement!*[191] How wrong I was. Lateantiquist saw that the Atherton essay on **Festus** had to be deleted right away. It had the same problem as the **Agnes of France** page mentioned above: *This article is a very close paraphrase of the relevant section of David Rohrbacher, The Historians of Late Antiquity.* But for Lateantiquist no one might ever have noticed that this essay was plagiarised. And that's one reason why putting your school essays and teaching notes in place of existing Wikipedia articles is a bad idea.

One of the very first complaints of political bias on Wikipedia concerned **Tony Blair**. The article as available on 31 July 2001 asserted: *While the 'rebranding' may have fooled some of the population, it should be noted in the interests of balance that the Blair administration was responsible for the loss of serious amounts of public money in (for example) the Millenium Dome fiasco...* and so on. Gareth Owen, a lover of Wikipedia from its infancy (he already had **The Beatles** and **Hobbits** to his credit: *Hobbits were essentially short, hairy footed versions of humans and lived in a part of Middle Earth called The Shire*) at first attempted to remonstrate on the Blair talk page. He then remarked on a mailing list that the article was *horribly biased*. Wales replied in person, admitting *I know virtually nothing of Tony Blair* but agreeing that the text was inappropriate. He suggested that a rewrite might read *Critics claim that Blair's rebranding strategy was superficial, and that his fundamental politics actually remain the same.*[192]

Why people love Wikipedia, if they happen to have an agenda in the world beyond Wikipedia that they are prepared to advance by hidden means, is that Wikipedia offers them unrivalled opportunities. Wikipedians have always known this, but it was in 2006 that the fact really came to public notice in the case that you may know as **USA Congressional staff edits to Wikipedia** but insiders call **wp:Congressional staffer edits**. The story broke in the *Sun* (a local newspaper of Lowell, Massachusetts), which was specially interested in Massachusetts congressman **Marty Meehan**'s biography:

'The staff of U. S. Rep Marty Meehan wiped out references to his broken term-limits pledge as well as information about his huge campaign war chest in an independent biography of the Lowell Democrat on a Web site that bills itself as the "world's largest encyclopedia," *The Sun* has learned. The Meehan alterations... represent just two of more than 1,000 changes made by congressional staffers at the U.S. House of Representatives in the past six months... Matt Vogel, Meehan's chief of staff, said he authorized an intern in July to replace existing Wikipedia content with a staff-written biography.'[193]

Meehan responded: 'I did not know that this change was being made at the time... Though the actual time spent on this issue amounted to 11 minutes... it was a waste of energy and an error in judgment on the part of my staff.' The Meehan biography had previously been extremely brief, and some pointedly unfriendly comments had been added to it anonymously in December 2004: *In the year 2000 when the Congressman ran for Congress, breaking his 1992 pledge, he called it a disservice to his constituents... This breaking of the pledge has been a controversial issue... Interestingly Congressman Meehan has one of the largest war-chests of all sitting Congressman. Some believe that this war-chest has become an obstacle to those wishing to challenge the sitting Congressman.* During those eleven minutes in July 2005 anonymous edits by the intern removed all of this, replacing it with a much longer and more favourable text (*His fiscally responsible voting record since then has earned him praise from citizen watchdog groups... Meehan has been a tireless advocate for economic development in Massachusetts*) which survived until, following the *Sun* news item, frantic vandalism and edit warring led eventually to another complete rewrite by a veteran Wikipedian named Neutrality.

Meehan's staff had, as he said, made an error of judgment. Congressman Joe Wilson's staffer, Emily Lawrimore, now demonstrated that there was a better way to do it. His biography, too, was quite inadequate. On Jimmy Wales's advice she put up an official biography at **Talk:Joe Wilson (U.S. politician)**. With Jimbo Wales's encouragement, a recent arrival named James S. worked on this to improve the article text. As a sad moral to this improving tale, James S., seemingly obsessed with **Depleted uranium** and **Capital punishment**, was soon the object of bans and blocks for political edit warring (*you do have a habit of slanting articles to the left*, he was gently told) and is no longer among us.

The Meehan edits were hot news among Wikipedians but they weren't scandalous; as Psm and John k afterwards observed on the talk page, the earlier version of the Meehan biography wasn't worth keeping. More surprising were certain others among the 'more than 1,000 changes made by congressional staffers'. Many of them had been immediately deleted as vandalism, including the claim that Representative **Eric Cantor** *smells of cow dung*, but there were plenty more serious changes that clearly had a political motivation. Representative **Gil Gutknecht**'s office had eliminated most of the existing text of his page and inserted his official biography, thus neatly omitting his soon-to-be-broken promise not to stand for re-election in 2006. At first the username Gutknecht01 was used, with the edit summary: *Edited on the authority of Congressman Gil Gutknecht's office.* The admin Jonathunder reverted the edit – it was clearly not neutral – and a fellow Wikipedian, Zscout370, issued a friendly warning about conflict of interest. Gutknecht01 fell silent, but the lesson hadn't been learned: further attempts to edit the article were made anonymously.

Soon afterwards investigations by Wikipedians brought to light comparable edits from computers at the CIA and the Department of Justice, including an expert opinion offered at **Talk:United States Marshals Service** (which was reverted as vandalism after two minutes):

Anyone applying to the Detention Enforcemnt Officer postion, Be Warned!!! You are treated as a second class citizen within the USMS. There is no union, and they expect you to kiss their a** just so you can hope to get a deputy spot... its a dead end job and it just plain sucks!

Also from the Department of Justice came a series of anonymous edits that removed information from Republican majority leader **Tom DeLay**'s biography about aspects of his increasing legal difficulties.[194] Next to be revealed were some not very reputable edits originating from Senators' offices and staff. These weren't limited to senatorial biographies. Someone in **Dianne Feinstein**'s office not only added an enormous list of 'awards' to her biography (removed by the admin Tom a month later) but also made the biography of her husband, **Richard C. Blum**, less exciting than it had previously been (the edit was reverted by an anonym some weeks later).

Some of the anonymous edits from congressional and goverment offices were made in good faith, but many represented blatant pushing of a political point of view. There really were over a thousand of them; it had taken a lot of time to correct them, to issue warnings, and in many cases to block the IP addresses. When the extent of the problem was revealed at least one inculpated official was brazen enough to blame Wikipedia's accessibility. 'They've got an edit provision on there for the sake of editing when things are not accurate,' said Senator **Norm Coleman**'s chief of staff, Erich Mische. 'I presume if they did not want people to edit, they wouldn't allow you to edit.' Mische or his staff had changed the description of Coleman as a college student from *liberal Democrat* to *activist Democrat* and then to *an active college student*. The heavy sentences, *Coleman campaigned in 2002 for the United States Senate, after being persuaded by Karl Rove not to run again for governor. Although Coleman tried to position himself as a moderate Republican candidate who would reach across party lines, his votes during his first year in office in 2003 lined up 98% of the time with President Bush, according to Congressional Quarterly*, had been rendered much lighter: *Coleman campaigned in 2002 for the United States Senate as a moderate Republican candidate who would reach across party lines.* Details of Coleman's interchanges with George Galloway in Senate subcommittee hearings were also rendered less neutral and easier on the potential voter's eye.

Mische is also cited for the disarming admission: 'When you put "edia" in there, it makes it sound as if this is a benign, objective piece of information.' He and his colleagues, he perhaps intended to add, had tried to show that it could be turned into something different.[195]

Wikipedia is often caught up in political infighting, and not only in the United States: it's nothing if not international. A televised debate between Nicolas Sarkozy and Ségolène Royal, in the evening of 2 May 2007, turned to nuclear power stations. 'You'll need to do some revision in this subject,' said Royal to Sarkozy. 'The European Pressurised Reactor is the third generation of nuclear stations, not the fourth.'[196] One minute later (as *PCInPact* tells the story) a surfer from Nancy in eastern France found the Wikipedia article **fr:Réacteur pressurisé européen**, clicked on 'edit', deleted *third generation* and inserted *fourth generation*. It is the only edit that this IP address has ever made. Two minutes later it was reverted by the well-named user Veilleur ('Unsleeping'), whose user page displays an eye in which is reflected a Wikipedia diffs page (one that highlights the differences between any two selected edits). Below this compelling image appears the warning: *I keep a close eye on IP (unregistered user) edits in order to eliminate vandalism and spam. I use a specially-designed program that allows me to watch dozens of edits at once and revert vandalism with a single click.* Two further attempts to insert the same information were reverted by Graoully, equally well-named (do you doubt me? Just say it aloud). Graoully added an edit summary: *Sarko n'est pas une source valable* ('Sarko isn't a reliable source'), and so was evidently well aware of what was going on, whether from the TV or from the talk page. Edit warring continued until, after an hour and a half, the word *third* now supported by a footnote, the article was semi-protected. During that short period it had undergone 50 back-and-forth edits, one of them traceable to the French Pacific territory of New Caledonia.

The clever argument by dedicated Sarkozians, in what soon became a lengthy talk page debate, that the EPR is *third generation in Europe but fourth generation in France* now seems to have devolved into a well-documented footnote which allows, at a stretch, the designation 'generation III+'. Royal may have lost the war, but at least she won this battle.

Was the first anonymous editor a Sarkozian? In the complex world of French politics this can't be assumed. The edit was certainly intended to make Royal appear to be mistaken. It was followed, almost immediately, by a comment posted on the left-wing newspaper *Libération*'s blog, rubbing in the fact that the Socialist candidate had got her facts wrong. In 2007 Royal had two problems (and her knowledge of third-generation reactors wasn't one of them). One problem was Sarkozy; the other was the endlessly fissile mass of left-wingers and Socialists, many of whom couldn't be persuaded to like her. On this debate, at any rate, the press was happy to chalk up a point for Royal; the rapid defence mounted by 'the encyclopedia that anyone can edit' earned it some praise.

Such incidents have happened often. Durova, veteran defender of Wikipedia, mentioned two cases in a web essay on the best way to correct falsehoods in Wikipedia articles. Between March and July 2007 an anonymous editor made 'gossipy edits to biographies, mostly of Ohio politicians' one of which was unfavourable to **Steve LaTourette** – and not only unfavourable but also false. 'For four months, Congressman LaTourette's staffers were aware of the falsehoods but did nothing to fix them because, as spokeswoman Deborah Setliff told the *Plain Dealer* of Cleveland, they feared a PR backlash if they edited the page': they were all too conscious of the recent controversy over congressional edits. Yet they could, like Joe Wilson's staffers, have found a way to deal with the problem.

The second story concerned malicious editing from which the intended victim managed to draw benefit. In 2006 an anonymous vandal had attacked the Wikipedia biography of Congresswoman Stephanie Herseth of South Dakota. Several false claims were added to the article including the completely untrue allegation that she was pregnant by a member of her staff. 'It's uncertain,' Durova added, 'whether the opposing campaign coordinated the vandalism, but shortly afterward its campaign manager sent an e-mail to several of the state's bloggers that cited the vandalized Wikipedia biography and added an accusation that Herseth was a "home-wrecker."' Rather than damaging Herseth's reputation, however, the tactic had backfired on Bruce Whalen, her challenger in the forthcoming election. The Rapid City Journal even called for a public apology from the Whalen campaign team. Herseth was triumphantly re-elected.

In comment afterwards Durova stated explicitly the Machiavellian potential of such incidents. For a PR manager 'it's a good idea to check in on the history files of your client's article from time to time. If a competitor made a black hat attack on the page – even if it only stayed live for one minute – that's something you may be able to leverage to your client's advantage.'[197]

Some people, then, love Wikipedia because they can push their political views on it – briefly and until someone notices. In retrospect, no new revelation of the vulnerability of Wikipedia to non-neutral edits emerged, even from the Congressional staffers affair. Wikipedia's vulnerability was already known; and, after all, every editor has a point of view. This just happened to be a group of editors with similar points of view. The real revelation was the childishness and lack of scruple of the politicians and their staffers: as Marty Meehan frankly said, such activities were 'a waste of energy and an error in judgment'. Sometimes such edits last minutes or hours, as the edits to **Gil Gutknecht** and **Norm Coleman** did; sometimes weeks, as with **Dianne Feinstein** and **Richard C. Blum**; sometimes months, like the revised **Marty Meehan** biography. They don't last forever, and they leave a bad smell: discussions on talk pages that never go away, bans, blocks and (in certain cases) press reports that damage the very cause that the editor aimed to support. It can't be known whether the publicity over Congressional edits ('Gutknecht joins Wikipedia tweakers') was a decisive factor for Gutknecht's 2006 re-election campaign. At any rate it's a fact that Gutknecht lost his election,[198] and it's a fact that Herseth won hers.

There's a curious paradox at the heart of Wikipedia. The articles, which are supposed to become definitive and stable, are in reality endlessly mutable; an added detail may very soon disappear again, and article histories are seldom visited. But the talk pages, which seem so obviously ephemeral and forgettable, are in reality permanent. However silly and inconsequential the talk may be, however potentially embarrassing to editors or to the people they are arguing about, it's preserved and displayed for years. It's because of this Wikipedia paradox that editing articles with a hidden motive, especially a political motive, is counter-productive in the long term.

David.Monniaux's interview with *Le Figaro*, at the time of the Sciences Po incident, served to bring to the attention of a wide audience a fact that Wikipedians knew only too well but that the press was only just getting to grips with. 'Politicians with a thirst for publicity, unknown artists, members of sects and political splinter movements regularly arrive on Wikipedia to rewrite history and promote their own ideas.'[199]

It was at the beginning of 2005, immediately after the 2004 Indian Ocean earthquake, that a new disaster assistance group created a page about itself on

Wikipedia with a link showing how to send it money. Wikipedians found it impossible to confirm from independent sources that this was a real charity, or to find out what it did with any money sent. The link was removed and the page was severely pruned. As an editor remarked in discussion, the group's only *claim to fame appears to be not being listed on a number of prominent charity directories*. Once revised after these investigations, the page inevitably turned from uncritical self-description into what was little more than *an attack page based on original research*. There was nothing for it but deletion. The unlucky Wikipedian who worked hardest on it was rewarded by fierce criticism on the group's news website. The hot-tempered arguments in the deletion talk pages remain for ever as a reminder that it's a bad idea to promote your organisation on a wiki.[200]

From time to time editors notice that links to a commercial site are multiplying across the Wikipedia world. Sometimes it's done in a simple way: an unimaginative firm will think of 50 articles slightly relevant to its business and add links to its website on all of them. There's another kind of spamming, too, the spreading of random links on quiet wikipedias in the hope of escaping human notice while improving the website's Google rating. Both of these methods can work for a short time, but once someone raises the alarm the cross-wiki timelords search out and remove every last link and block the insertion of others. The Wikimedia spam blacklist is said to be consulted by Google and Yahoo in compiling their own blacklists. Advertisers do themselves more harm than good by spamming Wikipedia.[201]

For some, no doubt, any publicity is good publicity; but it's a bad move to write about yourself on Wikipedia if you're extra-sensitive. In 2005 a new user named Israelbeach contributed to Wikipedia a biography of the Israeli PR writer, Joel Leyden, added his website Israelnewsagency.com to the list of Israeli newspapers and listed him as a 'significant writer' on the Fathers' rights movement. The biography read like a CV; my guess is that Leyden thought it would be useful in his career but hadn't fully realised that others could edit it. When information was added about former marriages, and doubt was thrown on whether his site could serve as a reliable source on the subject of himself – normal incidents in the course of developing someone's Wikipedia biography – he evidently began to wish the article didn't exist.

With the doubtful help of the non-notability rule it was, with difficulty, deleted. Reading the attacks on Wikipedia and Wikipedians that he has posted ever since, I hope that the Wikipedians on his target list are less easily bruised than he is, because Leyden doesn't pull his punches.

The last two cases appear to be naive attempts to make propaganda on Wikipedia. It doesn't end there. Raul654 towards the end of 2004 included in 'Raul's Laws of Wikipedia' the following item: *Wikipedia's steadily increasing popularity means that within the next year or two, we will begin to see organized corporate [astroturfing] campaigns*. Astroturfing is marketing that tries to make itself look like grassroots activity – just as astroturf tries to make itself look like grass. *Prediction confirmed, August 28, 2005*,[202] Raul claimed nine months later. Confirmation had arrived by a very strange route.

The story begins with a new user, Jon Hawk, who created an article about a pop star named **Jamie Kane**. The first version read:

James Kenton Kane (born 22 October 1982–2005) better known as Jamie Kane was a British pop musician and was a member of boyband Boy*d Upp. After the band split up, Kane launch a mildy successful solo career. He appeard on the covers of Top Of The Pops magazine and NME. Kane was the subject of several scandals in his last year. Kane died in a helicopter crash of the coast of the Netherlands.

Spelling aside, it wasn't a bad start. Another user, Daisy Mae, immediately added a link to the BBC web pages about Jamie Kane, and added the heartfelt edit summary: *I miss you Jamie xxx.*

Nine hours later Mholland slapped a disputed notice on the page, adding: *this is fiction, n'est pas?* Mholland was right: Kane never existed. He's a fictional character created by the BBC as part of an online virtual reality game. But the story didn't stop there: immediately afterwards the redlink left by Jon Hawk for the imaginary band **Boy*d Upp** was turned into a real article by an anonymous editor. This edit was traceable to a computer at BBC headquarters, and it was not the first time, nor the last, that the IP address concerned has been used for vandalism and the insertion of marketing material. At this stage Raul654 might have been forgiven for claiming that this very story confirmed his prediction about astroturfing. Other Wikipedians certainly leapt to that conclusion. They vociferously blamed the BBC for a 'viral marketing' campaign that had targeted the encyclopedia, and there was heated talk of blocks.

But it seems there had been no campaign after all. First off, Jon Hawk owned up: *Sadly I don't work for the BBC if that's what you're incinuating. I am mearly a British student.* He explained further, his spelling visibly improving:

Please do not use my edits to slander the BBC. If this were part of a viral campaign, the grammar of the article would almost certainly be better. I suspect the article would have been created at the same time as the game started also. Jamie Kane was mentioned on several blogs on Friday... I'm nothing more than a student. I'm sincerely apologetic for purposefully omitting the true nature of Jamie Kane... Evidence for the game's notability comes from the Guardian and Popjustice. Once again, sincere apologies, I assure you I will do no harm in future.

Then a new user named MattC confessed that the anonymous creation of **Boy*D Upp** had been his work:

I created the Boy*D Upp page from inside the BBC network on Friday evening after stumbling across the Jamie Kane entry linked from the Pop Justice forums. My action was in no way part of an orchestrated marketing campaign on behalf of the Jamie Kane project team nor was it intended for my page to be attributed to the BBC, which has been implied. It was nothing more than common garden vandalism for which I am sorry.

Uncle G rewrote the **Jamie Kane** page, and **Boy*d Upp** was reduced to a redirect. MattC (who had made anonymous edits before, he said) admitted: *I now better understand the community's passion about the Wikipedia project & have gathered an intimate knowledge of the article deletion process.* All was well, apparently. But did MattC really have no motive beyond fun? Could a student, even a British student, spell English as badly as Jon Hawk did, and if this was his first edit, how did he know so much about notability? Was Jon Hawk also Daisy Mae? Can Wikipedia, and the BBC's audience, rely on the Corporation's understanding of 'reality'?

Leaving those questions for others, the serious revelation for Wikipedia, and the real confirmation of Raul's Sixth Law of Wikipedia, came in a reader's comment to the report on *BoingBoing*.

'I can't say who I am, but I do work at a company that uses Wikipedia as a key part of online marketing strategies. That includes planting of viral information in entries, modification of entries to point to new promotional sites or "leaks" embedded in entries to test diffusion of information. Wikipedia is just a more transparent version of Myspace as far as some companies are concerned. We love it (evil laugh). On the other side, I love it from an academia/sociological standpoint, and I don't necessarily have a problem with it used as a viral marketing tool. After all, marketing is a form of information, with just a different end point in mind (consuming rather than learning).'[203]

Of course it happens. With every point that Wikipedia gains in Alexa.com's web traffic statistics, it's more than ever worthwhile to try to slant half-relevant pages in the direction of some marketing campaign. It's more than ever a challenge to Wikipedians to find the nefarious edits and root them out. This is a war with no end in sight.

The marketers and self-publicists are only two among many enemies besetting the path to Wikipedia's future neutrality. More difficult to deal with and often more time-consuming are those who insert nonsense because they believe it and they know it's important. And it might be true, of course. Nonsense was spread across an astonishing number of pages by former user Sadi Carnot, admirer of Georgi Gladyshev, the guru of human thermodynamics (which is all about falling in love, if I've got it right). This nonsense wasn't easy to strip out, and may still be encountered, but most of it has gone to a much more suitable place, A Human Thermodynamics Wiki.[204] Nonsense about the supposed complete version of the Greek alphabet was spread into many languages in 2006 by a user called Wikinger (and other names) who appeared to log in from various European service providers. *I switch between them as I want: I am tunnelling through them all, to cover my real country. But this is secret and you never get it. Your unholy efforts to get me caught and persecuted are futile*, Wikinger told me.[205] Wikinger was an admirer of the late **Anne Catherine Emmerich**, who, alone among twentieth century mortals, spoke the **Adamic language** apparently once spoken in the Garden of Eden. Even Emmerich did not know, I gather, that this almost-divine tongue is correctly to be written in the Greek alphabet plus eight letters, two of which were only otherwise employed in the Bactrian language of ancient Afghanistan. Ever since 2006 strange extra letters are to be found in tables of the Greek alphabet in certain wikipedias, and this is why. Tancarville, on the other hand, was an enthusiast (and, for all I know, a scion) of the Maltese nobility. He assiduously added articles to Wikipedia about hundreds of members of this none-too-exclusive club. Unluckily the nobility and notability of nearly all of them could only be verified by way of the genealogical works of Charles Gauci,[206] subject of a now-deleted article whose existence wasn't independent of the Wikipedia user Dr CA Gauci MD. Gauci's works may exist, but no Wikipedian except these two was able to find copies of them. The island's noble families has now been largely expelled from Wikipedia and Tancarville is indefinitely blocked.

There are even cloudier zones than the Maltese nobility. The Duchy of Pinica (*A sub-province of a fictional micronation!* wrote RickK dismissively), its Imperial Post and the Duchy of Natatoria (*'natatoria' is Latin for 'swimming-pools'*, as another Wikipedian pointed out)[207] were defended with dogged persistence by the surrealist editor Daniel C. Boyer, but they were eventually deleted from the Wikipedia world. Even the famous island of Porchesia has now gone. *Porchesia or also known as Porchess Island, is an island off the coast of Syria and Lebanon*, the Wikipedia article once read. *It is currently ruled by Lebanonese government.* Porchesia was created in November 2005 and survived on Wikipedia until the following September, when Danny reported on a mailing list: *I have just deleted an article, 'Porchesia'. Any admins are welcome to read the history... Problem is, there is no such place.*[208] Porchesia was so notable a hoax that it has surely earned a Wikipedia article in spite of its failure to exist. Another piece of pure fiction was the charming philosophy of *Harmonisme*, once to be found on the French Wikipedia. This, too, has now, sadly, been deleted.[209]

Good evening to you, wrote Lodewijk Vadacchino to a randomly-chosen user on the Serbo-Croat Wikipedia, *I am an Italian user. I would have need please that you translated from the English these two articles: Martin Weinek and*

Kaspar Capparoni. As the Kommissar Rex is a lot of succession in the Balkans it would be beautiful that these two actors would also have an article in Serbo-Croatian, I hope that you will help me. I thank you in advance. His request was successful; the two human stars of *Kommissar Rex*, a German TV show featuring the adventures of a police dog, are now suitably commemorated in Serbo-Croat. Lodewijk gave various other reasons on wikipedias in 67 (yes, 67) other languages: *I am creating an European fanclub on Martin Weinek and Kaspar Capparoni,* he claimed to a Danish victim. He occasionally had to pester as many as seven users before finding one sufficiently complaisant, but this never discouraged him. Lodewijk, incidentally, sometimes describes himself as Luigi I, Prince of Tirol; sometimes, possibly with greater precision, as *il rompiscatole d'Europa,* the ball-breaker of Europe. He has enthusiasms for **Lola Pagnani** and several other minor Italian and Austrian TV actors who, thanks to him, have been plastered across the Wikipedia world. *I had made to make this article both for gift of Christmas both because she is about to have a child,* he protested, after quietly removing the delete template that disfigured poor Lola on the Norwegian Wikipedia. When other editors compared notes, his importunities earned him a block on the Latin Wikipedia and a ticking-off from an administrator on the Italian one: *Don't ever again remove a deletion template placed by someone else... 'I wanted to give her a Christmas present' is not a good reason for starting a page... You must understand that such behaviour will get you blocked on other wikipedias.* It also got his favoured actors a bad name; it looked as though they or their agents had been spamming Wikipedia. This time it wasn't their fault, and Lola Pagnani survives in most of the wikipedias into which Lodewijk inserted her.

Armenian Genocide no longer carries the warning that Roy Rosenzweig described,[210] but the talk page (with its 18 archives) is headed by an eye-popping series of admonitions. *Under the discretionary sanctions imposed at wp:Requests for arbitration/Armenia-Azerbaijan 2, this article has been placed on a one-revert rule. Any editor who makes more than one revert (and this revert must be discussed on the talk page) in a 24-hour period will be blocked.*

Please edit cooperatively, and seek consensus and compromise rather than edit-war; and then take a deep breath and relax your eyebrows. If you are about ready to explode it is suggested that you stop for a minute and relax, because that indeed may happen after sifting through these heated debates; and then discussions on this talk page often lead to previous arguments being restated. Please read the recent comments, or look in the archives or FAQ section before contributing. Sadly it's evident that not every visitor considers these warnings before plunging in. Does the name of that arbitration page hint at a Byzantine world of paralegislative procedure, with endless discussion and all too little resolution? No impression could be truer, as a study based on **wp:Arbitration/Index/Cases** will confirm. Somewhere among these case notes are the names of Wikipedians who don't deserve to be there and the catch-titles of irresoluble conflicts in the world beyond Wikipedia. How did they ever decide 'Eastern European disputes' all at once? Wherein lay the 'Sarah Palin protection wheel war'? 'Homeopathy' and 'International Churches of Christ' may have been laid to rest but, like Jarndyce v. Jarndyce, **wp:Requests for arbitration/Scientology** will surely never die. Some of us love this metalegal rainforest; some of us occasionally enjoy observing it, peering through the barbed wire, seldom or never daring to enter (I once dipped a toe into **Macedonia (terminology)** but my guardian angel dragged me away); and many Wikipedians pray that they will never go that way at all.

The great ArbCom frequently reprimands, and occasionally demotes, naughty admins. Admins block naughty editors, and H. Jonat was one of the very first victims of this punishment: blockings and bans were rare in the early days. It's easy to identify vandalism, and vandalism will quickly lead to a block; edit warring will lead to a block; but there are many other forms of behaviour that have been known to lead to blocks. Examples have multiplied in this chapter with Tancarville, Wikinger and Israelbeach; I might add the several identities of PoetGuy.[211] Unlike all of these, Publicgirluk disturbed nothing in the encyclopedia except some of its editors. With revealing photographs on her user page she made clear her youthful attractiveness and her sexual enthusiasms. Sadly, rather like EssJay, Publicgirluk wasn't all she seemed to be. The photographs were discovered to be of a Swedish model (who merits a brief article on the Swedish Wikipedia, **sw:Linda Lust**); the identity of Publicgirluk in the world beyond Wikipedia has not been otherwise elucidated, so far as I know. It was Jimbo Wales, no less, who banned her.[212]

Some, after years of contributions, leave because it is evident to them that their contributions aren't welcome. This was the case with Sadi Carnot. Some, though their philosophies may be far from the mainstream, continue to contribute vigorously: I could name The Cunctator, Giano II and Daniel C. Boyer among these, and I might add Calmypal, who was also Arthur George Carrick, Woodrow and (new users found this confusing) sometimes called himself Wikipedia. He wanted to make a list of **Wikipedians by facial hair**, but it was deleted; he was the author of **Engime's Theory of Pure Absurdity**, also deleted; he is an honorary member of the Association of Inclusionist Wikipedians, and, as his user page asserts, *Calmypal is*.

It isn't easy being a Wikipedian. Raul654, in his Laws of Wikipedia, puts the difficulties in first place.

1. Much of Wikipedia's content, and all of the day to day functions are overseen by a small core of the most dedicated contributors. These users are the most valuable resource Wikipedia has. Corollary – Of these highly dedicated users who have left, the vast majority left as a result of trolls, vandals, and/or POV warriors – typically not as a result of any one particular user, but from the combined stress of dealing with many of them. Consequently, such problem users should be viewed as Wikipedia's biggest handicap.[213]

'Some even achieve fame of a sort on snarky Wikipedia anti-fansites,' writes Jonathan Dee. The harassment has been discussed by David Shankbone, a reporter and photographer who suffered it himself, for obscure reasons, after making sensible minor edits to the biography of the porn star **Michael Lucas (director)**.[214] Durova and SlimVirgin, high-profile Wikipedians, brave enough to court all kinds of controversy, are among those who have achieved this fame and have withstood the pressure of scurrilous attacks from the shadows beyond the encyclopedia. I have already mentioned some others whose names are bandied about on the wikifringes and who go on working: Raul654, Eloquence and Danny, Anthere and David.Monniaux are among them. Sam Blacketer keeps going too. The encyclopedia can do little to support them. No doubt they are all readers of the advice page **m:Wikistress**, though I'm sure they have never adopted method number 143 for dealing with the affliction: *Replace every image on Metapedia with this one*, advises Paradoctor. *Make sure they can't trace you, though.* The image is a beautiful close-up of a defecating seagull, seen from below.

Others have been unable to deal with the stress. As with those early academic Nupedians, many in more recent times have gradually dropped out, with or without an explanation. Katefan0 was among those driven away by harassment. Diderot was one who simply fell silent, and we don't know why.[215]

Chapter 7
Why you don't trust Wikipedia

Despite its flaws, the amateur-written encyclopedia has become the world's all-purpose information source. It's our new Delphic oracle.

Nicholas Carr, 'The Net is being carved up into information plantations'

THERE ARE GOOD reasons why you don't trust Wikipedia. Among these reasons is that you can't know why, or on what grounds, people make the edits that they do.

Some unexpected motives were recently revealed after a debate in the British House of Commons. To quote Cade Metz's succinct explanation in *The Register*, on 11 February 2009 during Prime Minister's Questions – 'a weekly session where the PM spends a half hour taking abuse from members of Parliament – [David] Cameron chastised [Gordon] Brown for a recent anecdote he spun about Titian. Brown had claimed that Titian lived to be 90 years old. But Cameron insisted he died at 86.'[216] If this reminds you of the Sarkozy–Royal dispute about the generations of nuclear reactors, you're right thus far; but in this case David Cameron's Conservative Central Office got involved in the Wikipedia editing and successfully demonstrated their skill (shared with several British political parties) at turning a conspiracy into a cock-up.

Not only was the exchange at *Prime Minister's Questions* a waste of time; it would still have been a waste of time even if Titian's age at death mattered to British political life. Titian died in 1576 and no one knows when he was born, as is explained at length in the main text of Wikipedia's **Titian** page. But the main text isn't everything. Until the morning of 11 February 2009 the infobox and first line of the Titian page summarised the vital dates as *c. 1485 – August 27, 1576*, which appears to justify Brown's claim and falsify Cameron's. Then the latest exchange in the House of Commons was discussed on Andrew Neil's BBC show *The Daily Politics*. Neil's researcher checked Wikipedia on the spot and calculated that Titian lived to 91. Laughter in the studio. OK so far?

At 12.29 on Wikipedia anonym A (origin unknown) changed the infobox and first line of **Titian** to *c. 1490 – August 27, 1576*, adding the edit summary: *Birth year corrected to that stated in text.* This was misleading: the text takes no firm position, and the truth rather seems to be that the edit favoured Cameron. Simultaneously, anonym B (traced by WikiScanner to Conservative Central Office), evidently listening to Neil's show, glanced at **Titian** on Wikipedia, saw that the not-yet-altered text favoured Gordon Brown, thought about it for five fatal minutes, then clicked on edit and changed the death date, in the infobox only, to *1572*, and meanwhile a colleague emailed *The Daily Politics* to say that they'd done their own research and Cameron was justified.[217] Not so: because of the five-minute delay between reading the article and editing it, they had undermined their party leader's stance on Titian by making the painter die at a mere 82. And now Wikipedians began to notice. *We have conflicting information on his year of death, with the infobox saying 1572 and the article's leader saying 1576, so which is right?* demanded TheRetroGuy; and at the same moment, at 12.36, Modernist reverted all the anonymous edits and restored *c. 1485 – August 27, 1576* to the infobox and first line.

That afternoon the talk page was busy, and anonym A boldly joined in the talk page discussion alongside the rest, but Sam Blacketer soon afterwards added a pointed warning: *Editors with a potential conflict of interest please note that journalists are already watching.* He added a link to the first online reaction to the story, Paul Waugh's blog piece *Has Cam made a Tit(ian) of himself?*[218] Waugh had done some quick research (or had a good memory). His article ends with a footnote: *The Tories have form on this kind of thing, of course. Channel 4 News found them out a few years back trying to amend the wiki entry for warthog poo. I kid you not.* That's nearly right. The article concerned is **Warthog**, and the edit in question from anonym B (possibly bored by recent labours devoted to **Conservative Christian Fellowship**) added the useful text: *they also smell of poo.* Whether they happen to be about warthogs or **Titian**, **Oliver Letwin** or **Anne Widdicombe**, this contributor's edits are not primarily intended to provide Wikipedia readers with full and correct information; and this contributor is not alone.

The story of an Englishman, a Scotsman and an Italian painter demonstrates the natural human desire for precise knowledge, a desire to which Wikipedia articles pander more often than they should, especially through their infoboxes. The body of the article is very hesitant on Titian's date of birth, but the infobox offers a figure. *This is further evidence of how infoboxes mislead*, said Johnbod on the talk page. *The info box is misleading and that should be changed. Its better to include no information than inaccurate information*, BritishWatcher agreed. The point was dismissed by others, but Johnbod and BritishWatcher are right after all. However frequently the **Titian** infoboxes changed, the infobox and first line always appeared more definite than the facts justify. The calculation reported by Andrew Neil shows that even a specialist researcher, even one who knows very well that precision is crucial, can easily ignore the *c.* and take the *1485* as gospel; very few will look further down the page to see what possible range the *c.* represents.

As hinted by Johnbod above, infoboxes are also not intended to provide full and correct information. If there's any doubt or difficulty of interpretation the infobox is sure to gloss over it. Many readers' eyes are drawn straight to them, and many biased and malicious editors target them for this reason. I could choose thousands of examples, but I'll take **Persian language**. When created in 2001 by Manning Bartlett (*an old-timer who has been here since the very, very early days*) the article claimed *over 30 million speakers* for Persian, and that, at least, was surely true. After some thousands of edits and expansions, an anonymous change to this article's infobox in October 2007 massively raised the number of speakers to *72 million native, 134 million total*, and also raised the language's 'world ranking' from 18th to 12th. The total has recently wandered even higher; it has also dropped as low as *54 million*. As I write, it stands at *60–80 million*. During this excitement the world ranking has slipped to twenty-second. In the equivalent article in French, ever since an infobox was first inserted on 15 December 2006, *80–110 million* have been claimed. In Spanish an infobox was added in May 2007 and *about 61.7–110 million* claimed; the higher of these two figures was recently removed. In Italian *71 million native, 110 million total* are claimed, with a world ranking of 19th. In January 2008 a new editor added an infobox to the Latin Wikipedia's article on Persian and claimed *134 million* speakers. In German the infobox claims *70 million native, 40 million as second language* (110 million total) but the text currently makes it *60 million as second language*. Which of these figures, if any, should be trusted?

Well, there is now a concerted attempt to increase the credibility of Wikipedia by documenting its statements. Any addition to a page risks being deleted (at least in theory; and it sometimes happens in practice) if it isn't accompanied by a reference to a reliable source. So perhaps, of all the possible figures for the number of speakers of Persian, the figures accompanied by footnotes are the ones that should be trusted? Far from it. During the single month of April 2009 **Persian language** claimed numbers of speakers ranging wildly from a low of *56 million* to the all-time high of *144 million*, ending at *60–80 million*. For nearly all of the month the same detailed footnote containing several references and sub-totals was attached to the item, as it still is. So which figure does the footnote support? If you add up the subtotals you get 59.5 million. Any figures above this, however convincingly footnoted, are in reality unsupported.

On just one occasion a more promising source was added to the **Persian language** statistical footnote. Unfortunately the added source was a Wikipedia mirror site; briefly the article was being made to serve, as if through a timewarp, as its own reference. This often happens and will go on happening. If you're aware that Wikipedia is mirrored (because its license permits this, and because others hope to increase their web visibility by borrowing its content) you know that articles found elsewhere that read like Wikipedia are almost certainly copies of Wikipedia. All well and good, and if you follow the footnote, you won't be misled. But those conditions don't always hold. You may not trouble to follow the footnote. Or you may believe, as some do, that the mirror sites are the originators (I have seen impassioned talk page denunciations, *this article is plagiarised from Answers.com!*). In such a case the footnote reference to a Wikipedia mirror might easily fool you.

References to Wikipedia mirror sites are not the only way to make Wikipedia verify itself. On 29 August 2008, after the draw for the UEFA Cup, a familiar and sometimes mischievous anonymous editor (we'll call this anonym C) went to the Wikipedia page on Manchester City's first-round opponents, the Cypriot football club **AC Omonia** and added the assertion that *a small but loyal group of fans are lovingly called 'The Zany Ones'. They like to wear hats made from discarded shoes and have a song about a little potato.* It was complete fantasy, and it stayed on the page for three weeks, until removed on 18 September by IrishPete as *obvious vandalism*. IrishPete had his fingers crossed here: the vandalism hadn't been obvious at all, until, as Manchester City travelled to Nicosia for the match, a *Daily Mirror* (– !) reporter copied the information into his match preview: their manager 'will not tolerate any slip-ups against the Cypriot side, whose fans are known as the "Zany Ones" and wear hats made from shoes'. 'By David Anderson from Nicosia', reads the byline, but, as Cade Metz observed in *The Register*, his research was done online.[219]

Let's assume it was after reading Anderson's piece that IrishPete was struck by the silliness of the information, found that it was also on Wikipedia, and removed it. Anyway, Wikipedia moved on. Next morning at 9.15, anonym C, happy with the experiment's success so far and having already boasted of his success on the chat site B3ta.com,[220] bravely returned to the Wikipedia page to add a factual section on the vandalism and its mirroring in the *Mirror*, with the edit summary: *Story about journalist relying on Wikipedia for facts.* But the hapless David Anderson, possibly a late riser, omitted to recheck his source before filing a story on the match itself. His story includes the claim that Omonia sent 'their fans – nicknamed the Zany Ones – completely wild'.[221] The repeated howler was noted by another anonymous Wikipedian, who added a footnote about it at 11.28 GMT. The eminent David Gerard (UK press contact for the Wikimedia Foundation, self-declared member of *at least five Wikipedia cabals*) looked in an hour later to insert a reference to B3ta.com and the edit summary: *It were b3ta wot dun it.* But admin Number57, unamused by all of this, removed the whole section early on 20 September, claiming it to be not appropriate. It returned once, and Number57 then protected the page on the grounds of repeated vandalism (one of the few occasions on which this accusation has been levelled at David Gerard).

And now we come to the uncanny bit. On 17 October 2008, long after the news story had died away and the page had calmed down, the false detail was re-inserted, quite seriously it seems, with a footnote reference to the *Daily Mirror* story. Number57 reverted it after six minutes, but the anonymous editor tried twice more (*why remove an external cited reference that is verifiable?*) driving Number57 at last to protect the page again. The story that spread from Wikipedia to the *Daily Mirror* was trying to return to Wikipedia with the *Mirror* as verification – and briefly succeeding.

Could it happen again? Of course it could. Let me begin with the name of the recently appointed (at the time of writing) German economic minister **de:Karl-Theodor zu Guttenberg**, or rather, to give him his full name as it appears on the first two lines of his biography in the German Wikipedia, *Karl-Theodor Maria Nikolaus Johann Jacob Philipp Franz Joseph Sylvester Freiherr von und zu Guttenberg.* There's a history of dispute on the talk page as to whether Wikipedia ought to be in the business of perpetuating silly names and titles of nobility for politicians in a democratic government. It may reflect irritation over this issue – or perhaps foreknowledge that Guttenberg's ministerial appointment was about to be announced – that at 20.40 on 8 February 2009 a certain anonymous Wikipedian decided the name would be all the better for an extra *Wilhelm.* Just seven minutes later the millstones of the German Wikipedia's new anti-vandal mechanism began to grind. In a system that Jimmy Wales is known to admire, latest edits are not publicly visible until checked by a trusted editor. In this case an admin named Gamma9, recently congratulated for having verified more recent edits than anyone else in 2008, glanced over the page and approved it, complete with *Wilhelm* and with several other minor innocuous additions.

Next morning Sebastian Fischer, on the news magazine *Der Spiegel* ('The Mirror' – !), wrote a profile of the new minister, with a paragraph presciently headed *'Nicht der Name zählt, sondern die Leistung'* ('It isn't the name but the achievement that matters') in which the subject's full and resonant name was recited and discussed. Working hastily, Fischer checked against his handiest and most reliable source – the German Wikipedia – and pasted the name into his text, complete with *Wilhelm*.[222] Fischer wasn't the only one: the Munich newspaper *Süddeutsche Zeitung* was among several other respected media that made the same little slip. So was the mass-circulation *Bild*.

The anonymous vandal confessed gleefully on the *Bild*-watching site Bildblog.de next day, generously supplying a reference to volume 110 of *Genealogisches Handbuch des Adels*, a truly reliable source.[223] *Wilhelm*, along with all of Guttenberg's real middle names, was removed from the Wikipedia article by Arcudaki (*a Minoan computer scientist*: there aren't many of those) at 13.23 on 9 February. Arcudaki clearly hadn't read Bildblog.de but may have suspected something; his edit summary, however, was the noncommittal *See talk*. The names were all restored four hours later by Steffen Kaufmann, and now we come to the uncanny bit (have I said that before?) Arcudaki, evidently still feeling uneasy about it, added a footnote reference to Fischer's article in *Der Spiegel* in which the names were all listed; and in this way, just as before, information that spread from Wikipedia to *Der Spiegel* was returning to Wikipedia with *Der Spiegel* as verification. This time it survived for more than 24 hours until, at 20.46 on 10 February, Tilmandralle deleted the *Wilhelm* for the last time. He forgot to remove the footnote: briefly it joined the ranks of the Wikipedia footnotes that don't support their text. Twenty minutes later Don-kun, with a silent smile, substituted for the *Der Spiegel* reference in this footnote the more accurate, instructive and amusing item at Bildblog.de.

So you don't trust Wikipedia when its facts are footnoted because the footnoted source could be mirroring Wikipedia. You don't trust the German Wikipedia, with its system of verification of edits before they go public – a system that might well spread to the English Wikipedia in the near future – because in such a small but important case as a vandalistic edit to the name of a German politician about to be promoted to cabinet rank, the system simply didn't work.

Whether it's of any use or not, you can be sure of one thing: Wikipedia pages will go on getting longer. As we'll see, there are several reasons quite specific to Wikipedia why articles get longer and longer, and most of those are bad reasons. In general, though, articles get longer because it's easier to go on writing than to compress what one has written; it's easier, many people find, to write than to edit what others have written; and it's easier to write than to get into a dispute over deleting what other people have written.

And, after all, the extra length is good, isn't it? It's better to have more information about a topic, isn't it? It's better to have more solid facts in a biography than fewer solid facts, isn't it? The **Sarah Palin** biography had been something of a backwater on Wikipedia until a certain fateful day, 28 August 2008, on which the article suddenly began to get bigger. At 8.10 on that day the new Wikipedian Young Trigg set to work on it, and in two spells of editing, occasionally interrupted and corrected by the more experienced Ferrylodge, added 600 words of meaty text. By the time he had completed his work at 13.30, he had earned the praise of Wikipedians. The **Sarah Palin** biography was looking much, much stronger. If the history is studied minutely it's noticeable that a few interesting details had disappeared, such as: *She admits that she used marijuana when it was legal in Alaska, but says that she did not like it.* On the other hand many interesting details were added, such as her ranking as *first runner-up* in a Miss Alaska beauty pageant in 1984, and the following more recent evaluation: *Fred Barnes praised Palin as a 'politician of eye-popping integrity' and referred to her rise as 'a great (and rare) story of how adherence to principle – especially to transparency and accountability in government – can produce political success'.* Among the Wikipedians who worked over the material after Young Trigg had finished, Wise added a link in the sentence I've just quoted and the edit summary: *Who is Fred Barnes? Had to look this up, so provided info.*

After this busy work the article was much fuller and was satisfyingly readable. That was lucky, because hours later, at 20.36, began a series of edits, at first anonymous, then by named editors, at first unsourced, then footnoted, at first reverted, then growing into a new and stable section, all about the breaking news that John McCain, Republican presidential candidate, would select Palin as his running mate.

In retrospect many people concluded that Young Trigg, the new Wikipedian, knew something that at that stage no one else in the world knew except John McCain and his closest advisers. It was widely assumed that Young Trigg worked for one of these, though he flatly denied it on his user page before bidding Wikipedia goodbye: *I will acknowledge that I volunteer for the McCain campaign... I did not know Palin was the nominee when I made my edits. (According to the Wall Street Journal, McCain didn't make up his mind until Thursday, hours after most of my edits.) If there's a politician out there hoping for appointments who want to hire me to edit their articles, maybe they will have the same luck.* According to the *Washington Post* a firm that trawls the internet looking for unusual business-related activity claimed to have remarked the busy traffic at Wikipedia's **Sarah Palin** page,[224] though in fact it was after her selection that the traffic increased massively: there were 7,000 edits in the next two weeks.

This was not the only unusually busy page. 'On August 22nd, the day before the Obama campaign officially named [Joe Biden] as the veep pick,' the *Post* noted, 'Biden's Wiki page garnered roughly 40 changes. Over the five days prior, users would make at least 111 other changes to his entry.' This was not the first time the Biden article had been in the news. At the time of the Congressional edits scandal, someone in Joe Biden's office slanted his biography in his favour by removing an old accusation of plagiarism. And that wasn't all; an edit from the same office altered the article on **Hamas**, which had recently won its majority in the Palestinian Legislative Council. Previously, with an attempt at balance, the text had read:

Hamas is engaged in social welfare activities as well as in violent activities to achieve its political goals. It is listed as a terrorist group by the European Union, Canada, the United States, Australia and Israel... Hamas affirms a right to engage in armed struggle... While during the election campaign Hamas dropped its call for the destruction of Israel from its manifesto, several Hamas candidates... called for Israel to be 'wiped off the map'.

The anonym from Biden's office adjusted this to read:

Hamas is notorious for engaging in violent activities to achieve its political goals. It is a terrorist group... Hamas affirms an indiscriminate right to murder innocent civilians... In the recent parliamentary elections, several Hamas candidates called for Israel to be 'wiped off the map'.

This was serious politically-motivated vandalism, but it was soon noticed. After just 15 minutes the older version was wisely restored by Zeq. Sadly Zeq has now been banned *till infinity* from Wikipedia after three further years of battling in the Wikipedia war zone of Israeli–Palestinian relations. He has been linked with the pro-Israeli Committee for Accuracy in Middle East Reporting in America (Camera) and its campaign to influence Israeli and Palestinian articles in Wikipedia; he offered it excellent and pointed advice, too long to quote here but well worth reading. His denunciation is a victory for the pro-Palestinian Electronic Intifada.[225] *Welcome to Wikipedia, where any biography can change every 5 minutes based the view of the person who write it,* he writes in his farewell message; *so for now goodbye.*

We can be hasty in our blocking. On 1 January 2007 'Wikipedia bans Qatar', the news media said; it was because persistent vandalism came from the single IP address that is used by the single internet provider for the whole country. On 7 December 2008 we blocked most domestic British users (although this strange incident was partly engineered by the Internet Watch Foundation which guards Britain's web morality). We Wikipedians are slightly worried about whether, by blocking the wrong people and not blocking the right people, we caused the global financial meltdown;[226] if you're worried too, look at the excitement around Mantanmoreland and **Naked short selling**, excitement that's clearly seen in *The Register*'s distorting mirror. We used to like Mantanmoreland but we don't any more. We have been known to block a whole neighbourhood in Salt Lake City because of a user we didn't like.[227] We have currently blocked anonymous edits from the whole Church of Scientology.[228] You don't trust us because you don't know – and we don't always know – whether we make the right choices when we ban and block. It helps the work to go on and makes some Wikipedians happy; that, at least, is good.

Young Trigg, who improved the **Sarah Palin** page, made another point in his palinode: *Every single cite to Fred Barnes has been scrubbed from the page* *by left-wing editors, even though Barnes wrote the first comprehensive national article about Governor Palin's political career and term as governor. No one is complaining about that, but it's the real scandal here.* You need make no final judgment on the reason for Young Trigg's interest in Sarah Palin: you still don't trust Wikipedia because, as the pages get longer and the editing gets busier, it's less and less easy to know whether the slant is fair. It's less and less easy for the ordinary reader to know by whom and for whom the additions and deletions are made. It's more and more evident that we Wikipedians, on our really bad days, behave like a primitive democracy, calling for the immediate ostracism of those on whom blame can be made to stick.

Ever since late 2001 it's been possible to attach a talk page to each and every Wikipedia article. Talk pages were originally intended for discussion, and where there was as yet nothing to talk about, there was no talk page. But anyone who has been watching the English Wikipedia for three years or more knows that nearly every article has now spawned a talk page. In most cases they aren't worth looking at because they contain no talk, only banners for two, three, four or more 'projects' that claim to have taken the article under their wing. People who want to read the article find these pages a waste of time; Wikipedians, unfortunately, often look at them, and may be tempted to take seriously the injunctions embedded in them. In most cases no human being has issued these injunctions. It may be that no human being has looked at the page at all. A *bot* has made an evaluation and given orders that its Wikipedian slaves are expected to fulfil. If an article is said to need an image, what can be done? Quick: find an image that a blind bot might think relevant and add it. If an article is said to belong to 'stub class' or 'start class', to which practically all of them are said to belong, what can be done? Easy: write more text. In these ways Wikipedia articles are gradually being steered into a resemblance to the web in general: the more text, the more pictures, the less relevance. And if an article doesn't have an infobox, sure as eggs are eggs, it wants one.

As an example, take the article I created about an M. R. James story,

Canon Alberic's Scrap-Book, and look at the banner on the talk page. Can this topic really be of 'mid importance' to WikiProject Novels? M. R. James and I are flattered. As regards quality, however, the article is classed as a stub, and, needless to say, in want of an infobox. Stub class is the very lowest grade. It *provides very little meaningful content; may be little more than a dictionary definition*, we are admonished on the project page. A little cavalier, I think, but how will I excuse myself to M. R. James's ghost if I and my article fail to improve our rating? So, to raise the article to start class, *any editing or additional material can be helpful. The provision of meaningful content should be a priority.* Would we then wish to try for class C? *Provision of references to reliable sources should be prioritised; the article will also need substantial improvements in content and organisation.* How will the bot know that the content has been improved? Never mind: assume that it's an unusually clever bot. We now aspire to class B, but things are clearly getting worse with my article: *a few aspects of content and style need to be addressed, and expert knowledge is increasingly needed. The inclusion of supporting materials should also be considered if practical, and the article checked for general compliance with the manual of style and related style guidelines.* Above class B, scarcely imaginable though this may be, are three more heavenly circles of which the highest is featured article status. When my article at last gets there *no further content additions should be necessary unless new information becomes available; further improvements to the prose quality are often possible.* One can, at a pinch, imagine the article **Ghost story** (also of mid importance, apparently) going through these stages of extension and improvement, but it's foolish and counter-productive to shepherd alongside it an article about a single short story in a hundred-year-old collection. On such a topic an encyclopedia article of three paragraphs with 11 internal links and three links to supporting material elsewhere on the web isn't an unpromising candidate for 'start class', it's lurking on the frontier of adequacy. Some would say it's too long already. Beyond a certain point additions will not be improvements: an encyclopedia reader, even a Wikipedia reader, needs conciseness, not indefinite extension.

The longer the article, the easier it is to hide from sight the sections that editors prefer not to emphasise. This certainly happens (it's what

Conservapedia calls 'Placement bias') although it happens most commonly for what most readers would agree are good reasons. If articles have 'Trivia' sections (which they aren't really supposed to any more) the 'Trivia' section comes at the end. That's the best place for it. If articles contain a few really salient facts, these go in the infobox and the introductory paragraph. That's potentially dangerous, as we've seen, but it's hard to deny that it's also useful. Now I'm going to borrow an example from Conservapedia:

'Readers expect the more important information to be first, and place more emphasis on the top part of an article. As an example of how this can be manipulated, Wikipedia's entry on former liberal Vice President Al Gore contains no mention of the drug charges against his son; these are only included within his son's own entry, which is rarely viewed. But Wikipedia's entry on conservative Vice President Dick Cheney prominently mentions his adult daughter's sexuality.'

When this was written (in October 2007) it was perfectly true. The first main section of the **Dick Cheney** article, headed 'Early life and family', included two sentences on the subject: *Mary is one of her father's top campaign aides and closest confidantes; she currently lives in Great Falls, Virginia with her longtime partner, Heather Poe. Mary's pregnancy and her sexual orientation as a lesbian became a source of public attention for Cheney during the 2004 election in light of the same-sex marriage debate.* As to Cheney it's not true currently: the two sentences are reduced to one, which is now almost the last sentence in a very long entry. (By contrast, the Conservapedia article on Cheney doesn't allude to the fact at all. This is, it might be said, another and more serious kind of bias, and a comment on the talk page points this out: 'I think in the interest of avoiding the pitfalls of wiki, one of which is leaving out facts which aren't convienent to the liberal mindset, we should strive to be inclusive with the truth.') As to Gore, Conservapedia scores a victory. Not only is the detail still not mentioned on the **Al Gore** page but the former page on his son has been deleted.

The page I started on **Canon Alberic's Scrap-Book** will never aspire to good article status, I suspect. If it did, one of the hurdles it would have to jump would be that of verifiability. The statements in Wikipedia articles are to be verifiable, which is why *references to reliable sources* are required for each assertion. While writing this I noticed that the article on the Greek playwright **Sophocles** risked demotion from good article status and I glanced at the discussion. It *does not meet the current standard of citation,* warned TonyTheTiger, who was advising on the problem. The issue seemed to be that the plot summary of the three 'Theban plays' didn't have any references to secondary sources.

I just tagged a short paragraph in the 'The Theban plays' section for you, Tony prompted. *Each sentence in that paragraph pretty much needs a source. Of course, it would be likely that they would have a common source because its coverage of a related topic. I would expect the reader to be able to look at all of those interesting facts and say yes WP told me a wp:RS* [reliable source] *where I can wp:V* [verify] *them. This is my basic problem.*

Why do we need to attribute a plot summary of Oedipus Tyrannos to anyone but Sophocles? demanded Akhilleus. He considered that the good article process was ridiculous and the ongoing review demonstrated one of its chief failings: the article was being evaluated mechanically, on issues such as the number of citations. Judging whether it was a good article seemed to have nothing to do with whether the article was actually good: in fact the process had made it worse by forcing editors to add a series of unnecessary and unhelpful citations.

Other editors, while betraying *little interest in the GA process,* were meanwhile trying to puzzle out what the rules required. *Tony insists that if Wikipedia... says that Oedipus Rex says x, we must have a footnote directing them to the play,* said Pmanderson. *Tony is in fact asking for even more than that,* Paul August corrected him. *He seems to be asking for us to cite a secondary source which says that Oedipus Rex says x.* And Tony himself returned to insist on this requirement: *Please find some source preferably secondary, but at worst primary so that each plot summary is sourced somehow.* Paul August still couldn't believe it: *Are you saying you want to see in the article something like: 'In Sophocles' Oedipus Rex, thus and so happens (source: Sophocles, Oedipus Rex)'? – You are holding the GA process up to ridicule,* Peter cohen said hotly. Before tempers could rise any further the admin Antandrus arrived, very much as Heracles does in the last scene of Sophocles' *Philoctetes,* and made a closing speech:

We have a general problem with overcitation. I've seen articles with many hundreds of citations, often of the most trivial and obvious matters... a common trend I see is a demand for citation not just of 'published opinion, counter-intuitive or controversial statements' but of very basic facts, that can be established by simple observation... Creating a plot summary, or noting that Oedipus Tyrannus is indeed set in Thebes, needs no citation; part of assuming good faith is presuming that our editors aren't making this stuff up.[229]

TonyTheTiger grasped at this branch and scrambled out of the quicksand into which he had been sinking. But forget Antandrus's intervention for a moment, because that wouldn't often happen. Instead let's just look again at Tony's main demand: *Please find some source preferably secondary, but at worst primary so that each plot summary is sourced somehow.* That's it in a nutshell. You don't trust Wikipedia because sometimes, especially in *good* and *featured* articles, the footnotes are there not because you need the citations, and not because the text was written with special reference to the items cited, but because the verifiability rule, as commonly interpreted by non-specialist editors, demands a certain density of citations and they were shoved in reluctantly to satisfy this rule.

You also don't trust Wikipedia because its 'reliable sources' rule demands secondary sources. Read Tony's words one more time: *preferably secondary, but at worst primary.* Could a more foolish and unhelpful requirement exist? Yet Tony isn't out of line: any Wikipedians who take this issue seriously are likely to interpret the rules as he does. The trouble with the avoidance of primary sources is that it's a one-size-fits-all rule that doesn't often fit. It is true that if primary sources are unpublished documents, it isn't helpful to cite them until you or someone else has first published them, because, until then, no one else can easily consult them to verify your claim. If primary sources are letters of Woodrow Wilson, or diplomatic documents surrounding the First World War, why not cite them? They have been published, and anyone can consult them as they can consult any other book. If primary sources are documents available online, why not cite them? They are more accessible than most books. But there's also the problem that in some disciplines the term 'primary sources' has a special meaning. In discussing **Diocletianic Persecution**, recently a candidate for featured article status, editors disagreed over whether Greek and Latin sources should be cited at all (even in translation). The compromise reached in discussion was that they can be cited as long as the citation has been copied from a nineteenth or twentieth century authority. It sounds silly; indeed it is extremely silly. The reason for it is that historians of the ancient world, a period from which very few real primary sources survive, use the term 'primary sources' loosely to mean Greek and Latin writings in general. That's it, then: you don't trust Wikipedia because certain editors don't dare to cite early sources for fear that their friends will call them primary; other editors (for fear of breaking the rule *no original research*) don't dare to cite the early sources they themselves have found, but only those chosen for them by a recent author. And you don't know whether they checked the reference.

So far we haven't said even as much as a typical Wikipedia talk page on the subject of the no original research policy. This rule, too, sounds silly at first, but Roy Rosenzweig saw immediately the necessity of something of the kind. 'Historians may find [it] surprising since we value original research above everything else, but it makes sense for a collaboratively created encyclopedia' and it's an essential accompaniment to the anonymity of Wikipedia articles. Rosenzweig likewise mourned the lost vigour of the old ninth edition of the *Britannica*, in which Algernon Charles Swinburne contributed and signed the article on John Keats: 'The "Ode to a Nightingale",' Swinburne wrote, 'one of the final masterpieces of human work in all time and for all ages, is immediately preceded in all editions now current by some of the most vulgar and fulsome doggerel ever whimpered by a vapid and effeminate rhymester in the sickly stage of whelphood.' This would hardly have done for an anonymous article weighted with the whole collective authority of *Britannica*; it was OK for an essay initialled by Swinburne, an essay which, although opinionated, had the solid information content that *Britannica* required. There are two good reasons why Wikipedia can't do that. First because the text is endlessly editable, and what Swinburne thought will not be what the next editor thinks. Second because it's anonymous: however high or low we rate the authority of Wikipedia, it couldn't reasonably be assigned to a statement of opinion as one-sided as Swinburne's in the sentence I've quoted. So Wikipedia has rules about this, and the rules are verifiability and no original research. 'How can the collectivity assess the validity of statements if there is no verification beyond the claim "I discovered this in my research"'[230] or 'this is my opinion'?

The rules about verifiability and no original research come into their own in the case of biographies of living people. Wikipedia has hundreds of thousands of these. As we've seen, they attract as much criticism as any other topic area and more than most. A proportion of the criticism comes from living people who have been unfairly described in their Wikipedia biographies, or, at least, think they have. Jimmy Wales's answer in one high-profile case was to strip the biography down to a bare minimum and to state the strict rule: *add back information only when it is... carefully sourced to mainstream reliable sources*. Shouldn't that always be the rule, he was asked? To save Wikipedia's neck, it should. Increasingly it is. And so, although on the subject of a well-known contemporary you might trust Wikipedia to guide you to the facts that no one disputes and that have been widely published in the press, you won't trust Wikipedia for information beyond that: if it's there at all, it's isn't because it's true, it's because no one's thought of taking it out yet. You might think of reposing added trust in the articles that are protected or semi-protected. But no, you don't trust those, because we've seen several cases already in which articles have been protected while containing obvious nonsense; and we noticed that on the first occasion on which Number57 protected **AC Omonia** it was not against vandalism but against embarrassing information involving Wikipedia. That has happened on biography pages too.

When the wise Antandrus succeeded in closing the debate about **Sophocles**, he didn't do it by agreeing with the specialist editors that TonyTheTiger's demands would produce a ridiculous result; instead he did it by finding a different Wikipedia policy that appeared to countermand those previously cited. Antandrus's chosen policy, *assume good faith*, is more or less irrelevant to the issue on which he appealed to it (but since the result was to ensure well-deserved good article status for Sophocles we'll say no more about this). The assume good faith policy is intended to cut out accusations of bias, self-interest and incompetence on talk pages. It has little to do with article content, thank goodness. If assuming good faith meant that biased and vandalistic additions were accepted without question into controversial articles, Wikipedia would be a lot less reliable than it is. Antandrus's method agrees perfectly with one of Jimmy Wales's dicta in his extended interview with Brian Lamb in 2004:

'Most of these rules have really a dual purpose:... the epistemological or intellectual purpose of saying this is what an encyclopedia should be like; there's also a social purpose which is somehow this rule helps us to get our work done collaboratively.'[231]

The official, openly-stated view of Wikipedia is that it's a work in progress. It isn't a reliable source and shouldn't be cited as if it were.

In evaluating Wikipedia as a tool for historians Roy Rosenzweig observed that 'the collective mode of composition in Wikipedia and the repeated invocation of the NPOV policy mean that it tends to avoid controversial stands of all kinds'; in spite of popular interest in 'lurid' and 'sensationalist' history, Wikipedia eschewed it. He took as an example the biography of President **Warren G. Harding**. When Rosenzweig looked at the article it cautiously warned of *innuendo* and *speculation* surrounding Harding's extramarital affairs, expressed doubt about his affair with Nan Britton, and insisted that there was *no scientific or legal basis* for the rumours of Harding's *mixed blood.*[232]

With its increased length Wikipedia has now found plenty of room for the lurid and sensationalist approaches to history that Rosenzweig expected (perhaps the early influence of MichaelTinkler and JHK has faded at last). The article **Pearl Harbor advance-knowledge debate**, for which Rosenzweig looked in vain, is now detailed enough for any conspiracy theorist. But a glance at the **Warren G. Harding** article today is depressing. Overall it's a lot longer. It's protected because of childish vandalism encouraged by *The Colbert Report* TV show, notably the repeated insertion of *Gangsta* as Harding's middle name. But on the matters raised by Rosenzweig it isn't consistently better than it was four years ago; it's just different. Back then the passage on Harding's debated ancestry was a long statement rooted in 1930s racial thought (and already heavily criticised on the talk page). Now it's all gone, replaced by the exiguous sentence: *One of Harding's great-grandmothers may have been African American.* It's footnoted, and the cited article is a useful one (recent, by a professional historian, written for a mass audience) but since Harding's immediate ancestors don't merit their own articles, and since the issue has been recently in the news (is Obama the first President of African descent or the second?), one short sentence isn't enough. Wikipedia ought to have more to say. Look at the discussion of Harding's affairs and the situation's quite different. The section 'Personal life' is all about them and extends to six paragraphs, which is perhaps an overdose since there are also now biographical articles on his two lovers and two illegitimate daughters; but this section is oddly focused (largely on the relevant papers and the attempts to keep them secret) and written in poor English. On Nan Britton we read that *according to Britton's book The President's Daughter, she and Senator Harding conceived a daughter, Elizabeth Ann, in January 1919, in his Senate office.* As for Elizabeth Ann, *during most of her life she shied from press coverage about her alleged birthright.* Four *citation needed* tags appear in this passage, which would, indeed, benefit from specialist attention. Four years after Rosenzweig looked at it, **Warren G. Harding** is still a work in progress, as is all of Wikipedia.

'It isn't worth reading yet, then,' according to one participant in a debate sparked by the **fr:Affaire Dreyfus** controversy, 'because I'm supposed to be expecting experts to improve it. I'm no expert: that's why I'm reading an encyclopedia... It's no use telling me Wikipedia has a lot of correct information, because I don't know which it is.'[233] On this matter the real problem, superficial as it may seem, is that encyclopedias are generally supposed to be reliable. Wikipedia calls itself an encyclopedia, and although it denies being a reliable source it looks like a reliable source. Does that mean it's our fault for being misled and treating it as if it were? No: it looks like a reliable source because it's designed like that. We're presented with a very distinctive web page – no advertising, no banner links; a near-monochrome design; a modest logo surrounded by purely textual in-site links, and, within the frame, an enyclopedia article that looks clinical, relevant, coherent, neutral and anonymous. What's more, the articles are supported by illustrations and diagrams; they have footnotes with precise citations of supporting material; they have external links (but never one that's sponsored) and bibliographies (but scarcely one that's inserted by a publisher). 'We're serious about this and we're not trying to deceive you,' the layout says. The impression is reinforced when we look around a bit. Behind each article – not showing up in the usual Google searches, just waiting for us to investigate if we want – there lurks a talk page that looks equally serious and works in a complementary way, with named comments and discussions that are much too boring to read but are clearly intended to help produce verifiability and neutrality in the article. There is often a banner confirming that this is what the page is for: *This is the talk page for discussing improvements to the x article. This is not a forum for general discussion about the article's subject... Article policies: No original research; Neutral point of view; Verifiability.* Just what we're looking for. In what else could reliability consist? Except, at a pinch, accuracy; except, where available, truth.

And there exactly lies the choice that Wikipedia has made. 'Articles on non-contentious topics are *usually* accurate,' Ira Matetsky writes carefully (my italics); 'articles on highly contentious articles are *usually* accurate *on basic facts*, but can be subject to bias and dispute with respect to the matters in controversy.'[234] But when those articles are accurate, they are accurate by chance, not by design. 'Excessive nerdiness isn't what's keeping Wikipedia from becoming the Net's killer resource. Accuracy is,' Paul Boutin concluded; he probably meant 'inaccuracy', and he was right at that.[235] Wikipedia's demand is not and has never been that its articles be accurate, still less that they be true.

'Can we all agree on what an apple is exactly, or the shades of the color green? Not easily. The wiki offered a way for people to actually decide in common,' wrote Marshall Poe. 'On Wikipedia, an apple is what the contributors say it is *right now*. You can try to change the definition by throwing in your own two cents, but the community... decides in the end... The community decides that two plus two equals four the same way it decides what an apple is: by consensus. Yes, that means that if the community changes its mind and decides that two plus two equals five, then two plus two does equal five.'

The Colbert Report put it more cuttingly and with equal precision: 'On Wikipedia, we can create a reality that we can all agree on – the reality we just agreed on.' 'The power of the community to decide,' Poe concluded, 'asks us to reexamine what we mean when we say that something is "true".' Yes, but the trouble is that most days you don't want to re-examine what you mean when you say that something is 'true'. Most days you want the truth.

Instead of demanding accuracy or truth, Wikipedia requires that statements in its articles be verifiable. If we look back a few pages we can see the results of this requirement playing out in practice. The anonymous editor who, after the immediate fuss over **AC Omonia** had died down, tried to add once again the fantasy details – the fans called the 'Zany Ones', the hats made out of shoes, the song about a potato – was absolutely on target in objecting: *Why remove an external cited reference that is verifiable?* According to Wikipedia's policies, that should have been all that was wanted. Accepting that David Anderson in Nicosia was a reliable source on AC Omonia – and why shouldn't he be? – the details were sourced and verifiable. Yes, they had been invented, and everyone including Number57 knew it, but they were verifiable. Hence, I suspect, Number57's failure to give any explanation when repeatedly deleting them. The explanation 'this is not true' is not admissible under Wikipedia's policies. I suspect Arcudaki had a strong feeling, when deleting all of Karl-Theodor zu Guttenberg's middle names from the biography page, that something in that long list was not true. But it would have done no good to say so; truth is not a policy on Wikipedia, not even the German Wikipedia. Hence the deletion was carried out with nothing more than a reference to the talk page, which conveniently contained some discussion about the fatuity of long noble names for democratic politicians. And when this deletion was reverted, Arcudaki (not having *Genealogisches Handbuch des Adels* to hand) had to fall back on citing *Der Spiegel* and thus rendering the information verifiable, albeit probably false. Verifiability was all that was required. Even on the following evening, after *Wilhelm* had at last been shown the door, Guttenberg's full name was briefly kept in limbo until an editor had managed to find a genealogical source that confirmed it.

By placing the emphasis on verifiability, and by insisting that not it but its sources must be reliable, Wikipedia tends to ensure, whether you wanted this or not, that it is never ahead of the consensus of opinion but always slightly behind it. This is because its reliable sources are bound to reflect the consensus; they are bound to suffer from normal publication lag; they are likely to be affected by the difficulty of getting unorthodox views into mainstream publication. For this reason you had better not trust Wikipedia for the most up-to-date views about drugs or other medical treatments. It may contain the most up-to-date views, but that's because the more practised editors have failed to remove them. Rockpocket wrote about this issue when giving advice on the talk page of a combative and dedicated therapist, one who was relatively new to Wikipedia:

I appreciate how frustrating it is [when] *one is on the opposing side of the pharmaceutical industry that has been entirely successful in colluding with science, medicine, media, government and God knows who else in* [order] *to establish the current establishment position on psychiatric illness. But you know what? Rightly or wrongly, its not Wikipedia's job to counter that view. Quite the opposite, it is our job to reflect it. That not to say that we can't report on the alternative, significant minority views. We can, and should, but we need to reflect them as a significant minority, even if that means we are propagating a myth.*

For this reason, even though Wikipedia is ahead with the news when something has happened, you won't rely on Wikipedia for the first news of what's about to happen. I can tell you now that when the end of the world is imminent an interesting discussion will kick off at **Talk:Risks to civilization, humans and planet Earth**. Watching the page itself, however, will be no help to you at all. Anonymous and unsourced edits will be made, and reverted; sourced edits will be made, and reverted; eventually the page will be protected, probably by J.delanoy. Then the lights will go out.

Chapter 8
Why you will trust Wikipedia

MEANWHILE THE REACH of Wikipedia seems likely to go on increasing. It is sufficiently demonstrated by Wikipedia's ranking among websites, currently standing at seventh according to Alexa.com. On the internet reach means power, and that can be demonstrated in several ways.

The press and online news sources talk about Wikipedia more than ever, and not only about the site's perceived faults, although there's still plenty of talk about those. Citations in this book have shown how insistent were the criticisms and dismissals in 2005 and 2006; they have shown how serious and nuanced the coverage is now becoming. It's no longer necessary for every news article to explain what Wikipedia is. It's now vanishingly rare for journalists to write as if they have never seen Wikipedia – back in 2005 that was still the norm – and it's uncommon for them to pretend that they don't edit it. Increasingly news reports and essays make the assumption that readers consult Wikipedia, even that they edit Wikipedia, and in any case that they care about omissions and bias. Wikipedia's importance as a news source is shown by the increasing likelihood that its coverage, its rapid changes and its errors will become news in the course of any big story, from the 2004 Indian Ocean earthquake and tsunami to the 2007 Virginia Tech massacre. On that occasion a local newspaper reported (and this was something new) that Wikipedia had 'emerged as the clearinghouse for detailed information on the event'.[236] And newspapers have if anything been slower to recognise the usefulness of Wikipedia than the world's law courts, which began to cite the encyclopedia as a source of terminology or background information in early 2003, albeit rarely at first. In some of these citations it was castigated as an unreliable source, but the number of mentions in court continue to increase to the point where Wikipedians now no longer attempt to list them all.[237] Most significantly, when the UK Intellectual Property Office ruled in 2007 in the Formula One trademark case, the judgment included this estimate:

'Wikipedia has sometimes suffered from the self-editing that is intrinsic to it, giving rise at times to potentially libellous statements. However, inherently, I cannot see that what is in Wikipedia is any less likely to be true than what is published in a book or on the websites of news organisations... I consider that the evidence from Wikipedia can be taken at face value.'[238]

In terms of Wikipedia's perceived power, more significant even than citations of the encyclopedia are the attempts to ban it or prevent its use. There was serious concern among Wikipedians, on 29 February 2004, that the United States Government was *claiming that it is illegal for any American to edit anything written by someone from one of several nations, including Iraq and Iran*, Vicki Rosenzweig reported. She disobediently edited the article **Yas-e-no** (about a Persian newspaper) *to make the point that that rule is oppressive, immoral, and will do nothing to harm the governments it is allegedly aimed at.* Had such a ruling ever been imposed as a practical regulation it could have crippled work on the English Wikipedia, which, international though it is, draws a large proportion of its active editors from the United States. In June 2004 Rosenzweig noted on her talk page that pressure from scientists had caused the ruling to be withdrawn. Simultanously China imposed its first block on Wikipedia. It lasted only two weeks, but was reimposed in October 2005 and has been in effect for long periods, sometimes affecting access to the whole site, sometimes only to the Chinese Wikipedia. The result has been to retard the growth of the Chinese Wikipedia and to give a big boost to *Baidu Baike*, a local online encyclopedia which shares some Wikipedia content but now has a great deal of its own.

One feature of Wikipedia that makes natural-born censors dislike it is that edits by any user are immediately visible to others (except on the German Wikipedia). *Baidu Baike* is not a wiki and lacks this feature. Another feature is its international range and its 'no censorship' rule. There can be in fact no such rule and there isn't, but the servers are housed at St. Petersburg, Florida, and the laws of Florida, with which the Wikimedia Foundation has to comply, are liberal. Foreign authorities have tried to be stricter, but with the exception of China they have seldom tried hard enough. In 2005 a German court attempted to stop Wikipedia publishing the real name of Tron, a truly notable computer hacker, because his parents wanted it concealed. The complexity of the internet put Wikipedia beyond the reach of this court's censorship. They shut down Wikipedia.de, a German site which at that time offered a portal to Wikipedia, but they had no way to get to de.wikipedia.org. Further attempts would have been pointless when (as *Ars Technica* reported at the time) Tron's real name already had 22,300 Google hits.[239]

In late 2007, in a second German case, the left-wing politician Katina Schubert complained that too much Nazi symbolism was visible on Wikipedia articles about the Nazi period. 'The extent and frequency of the symbols on it,' she complained, 'goes beyond what is needed for documentation and political education, in my view. This isn't about restricting freedom of opinion, it's about examining what the limits are... There are signs neo-Nazis are trying to take advantage of such structures, and this needs to be stopped in good time.'[240]

The argument turned on the German law permitting the display of Nazi symbols only for educational and record purposes. Schubert withdrew her complaint, before it reached court, after discussion with German Wikipedians; she surely realised that collectively they were highly unlikely to open the door to Nazi symbolism beyond what historical record required. The next such case was in the UK, where on 6 December 2008 the Internet Watch Foundation instructed internet providers to block access to the Wikipedia page on a 1976 record album, **Virgin Killer**, with an illustration of its original sleeve showing a young girl nude in a sexual pose. The IWF can censor without forethought and without any court order: 'Our core business is notice and takedown,' says its chief executive.[241] The issue was closely comparable to the Nazi symbolism complaint: the image was widely available elsewhere and it's used on Wikipedia as historical documentation, but internet images raise special fears. Schubert feared neo-Nazi propaganda; the IWF feared paedophilia. This time the blocking sparked a traffic surge via British proxies. Vandals were suddenly coming to Wikipedia from the same addresses as all other editors, and this caused Foundation servers to block access for many British domestic users. The IWF reversed its instruction after four days.

Its reach and power now pose a deadly danger to Wikipedia's competition. Even now this is sometimes seen as a two-horse race. I've quoted *Wales on Sunday* which, back in August 2001, made the obvious-seeming comparison between the 'official' *Britannica*, with its 'well-deserved reputation', and the new alternative of the 'homemade encyclopaedia' that was 'still an ongoing project'.[242] I've quoted Jimmy Wales in February of the same year: *Britannica's woes will only deepen. It's hard to compete against free volunteer projects... Of course, we aren't really making a dent in them yet.*[243] And I've quoted Clasqm in October 2001: *Forget Britannica... It was a great product in its time.*[244] We'll come back to the old horse. There are in fact many others in the race, among them the big foreign-language encyclopedias.

Brockhaus has been central to German cultural life since its first edition was completed in 1808. It was exactly 200 years later, in 2008, that the fateful announcement came: sales of the twenty-first edition were so disappointing that no more print versions would be produced. The latest two-DVD version, *Brockhaus Multimedial Premium*, is not to be despised at 19,500,000 words, but it's on sale at a mere €100 and the online version is free. That arrangement won't justify a new edition in any medium if experts have to be employed to write it. In any case, what money there is is going elsewhere. In June 2007 it was announced that the German Wikipedia would receive German state funding.

In Norway *Store norske leksikon* (a merger of two older encyclopedias) appeared in four successive editions between 1978 and 2003, the last one with considerable help from a charitable foundation. There will be no more. *Store norske leksikon* has been available online on subscription since 2000, but in 2009 it went over to free access and invites user contributions. No doubt the decision was prompted by the fact that it is no longer the biggest Norwegian encyclopedia. It has 150,000 articles; the Norwegian Wikipedia overtook it in January 2008 and now has well over 200,000 entries. In Denmark the venerable Gyldendal publishing house gave up producing its printed encyclopedia in 2006. *Den store danske* is now available free on the web, supported by advertising. At the foot of the page 'Michael Jackson', for example, which claims to be *verificeret*, is a selection of clickable links to buy books by Michael Jackson. It's a different Michael Jackson, but who cares?

The Danish Wikipedia currently claims 111,200 entries.

In France several publishers might claim to occupy the ground once trodden by the great *Encyclopédie*. The dictionary publishers, Larousse, brought out a ten-volume *Grand Larousse encyclopédique* in 1960–1964, but there will be no new print editions. Instead the Larousse website began in 2008 to offer, alongside the existing text, a space for new signed articles which (*Knol*-fashion) their authors, alone, are able to revise.[245] This plan may well have placed too much faith in the culturally conservative French critics of Wikipedia, who (like its American critics) spoke insistently but didn't represent the majority of the site's users. What was lacking in Larousse's business model, according to press reports during 2008, was a means of generating income.[246]

Even the one-volume *Quid*, a marvel of conciseness published in a new edition each year since 1963, lapsed in 2008. In the mid 1990s sales rose as high as 400,000, but they dropped precipitately in the last few years. The 2007 edition, the last so far and perhaps the last ever, claimed 2,500,000 facts on 2,176 pages for €32; it claimed to draw on 12,000 specialists, but also to be largely written by the founding editor, his wife and son. It bore the proud slogan *tout sur tout, tout de suite* 'everything about everything, fast'. Unluckily, as John Lichfield observed in the *Independent*, that's exactly what the internet claims to offer.[247] *Quid* is also available free online. A glance reveals the brevity that looked so good in print. On web pages space is cheap and Quid.fr looks cheaper, demanding a click to display each new short paragraph, each accompanied by a Club Med advertisement. I may be giving myself away here: the advertising is said in one source to be personalised, so perhaps I am identified as a target for Club Med and nothing else. The aim, at any rate, has been to finance the Quid.fr site through advertising, but it has never quite paid for itself.

Only the *Encyclopaedia Universalis*, a separately edited offshoot of the *Britannica* first published in 1968–1975, struggles on. Annual sales are down from 20,000 in the 1990s to 3,000 in 2007, it is said, but that was still enough to justify a sixth edition in January 2009, 30 volumes at €3,660. Wikipedia (in all languages) is now the eighth most visited website in France, according to a recent count, and it seems unlikely that the *Universalis* will run to a seventh edition.

The print version of *Encyclopedia Americana*, a *Brockhaus* offshoot with an independent history totalling nearly 200 years, is still selling, according to its publisher in 2008, but it's clear that the former annual editions have been abandoned ('the likelihood is there will not be the 2009 multivolume print version'[248] and this wasn't the first such announcement) while online sales target the institutional market only. If the *Americana* goes under, one result will be slightly less vandalism on Wikipedia: schools that no longer get *Americana* on subscription will have more reason to ensure that their access to Wikipedia isn't blocked.

Encarta, the descendant of the old *Funk & Wagnalls Encyclopedia*, spread across the globe at Microsoft's behest – there have been several foreign-language and national versions based on additional sources – but it will now spread no further. After toying with the idea of invited contributions, and after conceding free access to readers prepared to use the MSN search engine, Microsoft finally announced in March 2009 that *Encarta*, both DVD and online, was closing down. Ironically, having helped to bring the empire of the print encyclopedias to an end, *Encarta* had forgotten to create a business model for itself. Or perhaps, as Robert McHenry concluded, there was no need for one: *Encarta* served a lower purpose. 'Like many others of its sideline and ultimately abandoned products, *Encarta* was never anything to Microsoft but a tool. It turns out to be one they just don't need anymore.'[249]

Britannica is certainly still opposing any assumption (made as early as 2006 in a business school essay) that it is in crisis.[250] Its guns are sometimes trained on Google, which offers Wikipedia as a first response to ever more queries. 'Wikipedia!' Jorge Cauz of *Britannica* expostulated in early 2009. 'Is this the best they can do? Is this the best that the algorithm can do?'[251] The answer's simple: sites that demand money from the surfer, and don't give enough of it back to Google, aren't favoured, and *Britannica* can't afford enough of the sponsored links that would put it where Wikipedia is.

Jimmy Wales and Larry Sanger foresaw in 2001 that '*Britannica* would either have to become open content (and therefore have a moral justification to ask for volunteers) or become a pay service.'[252] Eight years later *Britannica* finally made its decision, and duly fell between the two stools. The 2008 incarnation of its website offers, to paying guests, full encyclopedia articles; it accepts edits submitted by registered and identified users, but these 'would have to be vetted by one of the company's staff or freelance editors before the changes were reflected on the live site.'[253] Thus users have to pay for the privilege of updating an encyclopedia that others have to pay to read. In parallel with all of this, the DVD boxed set *Britannica Deluxe 2009* – the equivalent of 32 volumes with additional multimedia content – is currently on offer at Amazon.com at $14.70.

Visitors to the online site can also read *Britannica* blogs including increasingly bad-tempered essays by Robert McHenry, former *Britannica* editor. Alongside him there's a weekly column *Liberal Media Bias: the worst of the week* and other explorations of liberal bias. Strange that there's no regular column on conservative bias – but perhaps the United States is lucky enough to suffer from only one of these two journalistic imbalances; or perhaps *Britannica* is making a pitch at Conservapedia's readers. I'm afraid that there may not be enough of them.

Having had a good look at Wikipedia and the expanding blogosphere, Nicholas Carr in 2005 attacked 'The Amorality of Web 2.0'. He foresaw that Wikipedia would have a negative effect on society because it would displace the professional alternatives that cost so much more to produce.[254] In 2006 he noted how well Wikipedia already performed on Google, and predicted with stunning accuracy how rapidly they would move towards the top.

'In the not too distant future, we may be living in a world where the default source of information about, well, pretty much everything will be a single and not altogether reliable amateur reference work. When critics point out the flaws in Wikipedia, its defenders are quick to respond, "It's only an encyclopedia; you don't use an encyclopedia as your only source." And that used to be true. In fact, after high school few people used encyclopedias at all, at least not regularly. But now, I'm not so sure. I'd wager that a heck of a lot of people searching the web do in fact use Wikipedia as their first and sole source, or at least their major source.'[255]

At New Year 2009 Carr repeated once again his survey of ten sample Wikipedia articles, and even he must have been slightly surprised to find that all ten had by that time reached first place among Google results.

'Congratulations, Wikipedians. You rule,' he concludes.[256]

We'll need to rely on Wikipedia in the future because the other sources of information are disappearing. Even if they hang on, they will fail to maintain their model of expert authorship and guaranteed authority.

In a recent *Britannica* blog, 'in the wake of the news that Encarta... was to be "euthanized"',[257] Robert McHenry revisited an old battle. He looked back to an explanation (published under Bill Gates's name) of the reasons for adjusting *Encarta* to national markets and to the neat scalpel work that McHenry himself had applied to this Gates argument.

The Bill Gates article had begun with a simple question. 'Did Thomas Edison invent the incandescent light bulb, or was it Sir Joseph Swan?' This was followed by the admission that while the US version of Encarta credited Edison alone and did not even mention Swan, the British version had an additional entry on Swan and gave him equal credit. According to the Gates article, this 'reflect[ed] a slightly different reality'.

'If you... ask "So, which one was it?"' McHenry continued, 'the answer seems to be "It depends on where you live." This is the "subjectivity" of "reality" in Bill's title.' The Microsoft editorial teams had developed their subjective approach to reality while localising Encarta for various national markets around the world. The Gates article then explored a second example of the same subjectivity: did the Scottish-American Alexander Graham Bell invent the telephone, or was it the Italian-American Antonio Meucci? To McHenry's horror, the article announced that while Bell was given the credit in other versions of Encarta, the Italian version, then in preparation, would emphasise Meucci's work, adding only that 'in 1876 another inventor, A.G. Bell, patented a similar device'. 'The Meucci claim is pressed as a matter of nationalistic pride by a few... hobbyists,' McHenry commented, 'but we also hear from Flat-Earthers from time to time. This is no instance of one "reality" having equal standing with another.'

Having dissected these two historical examples McHenry wondered how the Encarta editors proposed to deal with real conflicts in the modern world. What about Kashmir in the Indian and Pakistani versions? Would they prepare different versions for Greece and Turkey, so as to treat Cyprus differently; different versions for Israel and Syria; different versions for Spanish-speaking and Basque-speaking Spain? Different versions to deal with the variously preferred names of Macedonia and of the Falkland Islands?

To give credit where it's due, the Gates piece already foresaw that problems would arise when the different national versions of *Encarta* were all available online and people noticed that they were being fed different versions of reality. No solution was proposed. To give further credit where it's due, McHenry, who in general has little good to say about Wikipedia, admits 'that Wikipedia has improved upon the [Encarta] model, by allowing competing "realities" to battle it out right in the text, with all the world watching.'[258] It's an important point to which he could have given a few more words. I in turn admit that Wikipedia's very far from perfect on these matters, but it's a long way ahead of any *Encarta* model. This is precisely because the *Encarta* model was developed by software people who thought in terms of localisation, while the Wikipedia model was developed by a philosopher or two. On Wikipedia not only do the proponents of different 'realities' argue them out publicly; in addition, Wikipedia has set its face firmly against national editions; and in addition to that, every reader can immediately compare what the different language versions have to say on any issue and what the different talk pages have had to say about it. It's quite true that the language editions may sometimes differ unexpectedly on contentious issues – because they're edited independently, and the longed-for neutral point of view may be discovered in one place by one linguistic community and in another place by another – but the site makes it easy for every reader to watch what's happening. There is continual cross-fertilisation among the versions. And, finally, whether one likes it or not, English has attained the status of international language to the extent that, uncomfortable as it may often be, speakers of every language battle out their national realities in the English Wikipedia. This is exactly why the wikipedias need to go on being international (the argument is sometimes made that 'the English Wikipedia is for English speakers' but that argument was already lost in 2001).

This is also why Wikipedia needs to go on being multilingual: we need it to go on linking ideas and neutral points of view (if such they be) in as many languages as possible. As more than 250 language versions continue to grow, the difficulty in keeping up the interwiki links rapidly increases, in spite of the bots that continually work away at revising them. There is an endless succession of problems, small and large, in the translation of terms from one language to another. This is a basic feature of human language and even the projected new wiki devoted entirely to interwiki links can't make it disappear. But there must be no falling-off in interwiki links. The more multilingual Wikipedia becomes, the better, and the more multilingual editors it has, the better.

It's worrying, then, that the wikipedias in very small minority languages don't thrive as they might. In some cases, it must be admitted, they currently function as little more than toys for the few enthusiasts who insist that their local spoken dialect is a language and doggedly maintain, against almost all the evidence, that its speakers will one day want to use a big general encyclopedia in that language. In some cases the small wikipedias are almost the only general reading matter available in any published medium in a truly distinct language that struggles to survive from one generation of speakers to the next. And who can tell the two cases apart? The distinction may depend wholly on point of view.

The Wikimedia Foundation has already lowered the hurdle sufficiently for more than 250 encyclopedias. It could do more – if it happened to want to do so – by encouraging the smaller languages, particularly the ones that have failed to jump the hurdle individually, to combine. The variant model in which speakers of several languages and dialects, close neighbours, close relatives or cultural siblings, work together to produce a Wikipedia useful to all of them, tenuously exists already. To give one example (there are others) the Norman Wikipedia includes articles in the Guernsey, Jersey, Sark, Alderney and Cotentin dialects or languages, and is ready to find room for more. The pattern hasn't been encouraged, but it could be generalised to other small language communities, as was suggested for the many island languages of the Pacific by K. Kellogg-Smith, who is an admin in the Tok Pisin Wikipedia (in the lingua franca of Papua New Guinea).

As I see it, Kellogg-Smith began, *the problem here lies in the fact that the*

Wikipedia Administration currently only allows language-specific Wikipedias, not regional Wikipedias with regional editorial content. He saw no reason not to allow the creation of multilingual Polynesian, Melanesian, and Micronesian Wikipedias focusing on the languages, peoples, arts, customs and culture of the islands in those regions of the Pacific. In a regional wikipedia it would be easy to set up separate namespaces for articles about each nation. Other than the break with Wikipedia tradition and with the Foundation's current rules, could there be any good reason not to allow a Wikipedia Oceania or a Wikipedia Micronesia? *Niue, for example, is a Polynesian nation, and articles in both English and the Niuean language can certainly co-exist with articles about other Polynesian island nations in a 'Wikipedia Polynesia'... Chamorro, like Niuean, is a dying language, yet is still struggling to be heard. So is Hawaiian.* Kellogg-Smith pointed to the paucity of articles in the existing Hawaiian Wikipedia, dying because of a lack of interest on the part of native speakers.

In multilingual Wikipedias of this kind contributors would have a place to save the surviving scraps, no matter how small, of the history, culture, and language of these small nations and make it available in one convenient, internet-accessible location. Wasn't this what the Wikimedia Foundation was all about? If the underlying purpose was to bring knowledge to the world through the internet, small nations and their cultures would never be adequately documented and preserved in Wikipedia memory unless there was a break with the current policy of single-language Wikipedias. *Preserving whatever can be preserved now of the Niue language really is a cultural responsibility of everyone who has the capability and capacity to do so. And I believe that includes not only all of us as writers and editors in the Wikipedia community, but the Wikipedia Foundation and its Administration as well,* Kellogg-Smith concluded.[259]

'When Jimmy Wales says that the focus in the future will be quality not quantity,' wrote Dave Winer in 2006 in response to one of Wales's throwaway remarks on the wikifuture, 'this doesn't seem to translate to anything new in the work on Wikipedia. It's a very slippery subject, but an important one, because Wikipedia pages rank so high on the web. If they didn't, there would hardly be a reason to discuss. In the web before Wikipedia, every point of view had a chance, but Wikipedia tends toward centralization, toward one or two views prevailing, those that are represented by people who are willing to maintain a presence on Wikipedia.'[260] This states very well our increasing dependence on Wikipedia. I think it exaggerates the centralisation of Wikipedia and underestimates the range of opinions expressed on the site; perhaps Winer doesn't watch the same talk pages that I do. But what he describes is a real risk, no doubt of that. To guard against it we need Wikipedia to be as international as possible and as multilingual as possible, and we need Wikipedians themselves to go on being multilingual – to go on acting as ad hoc translators as well as editors. Or do we prefer to leave it to MI5 and the CIA to tell us what's being said on the Chinese, Persian and Arabic talk pages?

Increasingly Wikipedia will be the place where we look for confirmation – consolidation, let's say – of just-breaking news. It's sometimes the place where the news breaks, typically by way of anonymous edits reporting an event like the feminist **Andrea Dworkin**'s death in 2005 or the film director **Adrienne Shelly**'s murder in 2006; the latter information reached Wikipedia from a school IP address often used for vandalism. As a news source Wikipedia won't replace blogs, Twitter and other informal sites. What it will do, to some extent, is to take the place of newspapers. They have certainly begun to rely on it, and one reason they so often criticise Wikipedia is their nervous awareness of a question that's being asked: why read the newpapers when you can read their source?

Wikipedia editors tend to be aware of writing in an international medium that doesn't conform precisely to local taste – though local concessions are sometimes made. Wikipedia mentions the real name of **Tron (hacker)**, although his parents in Germany claimed a right to conceal it; the German Wikipedia currently follows their wishes but German readers can click the interwiki links to find out more. Wikipedia doesn't censor the *Virgin Killer* record cover, although Britain suspects child pornography in 2008 where in 1976 it did not. A certain Wikipedian didn't hesitate to report the death at

NBC studios on 13 June 2008 of the presenter **Tim Russert**. He collapsed at 1.40 pm (17.40 GMT), was rushed to hospital and was pronounced dead less than an hour later. NBC tried to keep back the news so as to notify his wife and son who were on holiday in Italy (whence Russert himself had just flown home). Long before NBC transmitted the news it was spreading across the web: Twitter knew about it and so did Wikipedia. The Russert biography was edited anonymously five times between 19.01 and 19.08 GMT to add the date of death and adjust the text. A couple of minutes later, two more anonymous edits from the same computer network reverted this information, but that didn't stick: the news was inserted again from a different source at 19.15. By 19.19 further text was being added, untidily, suggesting heart attack as the cause of death.

While the article was busy the talk page was filling up with discussions of the reliability of the death report and the exact cause (was diabetes a factor, or was he not diabetic after all? Was the long flight from Italy a factor?) A Wikipedian duly noted that the *New York Times* had the news at 19.32; another added the *Chicago Sun-Times*; but already at 19.29 a named editor, Harksaw, had added a footnote reference on the biography page to the *New York Post*'s website. That was perhaps the first 'press' report of Russert's death (whether based partly on Wikipedia is unknown). US television networks have a tradition of allowing the network for which the reporter worked to announce the death first. NBC was therefore the first of them to broadcast the news; it did so at 19.39. 'We were not prepared to say anything until all the family had heard,' said a spokeswoman. 'The last thing we wanted to do was to have the family discover this on the air... Before we reported it, I remember someone saying it's on Wikipedia.'

The earliest Wikipedia edits had come from a firm in Minnesota that provided web services to local NBC stations. 'A junior-level employee made updates to the Wikipedia page upon learning of Mr. Russert's passing, thinking it was public record,' the firm explained. They had 'taken the necessary measures with the employee'. 'Only minutes later, of course, none of this would matter,' wrote Noam Cohen of the *New York Times* in his report of the story... except to the sacked employee, he might have added. 'Even NBC News cannot protect the family of one of its own in that way,' reflected Cohen, aware that his own paper was one of those that had got in ahead of NBC. The *Times* may have done so because the *Post*, its local competitor, had taken the lead.[261]

Who on Wikipedia was first to announce the winner of the **United States presidential election, 2008**? CrazyC83, a little ahead of the game, claimed *CA for Obama - 44th President!!!* in an edit summary at 4.00 GMT on 5 November (11.00 pm on 4 November Washington time). Marlith added *Obama was selected as the presidential winner* to the introductory paragraph at 4.03. Two minutes later Hobie Hunter found a place in the text to insert the titles *President-Elect Obama and Vice President-Elect Biden*, and the edit summary once more claimed *Obama won!* and during the same minute Spliffy changed the first verb tense from *is* (*is the 56th consecutive quadrennial United States presidential election*) to *was*. Six minutes later it was Spliffy again who added a footnote reference for Marlith's important sentence, and the reference was to the BBC website. At 4.12 Turkeyphant pointed out that it was *the first time in U.S. history that an [African American] became president*, and Turkeyphant's edit summary, more concisely, reads: *black*. It was also at 4.03 that Steven Walling edited **Barack Obama** to name him *president-elect*, adding the edit summary: *CNN and NBC have called it!* Five minutes later Walling returned to add a footnote reference: this one was to the CNN website.

Noam Cohen, once more reporting in the *New York Times* on Wikipedia's emergence as a current news source, put the matter quite simply: 'at 11:03 p.m. Tuesday, Wikipedia called the election for Barack Obama.' Cohen went on to survey the feverish activity elsewhere on Wikipedia. As election returns flooded in, Wikipedians were updating charts, maps and texts minute by minute on the campaign article and also the candidates' biographies, both of which had reached featured article status.

'By midnight on the East Coast,' Cohen reported, 'two of the main contributors had agreed to edit alternately to avoid overwriting each others' work.' Using email he interviewed one of these two, Warfreak, who described himself as an 18-year-old from Sydney, Australia. 'It worked rather smoothly, I thought,' Warfreak commented. 'I covered it with results inflowing from interactive maps from CNN and The Associated Press, and I'm still doing so right now.' On the main article he added: 'It is a good source of information and [it] constantly changed as more results flowed in. In the future, the Internet will play a more important role in news media... overtaking print and televised media forms, which will make Wikipedia rather important.'

Cohen went on to discuss activity at **Talk:Barack Obama**: In accord with Wikipedia's usual transparency, there were public discussions over wording and what to include 'that can be read in all their tedious detail. Many pixels have been already been used to discuss whether Mr. Obama is technically the president-elect, even before the Electoral College has voted.' The editing spree, Cohen added, was 'repeated dozens of times over in the various Wikipedias in different languages'.[262]

Some of those other wikipedias, including the Italian one, were even quicker to give Obama victory; the Yoruba Wikipedia, on the other hand, didn't get round to changing the Obama entry until the next afternoon. The edit to **yo:Barack Obama** was made by Demmy, who didn't have the time or inclination to type the Yoruba accents on each vowel. No one has yet improved it.

As we rely more on Wikipedia for truly up-to-date information we'll need to be prepared to glance at the histories of edits and reverts; we'll need to glance at the talk pages, tedious as they undoubtedly are. If we do this we'll learn more than we could from a newspaper site. The newspapers had done their research in advance on whether to call Obama president-elect and on that matter they didn't waver, but, to take a case where previous research won't solve the dilemma, they vacillated for some hours on whether to give a cause of death on Tim Russert's obituary, and, if so, what cause to give. On the news websites the only version we can see is the latest; on Wikipedia we can go back and watch the discussion unfold, with references and links to the news sites when they offer something of use. That's equally true in cases where a mistake is made, as it was with the reported deaths of **Ted Kennedy** and **Robert Byrd**. The news sites made momentary errors in these cases too, but it's only on Wikipedia that we can still see when and why.

These examples are reminders that we'll be misinformed from time to time as we rely on Wikipedia – just as we will when relying on a newspaper. Sometimes we'll get the news before it happens, as with the death of **Aimé**

Césaire (mentioned earlier) and in the strange case of the **Chris Benoit double murder and suicide**, reported on Wikipedia 14 hours before the police knew of it, apparently because someone made a correct guess on the basis of very weak evidence.[263]

Sometimes we'll get news that no one very much wants. Although Conservapedians wanted to know about Albert Gore III's drug offence, in truth the incident wasn't enough to render the young man notable: it was only because of his father that he ever came to public notice and to Wikipedia's notice. The eighth attempt on Wikipedia to get consensus for deleting 'Al Gore III' was marginally more successful than the previous seven, and the article has now gone.[264] In similar ways, victims and participants in crimes that are possibly newsworthy but not, in the long term, notable are likely to appear briefly in Wikipedia, only to be deleted soon afterwards. Newyorkbrad (Ira Matetsky), in a series of essays on his experience of adminship at Wikipedia and on the site's present state and future prospects, gives several examples of news items that ought never to have become encyclopedic biographies, and, in the hands of wise admins, soon ceased to be so. One concerned a 13-year-old boy who was kidnapped and mistreated for four days before rescue. The search and rescue were newsworthy; his recovery became newsworthy; but he still deserved not to have a Wikipedia article about him. 'After a long discussion on the "deletion review" page my deletion... was upheld,' Newyorkbrad reports, and continues:

'Later that summer, policy was clarified to make it clear that in deciding whether to keep or delete a page, it is legitimate to take the effect of the page on its subject into account. But in spite of the deletion, [his] name still turns up on Wikipedia... despite my and others' having argued for removing it... Equally important, a Google search turns up not just a few but thousands of other hits with the same content.'

Newyorkbrad gives further examples of episodes in unlucky people's lives that 'Wikipedia did not need to, and no longer does, discuss'. Even where such items are deleted, he points out, the subjects aren't helped very much: 'the news coverage of their situations on fifty or five thousand other websites spreading the same gossip and showing the same disrespect for privacy and dignity are still out there'. Wikipedia is, as he puts it, a critically high-profile website. It looks authoritative; in spite of errors and uncertainties, in spite of disclaimers, it is authoritative. We, including the victims of such misfortune, are going to rely in the future on Wikipedians and their sense of proportion.[265]

But if we're going to rely on Wikipedia we need the site to remain free of commercial spam and we need there to be less vandalism. Google crawls Wikipedia ever more frequently; it seems there's now a measurable risk that Google will crawl a temporarily vandalised page. This happened recently with the **Barack Obama** page. At 4.44 on 19 February 2009 a named user (whose few previous edits had been not wholly nonsensical) replaced the whole text with the words *nigga nigga nigga*. At 4.46 J.delanoy, who usually seems to be around to deal with a mess of this kind, dealt with it. During those two minutes Google visited the page, and later in the same day, when anyone searched Google for 'Barack Obama', those words appeared as the 'snippet' or text sample of the page that appears with each Google result.[266] It's better if that doesn't happen.

Vandalism and spam aren't the fault of the servers, or the site itself, or the software. They are our fault as human beings. We're given access to the site, we're bored and stupid and we write childish and unpleasant things and leave a mess; we're greedy and we add links that we think will bring us money.

Vandalism could be quite largely prevented by insisting that users register before editing, but that's an extremely bad idea because great numbers of useful edits of all kinds, including the first reports of many major events, come from users who can't log in, don't want to, don't dare to, or think they haven't time. We really don't want to shut that material out. In any case, sites that insist on user registration can still get lots of vandalism of the more determined kind ('Liberal vandalism' as Conservapedia calls it) because people who really want to disrupt aren't discouraged by the few seconds it takes to get an account.

Vandalism could be quite largely prevented if we behaved better. There are those who can't resist the temptation to see if anything happens to them when they make a mess. On Wikipedia the great majority of such vandals are children, but equally childish edits often come from presumed adults including some with access to the US Congressional network and the Conservative Central Office computers. Several others cited in this book behaved no better. There are those who are hoping to amuse. There are those who, when offered the chance to inform others, prefer to shock or disgust them. It's safer to do these things online than to do them in a public place. Online you never come face to face with the people you're trying to amuse or disgust; you never meet the people who clear up your mess. You can sit at home and imagine their reactions. We can hope that there'll be less public vandalism, and less vandalism on Wikipedia, in a better future. We can hope that as Wikipedia becomes more important to schools teachers will get better at supervising its use – there's already a utility that helps them watch the contributions of their school IP address – but we can't be sure of any significant improvement.

That being so, we need Wikipedia to go on saving us from the consequences of our boredom, stupidity and greed – because we need Wikipedia's information, preferably without messes and distractions.

An unknown admin posted a comment on Slashdot in 2005, à propos of Larry Sanger's article on the history of Wikipedia, in response to the question of why spam doesn't flood the site. The answer covers vandalism as well as spam:

'Basically the transaction costs for healing Wikipedia are less than those to harm it, over a reasonable period of time. I am an admin and if I see vandalism to an article, it takes about ten total clicks to check that editor has vandalized other articles and made no positive contributions, block the IP address or username, and rollback all of the vandalism by that user. It takes more clicks if they edited a lot of articles quickly, but they had to spend much more time coming up with stupid crap to put in the articles, hitting edit, submit, etc. After being blocked, they have to be really persistent to keep coming back to vandalize. Some are, but luckily many more people are there to notice them and revert the vandalism. Its a beautiful thing.'[267]

This doesn't apply when Wikipedia vandalism is sparked by a TV broadcast, as when on the *The Colbert Report* in June 2008 Stephen Colbert described **Warren G. Harding** as a 'secret negro president' and sourced the claim by changing Harding's middle name to *Gangsta* in his Wikipedia biography. Vandals continually try to repeat the change unless the Harding article is protected, and protection has surely discouraged much-needed improvements. In January 2009 the plot of the NBC show *30 Rock* involved malicious editing of the **Janis Joplin** biography on Wikipedia, and viewers immediately started imitating the idea. We need Wikipedia to react quickly on these occasions, and, since Wikipedians' time could be better spent, we need to hope for fewer such occasions in the future.

'One type of malicious edit we examined,' report Fernanda B. Viégas and colleagues, 'is typically repaired within two minutes.'[268] Studies have shown how quickly most vandalism is reverted. But it's easy to watch for large changes in the size of a page. It's easy to watch for keywords such as obscenities that are often added in vandalism. It's much more difficult to detect vandalism when it consists of detailed changes in names or facts, because exactly the same changes could represent real corrections by a knowledgeable editor. Is it correct, or not, to say that someone has died? If we accept that Wikipedia may sometimes be the first source, we can't design an automatic system to check such edits. As we've seen, even humans have difficulty verifying them. It's not surprising that no one corrected the claim that **Tony Blair** was a Catholic (inserted in his biography at a time when he wasn't). It's not surprising that it took a long time to correct the false claim about the **Shimabara Rebellion** and the politically-motivated addition to the bibliography of **fr:Affaire Dreyfus**. What's surprising, in fact, is that even malicious changes of detail actually get corrected rather quickly. Roy Rosenzweig gave some examples:

'Over a two-year period, vandals defaced the Calvin Coolidge entry only ten times – almost all with obscenities or juvenile jottings that would have not misled any visitor to the site... The median time for repairing the damage was three minutes... Others have been more successful in slipping errors into the encyclopedia, including an invented history of Chesapeake, Virginia, describing it as a major importer of cow dung until it collapsed in one tremendous heap, which lasted on Wikipedia for a month.'[269]

Rosenzweig also cites the case of Alex Havalais, graduate director for the informatics school at the University at Buffalo and first in the line of experimental vandals that includes Shane Fitzgerald, Pierre Gourdain and colleagues. In August 2004 Havalais (using a named account, AlHalawi) inserted 13 small errors into Wikipedia entries, including the claim that the *well-known abolitionist Frederick Douglass made Syracuse his home for four years (1853–1857), and was the first African-American to be elected to a term on the city council.* All of these deliberate insertions were reverted within two and a half hours.[270] The one about Douglass lasted an hour and a half, and I hope AlHalawi felt really guilty when he saw CryptoDerk's edit summary: *Revert info about Douglass. Can you provide any reference? I can't find any after much searching.* In that case the transaction cost for healing Wikipedia was higher than the cost for experimenting on it.

So can we console ourselves, with Rosenzweig, with the reflection that 'vandalism generally has a short life on Wikipedia'? The answer is that we can't be complacent. Automatic and semi-automatic anti-vandal tools are being refined all the time: we rely on Wikipedians to watch the recent changes and to keep pages on personal watchlists, but although important and popular pages are likely to be on several lists, there are many pages that aren't even on one. Wikipedians may check their watchlists daily or several times a day, but even Wikipedians die, stop watching or go on holiday. We can only remind ourselves not to rely on Wikipedia (or any other source) without verification, and, faced with a surprising and undocumented assertion, to look at the article history and the talk page. If those rules are followed, Wikipedia vandalism, like planet Earth, is mostly harmless.

We will rely on Wikipedia more and more. With all its dangers, in some ways it will serve us better than its predecessors.

Nicholas Carr, whom I've quoted several times in this book, published a piece in *Atlantic* in July 2008 under the title 'Is Google Making Us Stupid?'[271] His answer was that work on the web (not just Google) is stultifying him, and, by extension, us in the sense that it's shortening our attention span. Where once we read books, now we read a bit of a web page and click on a hyperlink. We get the stuff we want, but that's partly because, in the process, we're lowering our expectations.

Carr's a persuasive fellow, but I will say in response that Wikipedia is one of those subdivisions of the web that doesn't make us as stupid as some other subdivisions do. As to reading Wikipedia, yes, how right he is! Reading Wikipedia is just like his description of using the web, albeit on a slightly smaller scale. We read half a page, we see a bluelink, we click on it and start reading another page. We forget the page we were reading. We'll never see it again. It's gone. Our thoughts have moved on. But reading Wikipedia is not the whole of our interaction with the site, because, as Jimmy Wales has so truly and so often said, 'Wikipedia will never be finished.'[272]

As I admitted in the prologue, any errors that I have noticed on Wikipedia and not corrected are my fault. When François Gèze (as reported by Daniel Garcia) noted the tendentious material at **fr:Affaire Dreyfus**, his response, conditioned by political life in the 1960s, was 'François Gèze told me that he'd contacted the Human Rights League immediately.' What a good idea! But not, perhaps, the best. Michel, in his comment on Daniel Garcia's blog, said so in revolutionary terms:

'When you come across something that you can correct or clarify it's up to you, knowledgeable citizen, to correct or improve it. Since you and François Gèze knew all about this book, all you had to do was correct the page, either stating the book's faults, or deleting the claim that it's a fundamental work. You don't even need to get an account: you just click on 'edit' and you can put the problem right in a minute. Your edit would have ensured that all future readers of fr:Affaire Dreyfus were better informed. You have a lot to learn about the collaborative Web, Daniel Garcia: you're still in the 19th century, when books and newspapers were the private hunting ground of learned editors and couldn't be corrected by their citizen readers.'[273]

Assouline, too, was in the nineteenth century. His fantasy of the invisible realms of Wikipedia was that 'a committee of "real" experts is of course there, watching from "up above" (the verticality of decision-making has not altogether been given up) to avoid collateral damage. Which regularly happens, none the less.'[274] As in the United States, in France too it was the cultural conservatives who didn't quite get Wikipedia. It was to make such readers comfortable that Larousse, as late as 2008, planned its encyclopedia website with the existing text of the encyclopedia 'inscribed in marble' on one side, not open to editing or to comment; on the other side a space for new signed articles displaying their authors' point of view. These, Larousse believed, would become magnets for the polemical topics that generate so much interest among surfers. The Holocaust, the Israel–Palestine conflict and global warming were offered as examples. While on Wikipedia these topics degenerate into battlegrounds, Larousse claimed, on its own website it would be able to organise multiple points of view and responses in parallel with a reference article. Somebody then reflected that the cure would be worse than the disease. The 'revisionist' view of the Holocaust can't be legally argued in public in France. In any case, is the full expression of extreme views on such topics what the reader of an encyclopedia page wants? Wouldn't that be far worse than Wikipedia, where, in the course of endless debate, an article eventually gets written that both sides can live with? Larousse therefore hastily added the proviso that *modérateurs* could reject a submission outright:[275] the censor and the 'verticality of decision-making' returned with a vengeance.

One of the more responsible ways to use Wikipedia in journalism and on television is to point out its inadequacies, errors and gaps and to suggest correcting them. The suggestion was made some years ago by Cathy Davidson of Duke University that 'if a journalist were to find something surprising on Wikipedia and the journalistic instincts suggested it was correct, the journalist might add that as an unsubstantiated Wiki-fact and invite comment', especially in the newspaper's online edition.[276] Davidson's initial idea is still recognisable in the Chicago Public Radio series *The Wikipedia Files*, in which creative artists are interviewed, faced with the Wikipedia page about them, and invited to improve it.[277]

Any gaps in Wikipedia – oh, yes, with only three million articles in English there are many, many gaps – any gaps that we notice are our fault too, at least, until we have done what we can to fill them. I wanted to know more about **Barbara Reynolds**, translator from Italian, so I started the page and filled in what I knew. Others have improved it. In the same way, Danny was curious about the American architectural sculptor **Lee Lawrie**, whose statue of Atlas is at the Rockefeller Center in New York. In December 2002 Danny created a two-line article. It was enough for someone else to get to work. The someone else was Carptrash 'who owned several books on Lawrie and who'd photographed his work not only at Rockefeller Center but also at the Capitol Building in Lincoln, Nebraska. Today, the Lawrie entry has grown from two sentences to several thorough paragraphs, a dozen photos, and a list of references,' as Daniel H. Pink tells the story. Kingturtle started a similar stub in November 2003 because he happened to wonder how many people are considered the father or mother of something.[278] **List of persons considered father or mother of a field** received 25 edits, by ten different editors, before the end of that year. Six years later it is a well-furnished list with 116 footnotes, and the parent of a series of specialised pages with similar titles.

With Barbara Reynolds, with Lee Lawrie and with the list of fathers and mothers, the editor who started the article had enough material for a stub, a very short article that still managed to give one or two good reasons to think that the subject was notable. That's the minimum. An article that fails to reach the minimum risks being deleted before anyone has time to make improvements. Even if we don't know enough for that, it's still possible to use Wikipedia as a means to finding more. In researching the contacts of the Greek prime minister **Eleftherios Venizelos** I found I needed to know a few details about a folk-music collector of the 1920s named Melpo Merlier. In the whole of Wikipedia I could find only three mentions of her name, all of them on the Greek Wikipedia, with no added information. There was very little to be found elsewhere on the web. The best I could do, around 14.00 on 13 October 2007, was to turn those three mentions into redlinks. There was just a chance that whoever came across one of them and knew something about Merlier would begin the article, turning my redlinks blue. I wasn't hopeful, and I was slightly amazed to get a message on my English Wikipedia user page less than two hours later, at 15.54: *A small article about Melpo Merlier is ready on greek wiki in case you are interested, since you added a red link. Greetings – Kalogeropoulos.* That, too, is wiki magic.

By those who don't want to rely on Wikipedia the anonymity of contributions is often held up as a rationale. Those familiar with literary and cultural history aren't likely to make this argument. Attaching names and qualifications to text has become the rule in modern academic writing, but it doesn't happen in other contexts and it happened much less in the recent past. Until the nineteenth century contributions to journals were mostly anonymous. The *Times Literary Supplement* kept up that tradition until 1974; *The Economist* still does. Reports in newspapers were nearly all anonymous until recently. In encyclopedias only the longer pieces are signed. In most of the big historical dictionaries like the *Oxford English Dictionary* even the longest articles, the ones that may have taken months of research, aren't signed. Of all the examples I've given, the *OED* offers the closest parallel to the way in which Wikipedia entries are built up. A long Wikipedia article is likely to be a compound of scraps of information selected and inserted by many editors, just as the individual quotations in any long *OED* entry were chosen and submitted by many readers. The *OED* entry would then be worked up by a single editor, or perhaps more than one; or perhaps by one at first, only to be revised by others long afterwards; and minor adaptations for style or consistency might be made by others still. The introductions and the lists of contributors give the names of a large proportion of those whose work has gone into the eventual *OED*, but not of all of them: some contributions were anonymous. In only a minority of cases is anything said of their qualifications. The readers have been self-selected volunteers whose full details haven't always been known. Andrew Lih, in discussing this comparison, cites the famous case of W. C. Minor, a major *OED* contributor who (as the editor, James Murray, eventually realised) was a convicted murderer confined for life to Broadmoor Asylum.[279] The parallel isn't perfect, of course. Contributors to the *OED* are, by contrast with Wikipedians, nearly always listed under their real names; in the *OED*, by contrast with Wikipedia, the user can't discover whose contributions went into which article. But it's close enough to show that Wikipedia's method isn't new.

Scholars and journalists have gradually moved towards real names and fully-stated qualifications in their publications; Wikipedia prefers the other way. 'There are two reasons I would put forward,' said Jimmy Wales in 2005 in the aftermath of the Seigenthaler incident. 'First, on the Internet, it's impossible to actually confirm people's identity in the first place, short of getting credit-card information. On any site it's very easy to come up with a fake identity, regardless. Second, there are definitely people working in Wikipedia who may have privacy reasons for not wanting their name on the site. For example, there are people working on Wikipedia from China, where the site is currently blocked. We have a contributor in Iran who has twice been told his name has been turned into the police for his work in Wikipedia.'[280]

There are two big differences between Wikipedia and most of the other cases of anonymity in publication. One is that in those other cases (with the partial exception of the *OED*) the general editor chose the contributors and knew their qualifications. The other is that the contributors expected to be paid. Wikipedia editors are almost wholly self-selected. Nearly all Wikipedia editors aren't paid and don't expect to be. Nice work if you can get it, they have sometimes said; because it's a known fact that a few who write on Wikipedia are paid, though not by Wikipedia.

No one can claim that Wikipedia, as a whole, is a 'reliable source'. Instead, accepting it as not the least reliable of online guides, and drawing thirstily on its footnotes and external links, we – I'm speaking now for myself and all the others, writers and journalists, scholars and scientists, who actually use Wikipedia already – judge each article for reliability on its merits. It comes to us on the authority not of Wikipedia but of its contributors. First, if necessary, we can consider its cogency as a whole. Then, if a detail is crucial to us, we can find out which editor added it and compare that editor's other contributions. We can ask on a talk page what justified the addition. We can judge whether that editor seems to have a hidden agenda or strange enthusiasms, or to be working for some government or organisation. At any rate we'll take the crucial detail as unreliable until we confirm it in an independent source. We'd do the same with the *OED*: if the quotation or dating is crucial, we'll check it (and occasionally find that the *OED* has misled us). We'll do the same with *Britannica* (and occasionally find that *Britannica* has misled us). We'll do the same with a newspaper: if some new detail matters to us, we won't believe it fully until confirmation turns up; we'll be aware that some news reports are more objective than others; and when reading a newspaper we'll place rather less reliance on what the motoring, wine and travel columnists say because we suspect that their rewards don't come exclusively from the publisher. In those cases, though, we can't go behind the editorial front to see where the single details originated.

More than most other sources of information, Wikipedia's editors are truly international. Any article bearing on world politics will have contributors from both sides, or all sides, of any argument, with long and heated discussions on its talk page. The most consistent participants will be pseudonymous, and the majority of these won't try to conceal their personal sympathies: in the long run that just doesn't work. Others will arrive wholly anonymously from IP addresses, but it's difficult to maintain an argument without a personality, even a pseudonymous one. The resulting Wikipedia article won't entirely satisfy any side, but all will be watching to ensure it doesn't get far out of line.

An example of Wikipedia's internationalism at work is seen in a recent controversy over articles of interest to Israeli contributors. The newspaper *Haaretz* reported a conference at which details on specific pages were discussed, including these:

'In demonstrating what he defined as problems, Eli Hacohen [of Tel Aviv University's Netvision Institute for Internet Studies] showed how Hamas is not defined as a terrorist organization in the first paragraph describing the organization [in the English Wikipedia]... Hacohen also documented his attempts to define Iran's president, Mahmoud Ahmadinejad, as a Holocaust-denier. Each time he included his remarks on Wikipedia, users and editors removed the reference – despite Ahmadinejad's frequent and public Holocaust denials. On a related entry, Hacohen also noted that Wikipedia defines David Irving – a known Holocaust denier – as a historian, although his credentials are recognized by no one but himself.'

Details in all these articles change with extreme frequency. We've heard of the Hamas article before in the context of anonymous vandalism from

Joe Biden's office. That naive attempt to make the introductory paragraph bluntly anti-Hamas was quickly repaired by Zeq. Currently, in spite of the *Haaretz* claim, the opening paragraphs of **Hamas** manage to strike a balance while including (as the opinion of certain governments) the phrase *terrorist organization*. I haven't identified Eli Hacohen's edits to **Mahmoud Ahmadinejad** – they were either anonymous or pseudonymous, and there have been thousands – but the article contains, in the introductory paragraphs, the words *He has also been condemned for describing the Holocaust as a myth, which has led to accusations of anti-semitism. In response to these criticisms, Ahmadinejad said "No, I am not anti-Jew, I respect them very much."* This passage is disarmingly clear, in spite of the *Haaretz* claim; it has four footnotes and is followed by lengthy discussion later in the article. The **David Irving** article defines Irving in the opening sentence, unarguably, as a *British writer specializing in the military history of World War II*; to this, in spite of the *Haaretz* claim, is attached a long footnote explaining why his self-definition as 'historian' has been widely disputed, and there is extended discussion of his revisionist writings on the Holocaust. I don't know exactly when Hacohen looked at these Wikipedia entries, but the relevant sections haven't changed significantly in recent months. So, assuming that he made specific and valid observations, my work suggests that *Haaretz* has reported them in a confused way. Sue Gardner, the Wikimedia Foundation's new executive director, who attended the conference, was perfectly justified in saying, as widely quoted, that she was 'quite comfortable' with Wikipedia's coverage in these cases. *Haaretz's* claim that 'errors' were found (a claim uncritically repeated by other commentators) seems, on the basis of these examples, to be embroidery.[281] On the same basis, Wikipedia, naturally enough, has done better than *Haaretz* at approximating an international view, if in these subject areas such a thing as an international view can be dreamed of.

Not only do we use Wikipedia: we needn't be ashamed to cite it. Not, of course, if a teacher or editor has ruled that Wikipedia must never be cited: in that case we'll plagiarise it and try not to get caught. In any case we'll use it as a way to find better sources, and those are the ones we'll quote and cite. Which is why Wikipedia is earning its place not in the bibliography but in the acknowledgments, alongside my partner, my kids, my professor and my agent.

In spite of all this, we're still not quite comfortable with the thing. A copy-editor (a regular at Testycopyeditors.org) will doubt the appropriateness of citing the encyclopedia that anyone can edit. An editor (a closet reader of *The Register*) will expect Wikipedia, if named at all, to be named with disdain. An agent will doubt whether a book about merely the seventh most popular website in the world will find a market. The consensus, even in 2009, may be that Wikipedia isn't quite mature yet. This consensus could just change with the story of the kidnapping in Afghanistan on 10 November 2008 and escape on 19 June 2009 of the *New York Times* reporter David Rohde, author of *Endgame: the betrayal and fall of Srebrenica*.

Two days after the kidnapping, Rohde's colleague Michael Moss, writing as Michaeljohnss, edited the Wikipedia biography of **David Rohde** to emphasise the pro-Muslim aspects of his work, the reporting on Guantánamo Bay and the work on the Srebrenica massacre. 'I knew from my jihad reporting that the captors would be very quick to get online and assess who he was and what he'd done, what his value to them might be,' Moss said later. 'I'd never edited a Wikipedia page before.' He was careful not to mention that Rohde used to work for the *Christian Science Monitor* because of the inconvenient word 'Christian' in that newspaper's title. Next day, for the first time, an anonymous user traced to Florida added the first news of the kidnapping. Moss deleted this an hour later and the same user promptly restored it, citing an Afghan news agency and adding the edit summary: *I have provided proof. Please don't remove sourced stuff.* At the next attempt, more sources were cited. This was an edit war that the *New York Times* couldn't fight alone, and the paper asked Jimmy Wales for help.

Wales in turn knew that whatever he did would attract attention. He enlisted the help of admins. At times they continued to revert, giving one good reason or another; at times the page was protected, but only for short periods so as not to attract attention. Most of the attempts to add the kidnap news continued to be anonymous; most were from Florida. 'We had no idea who it was,' Wales said afterwards. 'There was no way to reach out quietly and say "Dude, stop and think about this," and no way to know whether the intention was malicious.' The user's fields of interest are displayed unambiguously by other edits to pages such as **Exit Wounds**, **Transformers: Revenge of the Fallen** and **Murder of Bobby Kent**. A recent edit to **Characters in Resident Evil 4** is accompanied by the edit summary: *Saddler was blown up by a rocket. Krauser's left arm disintegrated after Ada killed her. Las Plagas only dies when the host dies. Grow the fuck up.*

After eight months Rohde and his translator, Tahir Ludin, escaped from a Taliban compound in Pakistan. The *New York Times* emailed Jimmy Wales at once, and he himself unprotected the page one last time at 15.57 on 20 June 2009. Half an hour later the same user from Florida inserted news of the kidnapping once more, with the brusque edit summary: *Is this enough proof you fucking retards? I was right. You were wrong.* 'From the early days of this ordeal,' said Bill Keller of the *New York Times*, 'the prevailing view among David's family, experts in kidnapping cases, officials of several governments and others we consulted was that going public could increase the danger. We decided to respect that advice.'[282] Fortunately up to 40 other news agencies that knew of the story agreed to the *Times*'s request for silence. Wikipedia was naturally the most difficult. Jimmy Wales confirmed that the site's cooperation had been a contentious issue. As so often, a convenient rule was discovered. 'We were really helped by the fact that [the news] hadn't appeared in a place we would regard as a reliable source,' he said afterwards. 'I would have had a really hard time with it if it had.'[283]

'Some may see this as censorship,' wrote Murad Ahmed soon afterwards at Tech Central, 'going against Wikipedia's ethos to freely release all information. But speaking as a biased journalist, I think this is an example of Wikipedia showing responsibility and understanding its power and importance in the digital age.' Comments posted in response to Ahmed's piece show that the sympathies of some readers would have been with the editor from Florida. 'Sorry, disagree. WikiFAIL. You think Afghan tribesmen are constantly checking to see if the guy's been mentioned in Wikipedia? Perhaps he can tell us now that he's free. Elsewise, it's just another jurnlistic arrogance,'[284] wrote PD, careless of Afghan reality.

Balancing David Rohde's right to survival with the demand for everyone to know everything they want wouldn't have been easy for any website the infant years of Web 2.0. On page 70, six weeks before news of the ohde kidnapping emerged, I wrote that no randomly-selected group of Wikipedians would ever agree on any political approach to any topic, still ss would they agree to say nothing about it – and this case disproves my rediction. The doubts of some commentators notwithstanding, in this case was for the best, and Murad Ahmed's claim, in the first words of the article st cited, may prove to have been justified:

'Wikipedia has grown up.'

Author's note

On the English Wikipedia I'm in the outer circle. I'm not an admin; I ha
been a fairly frequent editor. This means that under the heading 'Why v
love Wikipedia' some of the reasons I give are my own reasons. Some, c
the other hand, aren't. It's for you to judge whether in spite of my person
involvement I have managed to see Wikipedia as she really is, warts and a

Many of the quotations in this book are from Wikipedia articles ar
talk pages. Direct quotations from Wikipedia pages are italicised. Wikiped
page titles are bolded: typing the bolded text into a search box on t
English Wikipedia will find the page from which I have quoted. Wherev
reasonably possible I attribute text to the editor who originated it, and, if
matters, I give the date of the edit concerned. My claims should therefo
be easy to check. Those who want to follow my footsteps need to kno
that the earliest edits of Wikipedia pages, from 2001 and early 2002, m;
not be reliably accessible from page histories. They can sometimes be got
through user contributions, sometimes with the help of Archive.org. It's al
handy to know that talk about article deletions can often be found by typir
the article name into a Wikipedia search box; the deleted articles themselv
can't be found that way, but they sometimes survive elsewhere on the web
have done my best to give credit correctly, but the way that oversight wor
means that in controversial articles it's occasionally possible for text to
attributed to an editor who wasn't really responsible for it. If for this reaso
or through inadvertence, I have falsely credited any edits, I apologise no
and I'll correct the error at the first opportunity. Likewise if I have mistim
any edits: I have tried to be careful, but it's easy to get confused over t
interplay between GMT and the turning world.

Beyond the Wikimedia servers nearly everything I have quoted is onlin
or was when I quoted it. These quotations should be verifiable using a Goog
string search. I have sometimes adjusted punctuation in quotations but
have not adjusted spelling or grammar (God knows what my copy-edit
will do). [She didn't adjust spelling or grammar in quotations either.]

I have always used editors' Wikipedia usernames when citing their wo
on the site. This seemed to be the right thing to do, whether or not th

also make their real names public, because it is under these usernames that they choose to publish. Where they happen to have had more than one username I have usually, to simplify the story, fixed on one of them. With that exception, I, like the *New Yorker* in a famous case, haven't checked the real identities behind the usernames. I describe them as they describe themselves. However, a few Wikipedians whose edits are quoted in the text have also been employees of the Wikimedia Foundation, and it is giving away no secrets to identify these here: Jimbo Wales is of course Jimmy Wales; LMS is Larry Sanger; Danny is Daniel Wool; Eloquence is Erik Möller; Anthere is Florence Devouard. Also no secret is the identity of Fuzheado, whose work I draw on when looking at journalists' use of Wikipedia: he is Andrew Lih, author of *The Wikipedia Revolution*.

I have of course consulted *The Wikipedia Revolution*, which appeared as I was working on this book; I have also consulted a very different book with a very similar title, *La révolution Wikipédia* by Pierre Gourdain, Florence O'Kelly, Béatrice Roman-Amat, Delphine Soulas and Tassilo von Droste zu Hülshoff, published in 2007. My thanks to their authors; to all those listed in the bibliography, many of whose insights I have quoted; to Liz and Richard at Siduri Books, who have worked with impressive speed and efficiency; and to all the Wikipedia editors, named and unnamed, whose work I have drawn on.

Saint-Coutant, July 2009

Endnotes

1 Pliny the Younger, *Letters* 6.16, 6.20.

2 Pliny the Elder, *Natural History*, preface, 14.

3 See 'Encyclopaedia Britannica vs the Computer' at www.howtoknow.com/sidebar1.html

4 In Britannica numerical order, these are the 2nd, 3rd, 4th, 6th, 7th, 9th, 11th and 14th. The 5th and 8th were only partial revisions of the 4th and 7th. The 10th, 12th and 13th were reprints of the 9th and 11th with new supplements.

5 Robert McHenry, 'The Building of Britannica Online'

6 Douglas Adams, *Life, the Universe and Everything* in *The Hitchhiker's Guide to the Galaxy: A Trilogy in Four Parts* (London: Pan Books, 1992); Paul Boutin, 'Galaxy Quest'

7 Doug Wilson at groups.google.de/group/alt.bbs.internet/msg/154a6a552ca631af? R. L. Samuell at groups.google.com/group/comp.infosystems.interpedia/msg/05d4734a3d1a03a6?

8 Joseph M. Reagle, 'Wikipedia's heritage: vision, pragmatics, and happenstance'

9 At web.archive.org/web/20030414014355 and www.nupedia.com/pipermail/nupedia-l/2001-January/000676.html

10 At c2.com/cgi/wiki

11 At marc.info/?l=wikipedia-l&m=104216623605869&w=2

12 At Wikipedia:Announcements 2001

13 As observed by Paul Boutin, 'Galaxy Quest'

14 At osdir.com/ml/science.linguistics.wikipedia.misc/2002/msg03523.html

15 'Wikipedia Editor Larry Sanger resigns' (1 March 2002) at www.kuro5hin.org/story/2002/3/1/163730/6996

16 In this paragraph I have quoted selectively from three postings by Sanger (these are also my source for the remark by Wales). The full texts are at osdir.com/ml/science.linguistics.wikipedia.misc/2002/msg00552.html, osdir.com/ml/science.linguistics.wikipedia.misc/2002/msg01588.html, osdir.com/ml/science.linguistics.wikipedia.misc/2002/msg03500.html

17 Quotation from Steven Johnson, 'Populist Editing'. 'Editorial Policy Guidelines' at web.archive.org/web/20010607080354/www.nupedia.com/policy.shtml

18 At lists.wikimedia.org/pipermail/wikipedia-l/2001-October/000671.html

19 At osdir.com/ml/science.linguistics.wikipedia.misc/2002/msg03561.html

20 At lists.wikimedia.org/pipermail/wikipedia-l/2001-March/000048.html

21 At osdir.com/ml/science.linguistics.wikipedia.misc/2001-07/msg00029.html

22 See stats.wikimedia.org/EN/TablesDatabaseWords.htm

23 Brian Lamb, 'Jimmy Wales, Wikipedia Founder'

24 Pascale Vergereau, 'La fourmi devenue reine de l'encyclopédie' in *Ouest France* (13 January 2007)

25 See www.netsuus.com/informe-breve/especial-wikipedia

26 Dated 3 July 2006, now at :meta:Language committee/Archives/2006-09

27 *It is now widely agreed upon, that the creation of the Siberian language Wikipedia 2006 was based on a hoax,* according to :meta:List of Wikipedias. It was moved to sib.volgota.com, where it currently survives tenuously as a neighbour of the obsessively racial *Metapedia* at en.metapedia.org

28 The former Klingon wikipedia is now at klingon.wikia.com/, where a participant admits that *nothing has moved for a long time.*

29 Now at :meta:Requests for new languages/Wikipedia Serbo-Croatian

30 Distilled from a fragmented discussion at :meta:Requests for new languages/ Wikipedia Manchu 2

31 The talk pages can be found via :meta:Requests for new languages. The discussions of the committee are partly available at :meta:Language committee/ Archives (but GerardM's contributions are withheld from view).

32 At :meta:Language committee/Archives/2007-03

33 Quoted at Wikipedia:Announcements 2001

34 Quoted at History of Wikipedia footnote 39 (accessed 11 May 2009)

35 www.nytimes.com/2001/09/20/technology/circuits/20ENCY.html

36 Steven Johnson, 'Populist Editing'

37 lists.wikimedia.org/pipermail/wikipedia-l/2001-March/000044.html

38 osdir.com/ml/science.linguistics.wikipedia.misc/2001-07/msg00023.html

39 lists.wikimedia.org/pipermail/wikipedia-l/2001-October/000664.html

40 www.theregister.co.uk/2004/07/14/buckminster_fuller_stamp/

41 *Times Higher Education Supplement* (13 May 2005); business.timesonline. co.uk/tol/business/industry_sectors/public_sector/article522906.ece

42 Nicholas Carr, 'The Amorality of Web 2.0'

43 lists.wikimedia.org/pipermail/wikien-l/2005-October/030075.html

44 www.nature.com/nature/journal/v438/n7070/full/438890a.html

45 www.theregister.co.uk/2005/12/16/wikipedia_britannica_science_comparison/

46 At news.zdnet.com/2100-9588_22-146067.html

47 Nicholas Carr, '*Nature*'s Flawed Study'

48 At http://corporate.britannica.com/britannica_nature_response.pdf

49 www.usatoday.com/news/opinion/editorials/2005-11-29-wikipedia-edit_x.htm

50 Brian Lamb, 'Jimmy Wales, Wikipedia Founder'

51 www.nytimes.com/2005/12/11/business/media/11web.html

52 www.theregister.co.uk/2005/12/06/wikipedia_bio/

53 Chris Ayres, 'Kennedy theory forces internet rethink' at www.timesonline.co.uk/tol/news/world/us_and_americas/article754539.ece

54 Philippe Naughton, 'Editor Forces Wikipedia to Clean Up Its Act' at business.timesonline.co.uk/tol/business/industry_sectors/media/article754191.ece

55 Rhys Blakely, 'Wikipedia Founder Edits Himself' at business.timesonline.co.uk/tol/business/industry_sectors/technology/article774973.ece

56 Rosemary Righter, 'Unreliable (adj): Log On and See' at www.timesonline.co.uk/tol/comment/thunderer/article755331.ece

57 At www.heise.de/newsticker/Wikipedia-schrieb-Bertrand-Meyer-tot--/meldung/67895

58 Bertrand Meyer, 'Defense and Illustration of Wikipedia'

59 www.cest-off.com/?p=332

60 www.20minutes.fr/article/226089/France-Philippe-Manoeuvre-n-est-pas-mort.php

61 At fr:Wikipédia:Bulletin des administrateurs/2008/Semaine 19#Fausse annonce de la mort de Philippe Manoeuvre

62 At fr:Wikipédia:Bulletin des administrateurs/2008/Semaine 21#Grandes Manoeuvres, suite; also at fr:n:Wikipédia – poursuites judiciaires contre l'auteur d'une fausse nouvelle

63 At www.infos-du-net.com/actualite/13625-manoeuvre-mort-wikipedia.html

64 'J'étais dans le coaltar.' www.pcinpact.com/actu/news/43824-Philippe-Manoeuvre-Wikipedia-plaisantin-expl.htm

65 Frédérique Roussel, 'Wikipédia se trompe à tous vents' at www.liberation.fr/ecrans/0101106934-wikipedia-se-trompe-a-tous-vents

66 Alex Havalais, 'The Isuzu Experiment' (29 August 2004, revised 5 September 2004) at alex.halavais.net/the-isuzu-experiment/

67 Which was eventually published: Pierre Gourdain, Florence O'Kelly, Béatrice Roman-Amat, Delphine Soulas, Tassilo von Droste zu Hülshoff, *La révolution Wikipédia: les encyclopédies vont-elles mourir?*

68 No longer visible in the article history but reported at fr:Wikipédia:Vérificateur d'adresses IP/Requêtes/juillet 2007

69 See the history of fr:Discussion utilisateur:193.54.67.93

70 See fr:n:Quand des étudiants de Science Po vandalisent Wikipédia

71 Daniel Garcia, 'L'affaire Dreyfus' (30 November 2006) at www.livreshebdo.fr/weblog/webLogComments.aspx?idTxt=75&id=11

72 Pierre Assouline, 'L'affaire Wikipédia'

passouline.blog.lemonde.fr/2007/03/17/diderot-ne-meritait-pas-ca/
sponding to www.elpais.com/articulo/cultura/Wikipedia/siglo/XVIII/
epucul/20070316elpepicul_6/Tes

Assouline's question is *Peut-on écrire sans conséquence?* The part of his
sponse that I have translated is: *L'homme d'idées, celui qui travaille en principe
ns l'intelligence, devrait se sentir responsable de ce qu'il écrit au moment même
la création. Il ne devrait écrire qu'en pensant à n'avoir jamais à se renier ou à se
rocher l'une quelconque de ses phrases dans l'avenir, à n'en avoir pas honte, par-
là les modes et les régimes.* Pierre Assouline, *L'épuration des intellectuels* (Brussels:
omplexe, 1996) pp. 80–81

www.guardian.co.uk/technology/2006/jul/13/media.newmedia, www.
nonsandiego.com/uniontrib/20060923/news_lz1n23wiki.html

Didier Sanz, 'Wikipédia: encyclopédie sous haute surveillance'

www.conservapedia.com/index.php?title=Conservapedia%3ADesk%2FMiscell
y&diff=260943&oldid=260940

Compare Ed Brayton, 'Ladies and Gentlemen, Conservapedia' at scienceblogs.
m/dispatches/2007/02/ladies_and_gentlemen_conservap.php

See chak.volgota.com/index.php/Main_Page

See en.metapedia.org/wiki/Wikislavia

At fr.metapedia.org/w/index.php?title=Discussion_Utilisateur:Jaczewski&oldi
18360

David Wong, '5 Terrifying Bastardizations of the Wikipedia Model'

Quoted by Andrew Orlowski, 'A Thirst for Knowledge'

Roy Rosenzweig, 'Can History be Open Source? Wikipedia and the Future of
e Past'

Michael Singer, 'Free Encyclopedia Project Celebrates Year One' (16 January
02) at www.internetnews.com/bus-news/article.php/3531_956641

Roy Rosenzweig, 'Can History be Open Source? Wikipedia and the Future of
e Past'

'Wikipedia Editor Larry Sanger resigns' (1 March 2002) at www.kuro5hin.
g/story/2002/3/1/163730/6996

William Emigh, Susan C. Herring, 'Collaborative Authoring on the Web'

Jonathan Dee, 'All the News That's Fit to Print Out'

osdir.com/ml/science.linguistics.wikipedia.misc/2001-07/msg00034.html

Larry Sanger, 'The Early History of Nupedia and Wikipedia' part 2

At Wikipedia:Announcements 2001

At Wikipedia:Announcements 2001

www.livreshebdo.fr/weblog/webLogComments.aspx?idTxt=75&id=11

Pierre Assouline, 'L'affaire Wikipédia'

96 Nicholas Carr, 'The Net is being carved up into information plantations'

97 www.roughtype.com/archives/2006/08/the_oracle_of_w.php

98 Nicholas Carr, 'All hail the information triumvirate!'

99 Andrew Orlowski, 'Google Kicks Wikipedia in the Googlies' (14 December 2007) at www.theregister.co.uk/2007/12/14/googlepedia_announced/

100 www.telegraph.co.uk/news/worldnews/asia/southkorea/1404681/Japan-and South-Korea-fall-out-over-sea-with-no-name.html

101 www.telegraph.co.uk/news/uknews/1409951/Tebbit-will-stay-says-Tory-leader.html

102 www.theage.com.au/articles/2003/03/28/1048653848997.html

103 Donna Shaw, 'Wikipedia in the Newsroom'

104 www.theregister.co.uk/2009/05/07/wikipedia_jarre_hoax/

105 26 June 2007 at www.testycopyeditors.org/phpBB3/viewtopic.php?f=8&t=8178

106 Daniel H. Pink, 'The Book Stops Here'

107 Paul Boutin, 'Galaxy Quest'. I can't verify that *Britannica* doesn't have an entry on *Slate*, by the way. That information is on a need-to-know basis (*Britannica* needs to know my credit card number).

108 Donna Shaw, 'Wikipedia in the Newsroom'

109 The two articles, long since rewritten, are now called Socialist Alliance (England) and Scottish Labour Party (1976). See Wikipedia:Wikipedia press coverage 2003.

110 Links from www.lefigaro.fr/medias/2009/05/06/04002-20090506ARTFIG00627-des-journaux-pieges-par-une-fausse-citation-sur-wikipedia-.php

111 Shane Fitzgerald, 'Lazy Journalism Exposed by Online Hoax'. See also Talk:Maurice Jarre and Talk:Shane Fitzgerald (hoaxer)

112 See www.netmagellan.com/general/maurice-jarre-what-wikipedia-hoax-466.html

113 www.smh.com.au/national/obituaries/life-was-one-long-soundtrack-20090331-9i7f.html?page=-1

114 www.guardian.co.uk/film/2009/mar/31/maurice-jarre-obituary

115 www.joegratz.net/archives/2005/04/11/andrea-dworkin/

116 www.guardian.co.uk/news/blog/2005/apr/12/wikipediafirst

117 At fr:Wikipédia:Le Bistro/18 avril 2008#Philippe Manoeuvre

118 Perhaps the same text currently available at 24heures.blog.mongenie.com/index.php?idblogp=612343

119 www.20minutes.fr/article/224868/France-Wikipedia-enterre-Aime-Cesaire-avant-l-heure.php

120 voices.washingtonpost.com/capitol-briefing/2009/01/kennedy_the_latest_victim_of_w.html?hpid=topnews

121 lists.topica.com/lists/suber-fos/read/message.html?mid=1605194865&sort=c&start=8

122 At fr:Wikipédia:Le Bistro/10 avril 2007

123 Quoted by Gégé at passouline.blog.lemonde.fr/2007/01/09/laffaire-wikipedia/

124 Laure Endrizzi, *L'édition de référence libre et collaborative: le cas de Wikipedia.*

125 Keith Gerein, 'University Confronts Cheats in the Age of Wikipedia' at www.canada.com/technology/University+confronts+cheats+Wikipedia/1334881/story.html

126 Marie-Estelle Pech, 'Le copier-coller sur Internet irrite les profs' at www.lefigaro.fr/actualite/2007/04/10/01001-20070410ARTFIG90192-le_copier_coller_sur_internet_irrite_les_profs.php

127 Noam Cohen, 'A History Department Bans Citing Wikipedia as a Research Source'

128 Shaye J. D. Chen, as quoted in 'Professors Split on Wiki Debate' at www.thecrimson.com/article.aspx?ref=517305

129 Kristie Lu Stout, 'Wikipedia: the know-it-all Web site' at www.cnn.com/2003/TECH/internet/08/03/wikipedia/

130 Mills Kelly, 'Wikipedia in the Classroom' at edwired.org/?p=124, 'Why I won't get hired at Middlebury' at edwired.org/?p=126

131 Noam Cohen, 'A History Department Bans Citing Wikipedia as a Research Source'

132 osdir.com/ml/science.linguistics.wikipedia.misc/2001-08/index.html

133 lists.wikimedia.org/pipermail/wikien-l/2005-October/030075.html

134 Simon Waldman, 'Who knows?'

135 At Wikipedia:External peer review/Nature December 2005/Errors

136 Citing George Johnson, 'The Nitpicking of the Masses vs. the Authority of the Experts' (3 January 2006) at www.nytimes.com/2006/01/03/science/03comm.html?_r=1

137 See Wikipedia:Wikipedia Signpost/2006-01-30/Errors remedied

138 Judy Heim, 'Free the Encyclopedias!' (4 September 2001) at www.technologyreview.com/Infotech/12586/

139 Brian Lamb, 'Jimmy Wales, Wikipedia Founder'

140 Brian Lamb, 'Jimmy Wales, Wikipedia Founder'

141 Daniel H. Pink, 'The Book Stops Here'

142 Thomas Caywood, 'Answering Wikipedia's Call to Fill In the Blanks' (28 September 2006) at www.boston.com/news/local/articles/2006/09/28/answering_

wikipedias_call_to_fill_in_the_blanks/?page=1

43 Didier Sanz, 'Wikipédia: encyclopédie sous haute surveillance'

44 Reported at fr:n:600 000 articles sur la Wikipédia francophone

45 Pierre Gourdain and others, *La révolution Wikipédia*

46 At Wikipedia:Announcements 2001

47 Quoted by Marshall Poe, 'The Hive'

48 Quoted by Marshall Poe, 'The Hive'

49 At Talk:Alan Dershowitz/Archive 2

50 Roy Rosenzweig, 'Can History be Open Source?'

51 At User:Raul654/Raul's laws

52 Larry Sanger, 'The Early History of Nupedia and Wikipedia' part 2

53 www.indopedia.org/Talk:Silent_Ethnic_Cleansing.html

54 At m:Historical Wikipedia pages

55 These quotations are from a series of postings listed at lists.wikimedia.org/
pipermail/wikipedia-l/2002-September/date.html#4900

56 These examples and attached quotes are from the long list at
Wikipedia:Lamest edit wars

57 David Runciman, 'Like Boiling a Frog'

58 www.theregister.co.uk/2005/10/18/wikipedia_quality_problem/

59 Quoted by Roy Rosenzweig, 'Can History be Open Source?'

60 Paul Boutin, 'Galaxy Quest'

61 See eg User:RonaldMcWendys/Captûre Wines and the pages that link to it.

62 David Sarno, 'Wikipedia Wars Erupt' at www.latimes.com/
technology/la-ca-webscout30sep30,1,1815602.story?coll=la-headlines-
technology&ctrack=1&cset=true

63 Roy Rosenzweig, 'Can History be Open Source?'

64 David Runciman, 'Like Boiling a Frog'

65 Now at :m:Talk:Wiki is not paper

66 Now at www.wikipedia-watch.org/gifs/mtessjay.png

67 Stacy Schiff, 'Know It All: can Wikipedia conquer expertise?'

68 wikipediareview.com/index.php?showtopic=2778

69 Now at www.wikipedia-watch.org/gifs/wmessjay.png

70 As quoted by Brandt at wikipediareview.com/index.php?showtopic=2778

71 Stacy Schiff, 'Know It All: can Wikipedia conquer expertise?' as revised

72 As quoted at Essjay controversy

73 wikipediareview.com/index.php?showtopic=21101&st=80

74 See Wikipedia:Articles_for_deletion/David_Boothroyd, Wikipedia:Articles_
for_deletion/David_Boothroyd_(2nd_nomination) and Wikipedia:Articles_for_
deletion/Sam_Blacketer_controversy

175 See en.wikipedia.org/wiki/Wikipedia_talk:Arbitration_Committee/
Noticeboard/Archive_3#Resignation

176 Cade Metz, 'Sockpuppeting British politico resigns from Wikisupremecourt'
(26 May 2009) at www.theregister.co.uk/2009/05/26/wikipedia_westminster_
councillor/

177 James Tozer, 'Labour councillor David Boothroyd caught altering David
Cameron's Wikipedia entry' (8 June 2009) at www.dailymail.co.uk/news/
article-1191474/Labour-councillor-David-Boothroyd-caught-altering-David-
Camerons-Wikipedia-entry.html

178 As quoted by Aaron Swartz, 'Who Writes Wikipedia?'

179 Aaron Swartz, 'Who Writes Wikipedia?'

180 Aaron Swartz, 'Who Writes Wikipedia?'

181 Rhys Blakely, 'Wikipedia Founder Edits Himself' (20 December 2005)
at business.timesonline.co.uk/tol/business/industry_sectors/technology/
article774973.ece

182 'Student Reporters Expose "Royal" Sex Offender' (13 January 2006) at
abcnews.go.com/GMA/LegalCenter/story?id=1501916

183 Cara Page, 'Exclusive: Meet the Real Sir Walter Mitty' (11 April 2006) at
www.dailyrecord.co.uk/news/tm_objectid=16929538&method=full&siteid=6663
3&headline=meet-sir-walter-mitty--name_page.html

184 See Talk:Stephen Schwartz (journalist), Talk:Stephen Schwartz (journalist)/
old talk and www.wikitruth.info/index.php?title=Uncensored:Stephen_Schwartz

185 Cory Doctorow, 'Correcting the Record: Wikipedia vs The Register'

186 Pierre Assouline, 'L'affaire Wikipédia'

187 www.theatlantic.com/doc/200609/wikipedia

188 See Seth Finkelstein, 'I'm on Wikipedia: get me out of here' (28 September
2006) at www.guardian.co.uk/technology/2006/sep/28/wikipedia.web20

189 At Wikipedia:Articles for deletion/Seth Finkelstein

190 en.wikipedia.org/w/index.php?title=Special:Contributions&limit=500&targe
=67.111.218.66

191 en.wikipedia.org/w/index.php?title=Wikipedia_talk:WikiProject_Classical_
Greece_and_Rome&oldid=294628406

192 osdir.com/ml/science.linguistics.wikipedia.misc/2001-07/msg00038.html

193 Now at mediagiraffe.blogspot.com/2006/01/congressmans-staff-said-to-
ave.html

194 See n:United States Department of Justice workers among government
Wikipedia vandals

195 'Web site's entry on Coleman revised: Aide confirms his staff edited
biography, questions Wikipedia's accuracy' formerly at *Twincities.com*, quoted

partly from www.democraticunderground.com/discuss/duboard.php?az=view_all&address=160x16812, partly from n:Wikinews investigates Wikipedia usage by U.S. Senate staff members

196 www.ecrans.fr/Sur-Wikipedia-l-EPR-fait-faire-des.html

197 Durova, 'The Right Way To Correct Inaccurate Wikipedia Articles' and comment

198 'Gutknecht joins Wikipedia tweakers' in *Minneapolis-St. Paul Star Tribune* (16 August 2006) now at listserv.temple.edu/cgi-bin/wa?A2=ind0608&L=net-gold&P=46616

199 Didier Sanz, 'Wikipédia: encyclopédie sous haute surveillance'

200 Even when articles themselves have been deleted from Wikipedia, deletion discussions normally survive forever.

201 One such case is discussed at la:Disputatio Usoris:UV/2007#Spamming from Allcarparts

202 At User:Raul654/Raul's laws

203 Xeni Jardin, 'BBC Punks Wikipedia in Game Marketing Ploy?' at www.boingboing.net/2005/08/13/bbc-punks-wikipedia-.html

204 See Wikipedia:Articles for deletion/Human thermodynamics 2, Wikipedia:Articles for deletion/Human chemistry, Wikipedia:Articles for deletion/Georgi Gladyshev, Wikipedia:Administrators' noticeboard/Incidents/Sadi Carnot, www.eoht.info/page/Georgi+Gladyshev and www.eoht.info/account/Sadi-Carnot

205 At la:Disputatio Usoris:Andrew Dalby/Tabularium 1#Revert/Ban

206 See Wikipedia:Articles_for_deletion/Charles_Gauci, Wikipedia talk:Deletion policy/Maltese nobility, Wikipedia:Articles for deletion/Buttigieg De Piro (2nd nomination) and deletionpedia.dbatley.com/w/index.php?title=Category:Maltese_nobility

207 See en.wikipedia.org/w/index.php?title=Wikipedia:Votes_for_deletion_archive_May_2004&oldid=2881923

208 See uncyclopedia.wikia.com/wiki/Image:Porches.png and uncyclopedia.wikia.com/wiki/Image:Wikicaust.png

209 See fr:Wikipédia:Le Bistro/2 février 2006, fr:Discussion:Harmonisme/Suppression, fr:Wikipédia:Oracle/semaine 45 2005 and osdir.com/ml/org.wikimedia.france/2006-02/msg00014.html

210 Roy Rosenzweig, 'Can History be Open Source?'

211 www.encyclopediadramatica.com/PoetGuy, www.theregister.co.uk/2008/09/19/wikipedia_civil_servant_scandal/ and and www.wikinfo.org/index.php/User_talk:Taxwoman

212 See wikitruth.info/index.php?title=The_Sausage_Factory_and_the_

Sausage_Fest, User talk:Publicgirluk, Wikipedia:Administrators' noticeboard/ IncidentArchive138#Publicgirluk and wp:Publicgirluk photo debate

213 At User:Raul654/Raul's laws

214 David Shankbone, 'Nobody's Safe In Cyberspace'; Jonathan Dee, 'All the News That's Fit to Print Out'

215 Many such are listed at wp:Missing Wikipedians. A few of those who certainly will not return are listed at wp:Deceased Wikipedians.

216 Cade Metz, 'Prime Minister out-nonsensed by Conservative Wikifiddler' (11 February 2009) at www.theregister.co.uk/2009/02/11/wikimadness_uk_germany/

217 See Timrollpickering at en.wikipedia.org/w/index.php?title=Talk:Titian&diff =next&oldid=269990265

218 At waugh.standard.co.uk/2009/02/has-cam-made-a-titian-of-himself.html

219 David Anderson, 'New-look Manchester City Side Begin Their UEFA Cup Campaign in Earnest' (18 September 2009) at www.mirror.co.uk/sport/football/ manchester-city/2008/09/18/new-look-manchester-city-side-begin-their-uefa-cup-campaign-in-earnest-115875-20741334/; Cade Metz, 'Daily Mirror Trapped in Wikicirclejerk' (17 October 2008) at www.theregister.co.uk/2008/10/17/ wikipedia_and_the_mirror/

220 At www.b3ta.com/links/Lazy_Journalist

221 David Anderson, 'Omonia Nicosia 1–2 Manchester City: Goals start to flow for Jo' (19 September 2008) at www.mirror.co.uk/sport/football/match-reports/2008/09/19/omonia-nicosia-1-2-manchester-city-goals-start-to-flow-for-jo-115875-20743824/

222 Sebastian Fischer, 'Karl-Theodor zu Guttenberg: der Frankenblitz' (9 February 2009) at www.spiegel.de/politik/deutschland/0,1518,606315,00.html, with editorial note

223 'Wie ich Freiherr von Guttenberg zu Wilhelm machte' (10 February 2009) at www.bildblog.de/5704/wie-ich-freiherr-von-guttenberg-zu-wilhelm-machte/ and 'Wilhelm II' (11 February 2009) at www.bildblog.de/5731/wilhelm-ii/

224 Brian Krebs, 'Wikipedia Edits Forecast Vice Presidential Picks' (29 August 2008) at www.washingtonpost.com/wp-dyn/content/article/2008/08/29/ AR2008082902691.html

225 electronicintifada.net/downloads/pdf/080421-camera-wikipedia.pdf; David Shankbone, 'Nobody's Safe In Cyberspace'

226 www.dvorak.org/blog/2008/10/06/did-wikipedia-help-cause-the-financial-crisis/

227 www.theregister.co.uk/2008/12/03/patrick_byrne_cast/, www. theregister.co.uk/2008/10/01/wikipedia_and_naked_shorting/, www.forbes. com/2008/09/23/naked-shorting-trades-oped-cx_pb_0923byrne.html,

www.theregister.co.uk/2008/08/11/wikipedia_and_byrne_again/, www.
theregister.co.uk/2008/06/06/wikipedia_and_overstock_revisited/, www.
theregister.co.uk/2007/12/06/wikipedia_and_overstock/

228 www.theregister.co.uk/2009/05/29/wikipedia_bans_scientology/, www.
theregister.co.uk/2009/01/09/fresco_retires_from_wikipedia/, www.theregister.
co.uk/2008/02/06/the_cult_of_wikipedia/

229 At Talk:Sophocles/GA1

230 Roy Rosenzweig, 'Can History be Open Source?'

231 Brian Lamb, 'Jimmy Wales, Wikipedia Founder'

232 Roy Rosenzweig, 'Can History be Open Source?'

233 Christophe Ortoli at www.livreshebdo.fr/weblog/webLogComments.
aspx?idTxt=75&id=11

234 Ira Matetsky at volokh.com/posts/chain_1242098183.shtml

235 Paul Boutin, 'Galaxy Quest'

236 Noam Cohen, 'The Latest on Virginia Tech, From Wikipedia' (23
April 2007) at www.nytimes.com/2007/04/23/technology/23link.html?_
r=3&oref=slogin&oref=slogin

237 See Wikipedia:Wikipedia as a court source

238 'O-169-07: Trade Marks Act 1994: In the Matter of Application No.
2277746C by Formula One Licensing BV'

239 Peter Pollack, 'Court rejects family's suit in German Wikipedia case' (10
February 2006) at arstechnica.com/old/content/2006/02/6152.ars

240 Quoted by Lester Haines, 'German Wikipedia attacked over Nazi symbolism'
(7 December 2007) at www.theregister.co.uk/2007/12/07/wikipedia_
germany_charges/

241 Quoted by Tom Espiner, 'IWF chief: Why Wikipedia block went wrong' (20
February 2009) at news.zdnet.co.uk/internet/0,1000000097,39616171,00.htm

242 Quoted at History of Wikipedia footnote 39 (accessed 11 May 2009)

243 lists.wikimedia.org/pipermail/wikipedia-l/2001-March/000044.html

244 lists.wikimedia.org/pipermail/wikipedia-l/2001-October/000664.html

245 Laurent Suply, 'Larousse dans la bataille des encyclopédies en ligne' (13 May
2008) at www.lefigaro.fr/hightech/2008/05/13/01007-20080513ARTFIG00426-
larousse-dans-la-bataille-des-encyclopedies-en-ligne.php

246 'Vivre sur le net ou mourir!' (11 July 2008) at www.lefigaro.fr/
lefigaromagazine/2008/07/05/01006-20080705ARTFIG00591-vivre-sur-le-net-
ou-mourir-.php

247 John Lichfield, 'France's favourite encyclopaedia falls victim to Wikipedia'
(20 February 2008) at www.independent.co.uk/news/world/europe/frances-
favourite-encyclopaedia-falls-victim-to-wikipedia-784420.html

248 Quoted by Noam Cohen, 'Start Writing the Eulogies for Print Encyclopedias'

249 Robert McHenry, 'Encarta, R.I.P.' See also Tom Corddry, 'Encarta, R.I.P. (cont.)'

250 Shane Greenstein and Michelle Devereux, 'The Crisis at *Encyclopaedia Britannica*'

251 Quoted by Stephen Hutcheon, 'Watch out Wikipedia, here comes Britannic 2.0' (22 January 2009) at www.smh.com.au/news/technology/biztech/watch-out wikipedia-here-comes-britannica-20/2009/01/22/1232471469973.html

252 Larry Sanger at osdir.com/ml/science.linguistics.wikipedia.misc/2001-07/msg00023.html

253 Quoted by Stephen Hutcheon, 'Watch out Wikipedia, here comes Britannic 2.0' (22 January 2009) at www.smh.com.au/news/technology/biztech/watch-out wikipedia-here-comes-britannica-20/2009/01/22/1232471469973.html

254 Nicholas Carr, 'The Amorality of Web 2.0'

255 Nicholas Carr, 'Our New Delphic Oracle' (10 August 2006) at www.roughtype.com/archives/2006/08/the_oracle_of_w.php

256 Nicholas Carr, 'All hail the information triumvirate!'

257 Robert McHenry, 'Encarta, R.I.P.'

258 Robert McHenry, 'The Microsoft Way'

259 At meta:Requests for new languages/Wikipedia Niuean

260 At www.scripting.com/2006/08/09.html#When:2:56:30AM

261 Noam Cohen, 'Delaying News in the Era of the Internet'

262 Noam Cohen, 'Updating a Reference Site on the Fly'

263 spring.newsvine.com/_news/2007/06/29/808872-the-college-student-who-knew-about-the-benoit-murder-suicide-before-police

264 See wp:Articles for deletion/Al Gore III (8th nomination)

265 Ira Matetsky, 'Wikipedia, the Internet, and Diminished Privacy'

266 Bob Sullivan, 'Wikipedia, Google show Obama racial slur' at redtape.msnbc com/2009/02/wikipedia-googl.html

267 features.slashdot.org/comments.pl?sid=146479&threshold=1&commentsor =0&mode=thread&cid=12276095

268 Fernanda B. Viegas, Marvin Wattenberg, and Kushal Dave, 'Studying Cooperation and Conflict between Authors with History Flow Visualizations'

269 Roy Rosenzweig, 'Can History be Open Source?' citing chnm.gmu.edu/resources/essays/d/42#f45

270 Roy Rosenzweig, 'Can History be Open Source?' citing alex.halavais.net/the isuzu-experiment/

271 Nicholas Carr, 'Is Google making us stupid?'

272 Daniel H. Pink, 'The Book Stops Here'

73 Daniel Garcia, 'L'affaire Dreyfus' (30 November 2006) at www.livreshebdo.
/weblog/webLogComments.aspx?idTxt=75&id=11 with comments

74 Pierre Assouline, 'L'affaire Wikipédia'

75 Laurent Suply, 'Larousse dans la bataille des encyclopédies en ligne' (13 May
008) at www.lefigaro.fr/hightech/2008/05/13/01007-20080513ARTFIG00426-
rousse-dans-la-bataille-des-encyclopedies-en-ligne.php

76 Quoted by Donna Shaw, 'Wikipedia in the Newsroom'

77 apps.wbez.org/blog/?cat=243

78 Daniel H. Pink, 'The Book Stops Here'

79 Andrew Lih, *The Wikipedia Revolution* p. 71

80 Quoted at www.businessweek.com/technology/content/dec2005/
:20051214_441708.htm?chan=db

81 Cnaan Lipshitz, 'Wikipedia Editors: coverage of Israel "problematic"' (4
1ay 2009) at www.haaretz.com/hasen/spages/1082777.html; repeated by Robert
1cHenry, 'Wikipedia: playing the game' (11 May 2009) at www.britannica.com/
logs/2009/05/wikipedia-playing-the-game/

82 Dan Murphy, 'Rohde: media face tough choices in kidnap cases' (20 June
009) at features.csmonitor.com/globalnews/2009/06/20/rohde-media-face-
ugh-choices-in-kidnap-cases/

83 Richard Pérez-Peña, 'Keeping News of Kidnapping Off Wikipedia' (28 June
009) at www.nytimes.com/2009/06/29/technology/internet/29wiki.html

84 Murad Ahmed, 'Why Wikipedia was right to stop the revelation of David
ohde's kidnapping' (29 June 2009) at timesonline.typepad.com

Bibliography

Wikipedia

Pierre Assouline, 'L'affaire Wikipédia' (9 January 2007) at passouline.blog. lemonde.fr/2007/01/09/laffaire-wikipedia/

Nicolas Auray, Céline Poudat, Pascal Pons, 'Democratizing Scientific Vulgarization: the balance between cooperation and conflict in French Wikipedia' (2007) at www.obs.obercom.pt/index.php/obs/article/viewFile/152/109;

Paul Boutin, 'Galaxy Quest: Wikipedia is a Real-Life Hitchhiker's Guide: huge, nerdy, and imprecise' (3 May 2005) at www.slate.com/id/2117942;

Nicholas Carr, 'All hail the information triumvirate!' (22 January 2009) at www. roughtype.com/archives/2009/01/all_hail_the_in.php

Andrea Ciffolilli, 'Phantom authority, self-selective recruitment and retention of members in virtual communities: The case of Wikipedia' (11 November 2003) at 31.193.153.231/www/issues/issue8_12/ciffolilli/index.html

Noam Cohen, 'A History Department Bans Citing Wikipedia as a Research Source' (21 February 2007) at www.nytimes.com/2007/02/21/ education/21wikipedia.html

Noam Cohen, 'Delaying News in the Era of the Internet' (23 June 2008) at www. nytimes.com/2008/06/23/business/media/23link.html

Noam Cohen, 'Start Writing the Eulogies for Print Encyclopedias' (16 March 2008) at www.nytimes.com/2008/03/16/weekinreview/16ncohen.html?_r=1

Noam Cohen, 'Updating a Reference Site on the Fly' (10 November 2008) at www.nytimes.com/2008/11/10/technology/internet/10link.html

Jonathan Dee, 'All the News That's Fit to Print Out' (1 July 2007) at www. nytimes.com/2007/07/01/magazine/01WIKIPEDIA-t.html

Peter Denning, Jim Horning, David Parnas and Lauren Weinstein, 'Wikipedia Risks' (December 2005) at www.csl.sri.com/users/neumann/insiderisks05.html

Cory Doctorow, 'Correcting the Record: Wikipedia vs The Register' (11 January 2006) at www.boingboing.net/2006/01/11/correcting-the-recor.html

Durova, 'The Right Way To Fix Inaccurate Wikipedia Articles' (7 August 2007) at searchengineland.com/the-right-way-to-fix-inaccurate-wikipedia-articles-11877

William Emigh and Susan C. Herring, 'Collaborative Authoring on the Web: A Genre Analysis of Online Encyclopedias' (2005) at csdl.computer.org/comp/ proceedings/hicss/2005/2268 /04/22680099a.pdf

Shane Fitzgerald, 'Lazy Journalism Exposed by Online Hoax' (7 May 2009) at www.irishtimes.com/newspaper/opinion/2009/0507/1224246059241.html

Marc Foglia, *Wikipédia, média de la connaissance démocratique: quand le citoyen lambda devient encyclopédiste*. Limoges: FYP Édition, 2008

Pierre Gourdain, Florence O'Kelly, Béatrice Roman-Amat, Delphine Soulas, Tassilo von Droste zu Hülshoff, *La révolution Wikipédia: les encyclopédies vont-elle mourir?* Paris: Mille et Une Nuits, 2007

David A. Hoffman, Salil Mehra, 'Wikitruth Through Wikiorder' (9 April 2009) at papers.ssrn.com/sol3/papers.cfm?abstract_id=1354424

Todd Holloway, Miran Božičević, Katy Börner, 'Analyzing and Visualizing the Semantic Coverage of Wikipedia and Its Authors' (undated) at www.citebase.org fulltext?format=application/pdf&identifier=oai:arXiv.org:cs/0512085

Bernard Jacquemin, Aurélien Lauf, Céline Poudat, Martine Hurault-Plantet, Nicolas Auray, 'La fiabilité des informations sur le web: le cas Wikipédia' (30 May 2008) at hal.archives-ouvertes.fr/docs/00/28/35/69/PDF/JacqueminAl-Coria08-Final.pdf

Steven Johnson, 'Populist Editing' (9 December 2001) at www.nytimes.com/2001/12/09/magazine/09POPULIST.html

Brian Lamb, 'Jimmy Wales, Wikipedia Founder' (interview, 25 September 2005) at www.q-and-a.org/Transcript/?ProgramID=1042

Andrew Lih, *The Wikipedia Revolution*. London: Aurum Press, 2009

Robert McHenry, 'The Faith-Based Encyclopedia' (15 November 2004) at www.techcentralstation.com/ [search on 'faith-based']

Ira Matetsky (Newyorkbrad), series of essays including 'Some First Thoughts on Wikipedia', 'Wikipedia, the Internet, and Diminished Privacy', 'Wikipedia and the Biography Problem' and 'Wikipedia: who runs the place?' (May 2009) at volokh.com/posts/chain_1242098183.shtml

Bertrand Meyer, 'Defense and Illustration of Wikipedia' (January 2006) at www.eiffel.com/general/column/2006/January.html

Cade Metz, 'Wikipedia Black Helicopters Circle Utah's Traverse Mountain' (6 December 2007) at www.theregister.co.uk/2007/12/06/wikipedia_and_overstock

Andrew Orlowski, 'A Thirst for Knowledge' (13 April 2006) at www.guardian.co.uk/technology/2006/apr/13/wikipedia.web20

Daniel H. Pink, 'The Book Stops Here' (March 2005) at www.wired.com/wired/archive/13.03/wiki.html?pg=1&topic=wiki&topic_set=

Marshall Poe, 'The Hive' (September 2006) at www.theatlantic.com/doc/200609/wikipedia

Anita Ramasastry, 'Is an Online Encyclopedia, Such as Wikipedia, Immune From Libel Suits?' (12 December 2005) at writ.news.findlaw.com/ramasastry/20051212.html

Joseph Reagle, 'Wikipedia: the happy accident' in *Interactions* vol. 16 no. 3 (May/June 2009)

Roy Rosenzweig, 'Can History be Open Source? Wikipedia and the Future of the Past' in *Journal of American History* vol. 93 (2006) pp. 117-46; also at chnm.gmu.edu/resources/essays/d/42

David Runciman, 'Like Boiling a Frog' (28 May 2009) at www.lrb.co.uk/v31/n10/runc01_.html

Larry Sanger, 'The Early History of Nupedia and Wikipedia' (18-19 April 2005) at features.slashdot.org/features/05/04/18/164213.shtml?tid=95 and features.slashdot.org/article.pl?sid=05/04/19/1746205&tid=95

Didier Sanz, 'Wikipédia: encyclopédie sous haute surveillance' (17 January 2007) at www.lefigaro.fr/hightech/2007/01/17/01007-20070117ARTFIG90183-wikipedia_encyclopedie_sous_haute_surveillance.php

Stacy Schiff, 'Know It All: can Wikipedia conquer expertise?' (31 July 2006, revised 5 March 2007) at www.newyorker.com/archive/2006/07/31/060731fa_fact

David Shankbone, 'Nobody's Safe In Cyberspace' (June 2008) at www.brooklynrail.org/2008/06/express/nobodys-safe-in-cyber-space

Donna Shaw, 'Wikipedia in the Newsroom' (February/March 2008) at www.ajr.org/Article.asp?id=4461

Aaron Swartz, 'Who Writes Wikipedia?' (4 September 2006) at www.aaronsw.com/weblog/whowriteswikipedia

Fernanda B. Viégas, Martin Wattenberg, Kushal Dave, 'Studying Cooperation and Conflict Between Authors with History Flow Visualizations' (2004) at alumni.media.mit.edu/~fviegas/papers/history_flow.pdf

Simon Waldman, 'Who knows?' (26 October 2004) at www.guardian.co.uk/technology/2004/oct/26/g2.onlinesupplement

Gabriel Weaver, Barbara Strickland, Gregory Crane, 'Quantifying the Accuracy of Relational Statements in Wikipedia: a methodology' in *Proceedings of the 6th ACM/IEEE-CS Joint Conference on Digital Libraries* (New York: ACM, 2006)

Watching Wikipedia

Boingboing, www.boingboing.net

The Register, www.theregister.co.uk

wp:Press coverage

wp:Wikipedia as a press source

fr:Wikipédia:Revue de presse

de:wp:Artikel mit Wikipediazitaten

de:wp:Pressespiegel

BJAODN ('Bad Jokes and Other Deleted Nonsense'), www.bjaodn.org

Deletionpedia, deletionpedia.dbatley.com

Encyclopedia Dramatica, encyclopediadramatica.com

The Wikipedia Blog, www.enotes.com/blogs/wikipedia/

Wikipedia Review, wikipediareview.com/blog/

Wikipedia Watch, www.wikipedia-watch.org

Wikitruth, www.wikitruth.info

Wikipedia in teaching

wp:School and university projects

fr:Wikipédia:Projets pédagogiques

pt:wp:Projetos/Escolares e universitários

Robert E. Cummings, *Lazy Virtues: Teaching Writing in the Age of Wikipedia*. Vanderbilt University Press, 2009

Laure Endrizzi, *L'édition de référence libre et collaborative: le cas de Wikipedia*. Lyon: Institut National de Recherche Pédagogique, 2006 and at www.inrp.fr/vst/ Dossiers/Wikipedia/sommaire.htm

Christopher Miller, 'Strange Facts in the History Classroom: or how I learned to stop worrying and love the *Wiki(pedia)*' (May 2007) at www.historians.org/ perspectives/issues/2007/0705/0705vie1.cfm

'Featured Content from Schools and Universities' at wp:Wikipedia Signpost/2008-05-09/Dispatches

'Wikipédia et éducation: un exemple de réconciliation' (16 February 2009) at www.framablog.org/index.php/post/2009/02/16/wikipedia-education-exemple-projet-pedagogique-1

Wikipedia: how to do it

Sébastien Blondeel, *Wikipédia, comprendre et participer*. Paris: Eyrolles, 2006

John Broughton, *Wikipedia: the missing manual*. Sebastopol, California: O'Reilly Media, 2008

Florence Devouard, Guillaume Paumier, *Wikipédia: découvrir, utiliser, contribuer*. Grenoble: Presses Universitaires de Grenoble, 2009

Phoebe Matthews, Charles Yates, Ben Ayers, *How Wikipedia Works, and how you can be a part of it*. No Starch Press, 2008

Web 2.0

Nicholas Carr, 'The Amorality of Web 2.0' (3 October 2005) at www.roughtype. com/archives/2005/10/the_amorality_o.php

Nicholas Carr, 'The Net is being carved up into information plantations' (17 May 2007) at www.guardian.co.uk/technology/2007/may/17/media.newmedia

Nicholas Carr, 'Is Google making us stupid?' (July 2008) at www.theatlantic.com/doc/200807/google

Erik Möller, *Die heimliche Medienrevolution - Wie Weblogs, Wikis und freie Software die Welt verändern*. Hanover: Heinz Heise, 2006. 2nd ed.

Don Tapscott, *Wikinomics: how mass collaboration changes everything*. New York: Portfolio, 2006

Other encyclopedias

Ronna Abramson, "Look under 'M' for Mess" in *Industry Standard* (9 April 2001) p. 56

Nicholas Carr, '*Nature*'s Flawed Study of Wikipedia's Quality' (16 February 2006) at www.roughtype.com/archives/2006/02/community_and_h.php

Tom Corddry, 'Encarta, R.I.P (cont.)' (3 April 2009) at www.britannica.com/blogs/2009/04/encarta-rip-cont-a-reply-from-tom-corddry/

Annie Ferfant, *Encyclopédisme et savoir: du papier au numérique*. Lyon: Institut National de Recherche Pédagogique, 2006 and at www.inrp.fr/vst/Dossiers/Savoir_encyclopedique/sommaire.htm

Jim Giles, 'Internet Encyclopaedias Go Head to Head' in *Nature* vol. 438 (2005) pp. 900-901; see also 'Wiki's wild world' (15 December 2005) at www.nature.com/nature/journal/v438/n7070/full/438890a.html and supplementary items linked at www.nature.com/nature/journal/v438/n7070/full/438900a.html http://www.nature.com/nature/journal/v438/n7070/extref/438900a-s1.doc

Shane Greenstein and Michelle Devereux, 'The Crisis at Encyclopaedia Britannica' (2006) at www.kellogg.northwestern.edu/faculty/greenstein/images/htm/Research/Cases/EncyclopaediaBritannica.pdf

Lester Haines, 'Need Hard Facts? Try Conservapedia' (20 June 2007) at www.theregister.co.uk/2007/06/20/conservapedia/

Robert McHenry, 'The Microsoft Way' (undated) at www.howtoknow.com/contragates.html

Robert McHenry, 'The Building of Britannica Online' (2003) at www.howtoknow.com/BOL1.html

Robert McHenry, 'Encarta, R.I.P.' (2 April 2009) at www.britannica.com/blogs/2009/04/encarta-rip/

Fred Moody, *I Sing the Body Electric: A Year with Microsoft on the Multimedia Frontier* (New York, 1995) pp. 6–17 [on *Encarta*]

Joseph M. Reagle, 'Wikipedia's heritage: vision, pragmatics, and happenstance' (undated) at reagle.org/joseph/2005/historical/digital-works.html

Larry Sanger, 'Britannica or Nupedia? The Future of Free Encyclopedias' (25 July 2001) at www.kuro5hin.org/story/2001/7/25/103136/121

David Wong, '5 Terrifying Bastardizations of the Wikipedia Model' (11 May 2009) at www.cracked.com/article_17341_5-terrifying-bastardizations-wikipedia-model.html

May Wong, 'Pity the Poor Encyclopedia' (9 March 2004) at www.cbsnews.com/stories/2004/03/09/print/main604937.shtml

ndex of usernames

General index